FOLGER DOCUMENTS
OF TUDOR AND STUART CIVILIZATION

THIS volume is one of a series of publications of Tudor and Stuart documents that the Folger Library proposes to bring out. These documents will consist of hitherto unprinted manuscripts as well as reprints of rare books in the Folger Library. An effort will be made to choose significant items that will throw light on the social and intellectual background of the period from 1485 to 1715. In response to almost unanimous requests of interested historians, the spelling, punctuation, and capitalization will be modernized in printed texts. In some cases, where the original printing is clear and easily read, texts may be photographically reproduced. The Folger Library is prepared to supply microfilm of original texts to scholars who require a facsimile.

Folger Documents of Tudor and Stuart Civi

THE CHRONICLE AN

POLITICAL PAPERS

OF KING EDWARD V

THE CHRONICLE *and* POLITICAL PAPERS *of* KING EDWARD VI

EDITED BY

W. K. *Jordan*

Leroy B. Williams Professor of History
and Political Science, Harvard University

PUBLISHED FOR

The Folger Shakespeare Library

BY

CORNELL UNIVERSITY PRESS

Ithaca, New York

CORNELL UNIVERSITY PRESS

First published 1966

Library of Congress Catalog Card Number: 65-27564

PRINTED IN THE UNITED STATES OF AMERICA
BY VAIL-BALLOU PRESS, INC.

PREFACE

THE editor finds himself indebted to many friends and colleagues who have lent invaluable assistance in the editing of these materials.

Mr. C. E. Wright, Deputy Keeper of Manuscripts at the British Museum, has provided valued and trenchant advice on the history of the manuscript, as has my former student, Professor F. Smith Fussner of Reed College. Mr. H. D. Molesworth, Keeper in the Victoria and Albert Museum, has kindly given me his expert judgment on the traveling coffer now happily in his care, which once belonged to Edward VI, while Mr. S. W. Wolsey (of the firm of Wolsey (Antiques) Ltd., London), who found the coffer, has been most generous in helping with the identification. Mr. F. G. Emmison, the County Archivist for Essex, has given me numerous helpful suggestions drawn from his great learning in sixteenth-century matters. The Marquess of Ailesbury has placed me in his debt by his kindness in exploring with me the region in which the Seymour family was seated and in which the Lord Protector was building a great house at the time of his fall from power. Miss Carolyn Merion has lent considerable assistance in establishing the text of certain of these pieces. Miss Virginia A. LaMar, of the Folger Shakespeare Library, has been discerning as well as learned in the editing of the manuscript of this volume, while displaying great patience with its editor. But my great indebtedness is to Madeleine Rowse Gleason (Mrs. Sidney Gleason), whose enthusiasm and whose skill and accuracy have made great contribution to this work as to other studies over the past twenty years and more. In particular, Mrs. Gleason has compiled the index, typed the manuscript in its various stages, and as a philologist has lent invaluable assistance in the identification of obscure and inaccurately rendered place and family names.

W. K. JORDAN

Cambridge, Massachusetts
November, 1964

CONTENTS

INTRODUCTION

THIS work sets out the text of seven political papers composed by Edward VI, presumably for his own edification and, in several cases, quite clearly as "position papers" in which his own sentiments and policy on important matters of state are intimately and revealingly disclosed. It has been our effort to provide an exact rendering of the manuscripts of these essays, within certain conventions established by the Folger Shakespeare Library for the series of which this volume is part. Spellings have throughout been modernized and the young King's punctuation has on occasion been lightly touched. Archaic words have usually been retained, with clarification in the notes when that seemed desirable. Foreign spellings of place names and family names have in most cases been anglicized and when obscure identified, though the careful reader of the notes will discover not a few instances where we have had to confess failure of identification. The difficulty is that much of the King's intimate knowledge of the course of events on the Continent was derived in conversation, in one period of rather more than a year quite evidently principally from the French ambassador at his court, and the spelling of a name or a place was set down from memory by Edward with no more than a phonetic approximation of accuracy. The King's ear was good, his Latin excellent, and his French highly competent, but some extraordinary renderings nonetheless enliven the manuscript, and we fear that a few Flemish hamlets bravely stormed by the French, and perhaps as many brave but junior officers killed or captured in these engagements, must remain unidentified.

All matter in the text following set in square brackets is an addition, elucidation, or speculation of the editor. Words and phrases set in parentheses are additions, corrections, or deletions in the King's own hand (described in our italics), or in a few evident instances follow his own use of the parenthetical symbols. The form *Marquis* has been adopted for both English and French nobility of the rank; *Mons.* is the style adopted for the French gentry; and *Mr.* has been retained, though the meaning in Edward's use was of course *Master* rather than *Mister.* In the very nature of the case, the notes supplied for the text of the *Chronicle* are numerous, but an effort has been made to keep them terse. In an effort to keep the number of notes under a reasonable control, the following working principle has been established: biographical notes will not be provided ordinarily for the greater servants of the Crown when adequate notices may be found in the *Dictionary of National Biography,* and identifications will not usually be made of obscure persons who are mentioned by the King only in passing. The *Index* is long and is meant to be full, supplying in many instances materials not to be found in the notes and thereby saving them from tedious repetitive matter.

Since we are dealing with a royal personage, only the briefest of biographical material needs here be presented, particularly since we are now engaged in preparing a history of the reign. Fairly full and easily available accounts of this short life may be found in S. L. Lee's notice in the *Dictionary of National Biography* and, as part of a longer narrative, in A. F. Pollard's extended essay, *England under Protector Somerset.*

Edward was born at Hampton Court on October 12, 1537, the son of Henry VIII and Jane Seymour, the mother dying some days later. Here was the male heir which the House of Tudor so desperately required and to secure whose birth so much of dislocation and revolution had been undertaken by an imperious monarch. Every possible safeguard was thrown about the infant, even the christening being performed under conditions approaching informal martial law in order to exclude the risk of infection. As Edward himself later remarked in the *Chronicle* (p. 3), he was brought up "among the women" until the age of six, when Richard Cox was summoned to be his first tutor in July, 1544. It is significant that Cox, who had been educated at Cambridge, had long been strongly Protestant in his sympathies. He had enjoyed a distinguished career as headmaster of Eton and was an intimate of Archbishop Cranmer, who very probably recommended him to the King. Cox's tutorship was continued until early 1550. An excellent Latinist, a patristic scholar of some reputation, and a skillful administrator, Cox was to lay the foundations for the remarkable education of the young Prince and King.

Closely associated with Cox in this precious task of education was Sir John Cheke (1514–1557), who since 1540 had served as the first Regius Professor of Greek at Oxford and who was the most brilliant of the notable group of humanists to be found in the two universities, so many of whom were called upon to render public service during the brief reign of Edward VI. Cheke's influence over the young Prince was very great, and it was he who grounded him so thoroughly in Greek and Latin classics, who insisted on meticulous penmanship, and who encouraged him to develop the habit of constant writing as a means of self-expression as well as for academic discipline. Other and lesser men taught the boy French, music, and riskless sports, but it was Cheke and Cox who remained his masters, who shaped his style, and who gave to him such an extraordinary and humane education. Few monarchs in history have been as well equipped for their task as was Edward VI: he stood as a prince who would have delighted the fastidious and demanding taste of Erasmus.

Cheke and Cox likewise very sensibly arranged that the young Prince and King should gain experience in humanity by sharing his upbringing and some aspects of his formal education with well-born youths of his own age, at least fourteen of whom have been fairly certainly identified and most of whom were sons of peers of the realm. But of this group Edward became the fast friend of only one, Barnaby Fitzpatrick, son of an obscure Irish peer, with whom to the end of his life the King spoke with freedom and candor and to whom, while Barnaby was completing his education at the French court, he wrote a series of remarkable letters—strangely mixed in temper and mood—in part the bubbling confidences of boy to boy and in part the imperious dicta of a Tudor sovereign addressing a subject.

Some of the fruits, as well as a clear indication of the educational method of Cox and Cheke, may be found in the academic exercises written by Edward, numbering well over one hundred, now preserved in the British Museum (Harl. MS. 5087, Addit. MS. 4724). These Latin and Greek compositions and declamations mostly date from September, 1548, to July, 1552. They will be more fully discussed in the later work on which the editor is engaged, but it may be said here that they deal with a great variety of topics—classical, religious, political, and moral—almost certainly following the method prescribed by Erasmus but concentrated on completing the education of a remarkable boy already a king when the exercises were composed. These essays demonstrate as well a brilliantly competent mastery of the Latin language, an easy and impressive knowledge of Greek, and, in several rather ambitious religious exercises, a very nearly idiomatic command of French. As one examines these highly formal documents, there is a sense that until about May, 1551, they were composed for the scrutiny and criticism of the tutors, while thereafter the King was completing the shaping and polishing of his style and his grasp of the logical processes of presentation principally on his own initiative and for his own purposes. So, too, in his most important composition, the *Chronicle*, this same transition in the nature and purpose of composition may be observed, though in this instance what may be described as the arrival of intellectual maturity was to occur about a year earlier.

The Chronicle

The principal of the writings of Edward VI is a political or state diary extending nominally from the record of his birth and early years to the abrupt termination on November 28, 1552, a short while before the onset of his fatal illness, but in a detailed and more informal style covering the period from March 24, 1550, to the end. Edward himself entitled the document in two places his "Chronicle," though the word was carefully lined through, presumably by his hand, on the page which would normally bear the final name of a work probably still in progress. In the other place the same title is used at the outset of the contemporaneous entries. Bishop Burnet called the work a "Journal," a word not used in this sense in the mid-sixteenth century and not in any event fully expressing the content and form of the document itself. Perhaps the most accurate title which could be imposed on what is formally a title-less work would be "Political Diary," but "Diary" was a word likewise not known in the author's time and conveys a sense of personal and intimate jottings not to be found in this sternly sober recital of events. Perhaps, therefore, Edward's own somewhat wavering choice of *Chronicle* may be restored as setting out most accurately the nature of the document which follows.

The manuscript of the *Chronicle*, containing sixty-eight leaves, is to be found in the British Museum, Cotton MSS., Nero, C, x. It is bound with certain of Edward's other writings and exercises and is prefaced by a beautifully wrought, though unfinished, rendering of the royal arms. The manuscript remained in the Royal Library until about 1616, having been seen there by Bishop James Montagu, probably in connection with his work in editing and translating the political works of James I. It came, as did so many other priceless manuscripts, into the hands of the great antiquary and collector, Sir Robert Bruce Cotton, who for many years had free access to the state papers and whose library came ultimately to contain more than one hundred volumes of state documents, almost all concentrated in the period 1509–1615. Cotton was in difficulties in late 1615, when he was examined by the Privy Council and for a short time imprisoned because of the aid and advice which he had given to Robert Carr (Earl of Somerset), but he continued to enjoy James's confidence and retained at least some measure of royal favor for the remainder of the reign. The manuscript on its flyleaf bears Cotton's signature in the form "Ro: Cotton Bruceus," but this establishes no more than that the materials had come into the great collector's hands sometime before his death in 1631. Another inscription on the flyleaf suggests that Dugdale consulted the volume in Cotton's library in *ca.* 1652, while Thomas Fuller, when preparing his *Church History,* sometime before 1655, saw the manuscript in the Cotton Library "by the favour of Sir Thomas Cotton," Sir Robert's son and heir. The Cotton Library was acquired by purchase in 1707 by act of Parliament as the foundation for a national library, and the manuscript passed with the rest of Cotton's huge collection to the British Museum on its founding in 1753.

Edward's *Chronicle* was first published by Bishop Burnet in his *History of the Reformation* (3 vols., 1679–1719), of which the best and most easily available edition is that so elaborately edited by Pocock and published by the Clarendon Press in 1865. Great as Burnet's contribution to English historiography is, the text thus published, in form as part of an appendix of sources for the *History,* must be described as inexact and careless, while the utility of the rendering is gravely weakened by the failure to provide notes. This text should not be used by any student engaged in serious historical scholarship.[1]

Very different indeed is the other available printed text, published in 1857–1858 by John Gough Nichols (1806–1873) for the Roxburghe Club under the title, *Literary Remains of King Edward the Sixth*. Like all of Nichols' many editorial contributions,[2] the rendering is careful, perceptive, and on the whole accurate. Moreover, Nichols provided elaborate annotations and documentation, useful to the modern student, though, as was always the case with this really great antiquary, the notes tend to be heavily overladen with source materials often only remotely apposite to the question immediately at hand. This edition has recently been reproduced by photographic process (2 vols., New York [1963–1964]).

The young King, who was such a delight to his learned tutors,

[1] As much must be said for another very rare edition, issued in 120 "large paper and 400 small paper copies" by the Clarendon Historical Society, Edinburgh, 1884–1885 (new ser., nos. I–VI). The text is unreliable, there are none save a few textual notes, and the name of the editor is not given.

[2] Nichols' great contribution to English historical scholarship has never been sufficiently acknowledged. A native of London, educated at the Merchant Taylors' School, he was born into a publishing family with pronounced scholarly interests. Entering the family firm in 1824, his first task was to complete the work begun by his grandfather (John Nichols) and published under the title, *The Progresses of James I*. Nichols was over a long career continuously active in literary and historical affairs, serving for many years as an editor of the *Gentleman's Magazine*, helping with the founding of the Camden Society, to which he contributed many of the early and still valuable volumes, and assisting in the work of the Surtees Society. In all, there are upwards of thirty titles which bear his name as author or editor, his tastes and interests ranging widely over historical, antiquarian, architectural, and, above all, biographical matters. His consuming interest was in getting the sources for English history published. His contribution must on the whole be described as that of a learned antiquary, but his skill, prudence, and integrity as an editor introduced new canons in English historical scholarship. Had Nichols lived a generation later, he would have made the ideal editor of the *Dictionary of National Biography*.

Introduction

is likewise a joy to a modern editor and reader. In a generation
in which the English hand in both public and private documents
suffered its ultimate deterioration, one is almost startled to find
in the *Chronicle*, as in all his other exercises and writings, a
bold, clear, and beautiful Italianate hand which is in the main
almost as clean and legible as typescript. Edward had been
splendidly drilled by Cheke and his other masters, and there is
abundant evidence of an almost physical pride in composition,
beauty of penmanship, and polish of the material. In no more
than a score of places is there doubt of the King's spelling or
meaning, and in most of these the difficulty arises either from
damage to the document itself or from the King's own insertions
or overscoring.

We have spoken of the quality and the depth of the young
King's education. His exercises and declamations not only reveal
an impressive grasp of language, considerable logical powers,
and liberality of knowledge, but they exhibit as well a literary
style of some distinction and polish. This last cannot of course
be claimed for the *Chronicle*, which is in the very nature of the
case terse, telegraphic, and meant to be reminiscent rather than
expository. Nonetheless, it will be observed that the boy loved
words, savored them, and used them with considerable skill and
linguistic daring. He was also a coiner of words, a good many of
which have endured in our usage. We may well not have noted
them all, but at least fifteen of his words antedate the first cita-
tion found by the editors of the *New English Dictionary* or are
cited by that magnificently useful work as being the first usage.
There was in him, then, a remarkable fertility of expression, just
as there was great perceptivity and trenchant powers of expression.

The *Chronicle* derives its great interest and importance not
only from the subject matter itself and from its significance as
an historical source, but because it is quite un-self-consciously
the clear and moving record of the shaping and maturing of a

precocious mind and temperament. One observes in it, indeed, the successful struggle of a tightly disciplined, steadily observed, and anxiously guarded child, who was also a sovereign, to attain independence of habits and personality, and—since he was, in the whole meaning of the word, a Tudor—to reach out for the essential elements of power. One has constantly to remind himself that the composition of this work in its diary form was begun when Edward VI was aged twelve years and five months, and that at its somewhat forbidding last entry he was aged no more than fifteen years and one month. The whole weight of the evidence which the text supplies, and on which we comment in the notes, suggests that the young King stood ready to grasp the reins of power just as he was stricken with tuberculosis, a debilitating and shortly a fatal illness. The evidence of the *Chronicle* and of the other papers here published would also suggest that few sovereigns of his years have ever possessed a clearer sense of direction, of tasks to be accomplished, than did this young monarch, or to have been endowed with greater resources wherewith to secure their accomplishment.

Internal evidence suggests that the *Chronicle* was begun as an exercise with his tutors, very possibly at about the time of his coronation. The composition may well have been begun originally at note 5, page 4, the wholly conventional sketch of his birth and childhood having been added later. The presentation and the material dealt with are rather stiff and hackneyed, though by no means devoid of interest, until March, 1550, when greater informality, far greater concern with immediate matters and details, and a more vigorous and personal style begin to mark the work. The *Chronicle* was becoming his own and was ceasing to be an exercise over which his tutors doubtless maintained a benevolent but still critical concern. Not many months later, in the summer of 1550, not only do the entries tend to become longer, to cover a wider spectrum of interest, and to be expressed more informally, but one begins to see clear evidences of concern with policy as well as with the details of administration. It is significant that, to gauge it very roughly, the contents of the *Chronicle* to July 1, 1550, occupy only a fourth of the whole bulk of the document. From about this date forward there is an impressive regard displayed not only for the persons and activities immediately around the King, but for larger problems of finance, foreign affairs, and administration which betoken the precocious maturity of the boy still not quite thirteen years of age. This maturity may be said to have ripened, to have been substantially completed, in early 1552 (see entries March 3 and 9, 1552, and accompanying notes as instances), when the King was bringing important recommendations before the Council, whose debates he was now following with close attention, and when there was being framed in his own mind a program of major reorganization of the Council and its conduct of business. A further, and final, transition in the King's interests and concerns occurs in May–June, 1552, when he began to follow in detail the course of the interminable war between France and the Empire, drawing on sources, some of which remain obscure, quite beyond the flow of information reaching the Council from the English ambassadors abroad. So great and absorbing did this concern become that it tends in the final months to dwarf and obscure his recital of domestic affairs. But on every count it seems clear that the King was at the point of assuming power when a fatal illness overcame him in early 1553.

The King was evidently faithful in his habits of composition in the preparation of the *Chronicle,* most entries apparently having been set down on the date formally indicated. This is suggested by the fact that in a number of instances facts were somewhat erroneously stated on the basis of knowledge in hand on the day of writing, with correction or enlargement of the entry in later passages. The reader will also observe that each month Edward seems to have tidied and completed his *Chronicle,* with the result that a great many entries occur out of chronological sequence. This is particularly true in his discussion of European diplomatic and military events, which tend to be set down as of the date of occurrence as the news reached him and are presented as *post scripta* for the month or other period involved. After some uncertainty, it has been decided to follow the chronology of the manuscript faithfully and to resist the temptation to present the whole in chronological order.

Surely in English history, and very possibly in European history, there is no historical source quite of the nature of the *Chronicle* of Edward VI. It is in part private diary, in part an educational exercise, and in part considered notes on policy and administration. The document stands as one of the major sources for our knowledge of the entire reign and not infrequently constitutes our only source of information for events of considerable significance. At all points where it may be tested the *Chronicle* is surprisingly reliable and the whole of it is marked by an extraordinary, an almost frightening, objectivity as events and men are described and discussed. It is evident that from the age of about thirteen onward the King was watching the course of government and of policy with an observing, an independent, and an increasingly critical eye; that at a very early age he was already working assiduously to prepare himself for the responsibilities which it was assumed lay just ahead for him. When one reflects on the indolence and sheer indifference to public events which marked the early years of his father's reign, one finds much that is in decided contrast between these two Tudors. Edward was in temperament, in ability, and in capacity for noting and mastering detail much more akin to his great sister than to the tempestuous human being who was his father.

As the reader of our notes will at once observe, most of the events, the decisions, and the apprehensions recorded by the King may be verified and found in fuller form in the *Acts of the Privy Council*, the *State Papers Domestic*, and the *State Papers*

Introduction

Foreign. This means, of course, that the King from a very tender age was seeing and was digesting the flow of data with which his government was informed and on the basis of which it was laying out the course of policy. But the King's information, particularly on foreign affairs and military events abroad, on occasion went far beyond the official documents available to us, presumably being derived from his conversations with envoys accredited to him, from his day-to-day meetings with Petre and Cecil, very possibly from that strange humanist, William Thomas,[3] and in a few cases from quite uncertain sources.

[3] William Thomas, of Welsh origin, was probably educated at Oxford. He left England in 1545, probably because of his advanced Protestant views, though also under suspicion of having defrauded his patron, Sir Anthony Browne. Thomas spent four formative years abroad, mostly in Italy. He wrote a defense of Henry VIII after that monarch's death and likewise compiled an Italian grammar of considerable utility. Then, just before his return to England, Thomas wrote an interesting history of Italy for the English audience, recently republished in this series by Professor George B. Parks (Cornell University Press, 1963).

Thomas wrote easily and well, but all his works suffer from conventional superficiality and a certain glibness. In April, 1550, he gained an appointment as clerk of the Council and a year later was one of Northampton's retinue when that peer proceeded abroad to negotiate the marriage treaty with France. He gained indirect access to Edward VI in late 1550, probably through the offices of Sir Nicholas Throckmorton, then a knight of the Privy Chamber, setting before Edward eighty-five political topics, in the form of questions, any one of which he undertook fully to expound upon request. These topics covered a wide range of political theory, military policy, and statecraft, there being, significantly, only one on religion (Cotton MSS., Titus, B, ii). He likewise prepared six of these political discourses (Cotton MSS., Vespasian, D, xviii) which were almost certainly proffered to the King. One piece particularly, "touching the reformation of the coinage," was in the King's hands while this question was before the Council. In it Thomas urged the high necessity for a restoration of the purity of the coinage, advising that a modest profit of 5 per cent be taken on the re-coinage, and that this be at once invested in additional lands for the Crown. There is some evidence that Edward was influenced by Thomas' papers, and it seems likely that the form, though not the content, of the political and economic memoranda which we print (nos. I–V) may owe something to this shadowy and interesting figure. Thomas was not a considerable thinker, though his writings are embellished with quotations from the

Introduction

As one reads and contemplates the *Chronicle,* which in a very true sense is a record of what interested the young King, a considerable revision of the traditional assessment of his character and personality emerges. His deepest and most persistent concern is evidently with the reform of the whole process of conciliar government, with the dull but essential tasks of administration. Here he had ideas that were his own, and it can be said with conviction that a reform of administration was in hand when he was stricken with his final illness. It is equally clear that he had an intelligent and active interest in the fiscal problems of his government, was searching out the causes for the ruinous inflationary process then under way, and was not without influence in bringing to an end the disgraceful course of debasement of the coinage which his father had begun and his own ministers had completed. He was ardently interested as well in the larger implications of European diplomacy, following even day-to-day events abroad, during those months when Northumberland's policy was paralyzed by an ineptitude mixed with fear. Further, his excited interest in the clashes of the Emperor and the faithless Maurice, of Henry II and the Emperor, and in obscure skirmishes outside the walled citadels of Italy suggest a martial ardor which, had he lived long enough to assume power, might have embarked England once more on dangerous waters. And, finally, there is overwhelming evidence in the *Chronicle* and in the political papers of the young monarch's deep concern with the economic and social dislocations of his generation. In this whole area of his thought it seems certain that he had absorbed from Somerset, from Latimer, whose preaching greatly influenced him, from Hales, and from

classical authors and from Machiavelli, on whom he seems to have modeled his political thought. Perhaps the most interesting and important fact is that we have here certain evidence that the King was seeking independent advice and had already learned that he must arrive at his own judgments. We shall treat Thomas' thought and his rather hazy and most transitory influence on the King fully in another study.

others the whole general moral tradition of the Commonwealth Party. Edward VI wanted reforms, and he wanted a larger measure of social justice within his realm. Such warmth and zeal as there is in his writings is principally concerned with these matters, with policies which in point of fact had destroyed his uncle when he alienated the support of the dominant landed classes. England would have been an exciting realm indeed had Edward VI lived; it just possibly might have been a better dwelling place for men.

But a careful reading of the *Chronicle* enforces a still more important revision of our estimate of the King, his interests, and his aspirations for England. There is little evidence indeed in these pages of religious warmth, much less of zeal, or that he was much concerned about religious matters save as they touched his supremacy and his ultimate sovereignty. Advanced Protestant he undoubtedly was; genuinely and deeply pious other evidence would suggest him to be; but the root concern as evinced in the *Chronicle* is with the control of the structure of ecclesiastical power. There is in point of fact little notice of religious matters at all, not more than five per cent of the whole work being so concerned and well over half of that meager proportion being directed actually to purely administrative questions. Once again the young King's concern seems amazingly similar to that cool and secular spirit with which his sister was a decade later to fasten ecclesiastical policy in a firm Erastian grip. In the end it is true that this frail and dying boy fell victim to the threat of Northumberland's demoniacal persuasions. But from what we can deduce from the writings of Edward VI, one is led to wonder whether the King in his dying effort to set Mary's succession aside was not moved rather more by the already well-exhibited obsessive and fanatical Catholicism of his elder sister than by the objective fact of her faith. We simply cannot know, but the King may have understood her well enough to sense that she would in fact make a disastrously bad queen for the realm which death was snatching from his grasp.

The internal evidence of the *Chronicle* does, then, not settle all questions relating to the character of this remarkable and precocious boy. One such question remains about which there is a brooding uncertainty: the nature of his personality. This is a cold, harsh, and perhaps overly-disciplined document. There is almost nothing of personal warmth, of boyish affection, of youthful preoccupation to be discerned in it. The death of his Seymour grandmother goes unnoticed, though two days earlier (October 16, 1550) the King had returned to Westminster. The execution of Somerset, his own uncle and his head of state, is dismissed with a cold and terse comment exhibiting no emotion whatsoever. The earlier destruction of Thomas Seymour, deserved though it was, is harshly noted, even though that engaging rogue had sought to subvert the boy with pocket money and furtive backstairs plotting. There are only two references in the whole work to Elizabeth, not many years older than he, and these are merely passing comments. Only in his relations with Barnaby Fitzpatrick, expressed principally in the King's letters, and in his evident pleasure in the visit to England of the Marshal St. André is boyish pleasure expressed, is the steel of self-discipline for a moment relaxed. Only rarely, then, does the boy express excitement and enthusiasm, even in this his private journal. He had been disciplined and rigorously trained for the great office which he held. He had seen plots and counterplots around him, and he held neither Somerset nor Northumberland in full esteem or confidence. The young King was not fearful, but he was always alert, and he was almost invariably suspicious of men and their motives. Almost pathetic are the references to his desk, which he could lock and to which he could safely entrust the pages of his *Chronicle* and the state papers on which he loved to work.[4] The tutors selected with such shrewd

[4] A traveling coffer presented in 1958 by the British Antique Dealers' Association to the Victoria and Albert Museum is very possibly the desk

care by Henry VIII had made a king; they had also destroyed a boy.

The Political Papers

I. Discourse on the Reform of Abuses in Church and State (April?, 1551)

This essay, in the King's hand, is also found in the Cotton MSS. (Nero, C, x, ff. 113–117). It is evidently unfinished, has been left somewhat unpolished, and was very possibly conceived of as a quite detailed state paper on the principal social and economic problems of the age. Bishop Burnet has suggested, probably correctly, that it may have been inspired by Martin Bucer's *De Regno Christi,* presented to the King in manuscript as a New Year's gift in 1550–1551.[5] Bucer's treatise was principally concerned with the further reforms required by the Church and with the imperative need for the imposition of discipline on Christ's Church on earth. The brief, and trivial, discussion lent by Bucer to temporal matters is wholly conventional and quite incidental to his fervent plea for a church so reformed as to be consonant with Continental models.

Internal evidence makes it clear that Edward's work was composed during the parliamentary session extending from January 23 to April 15, 1551, and probably toward its close. The very brief and somewhat hackneyed preliminary section dealing with ecclesiastical matters may indeed have been inspired

---

or chest in which Edward locked away his writings. The attribution of the piece to Edward VI seems beyond question; there is a key, and the chest would quite perfectly have met the needs of the young King who was, as the *Chronicle* records, so frequently removing from one royal residence to another. It will also be recalled that in the mid-sixteenth century the term "desk" was quite as much used for a repository for writing materials as for the surface on which one wrote.

[5] The work was first published at Basle in 1557, while a French translation appeared in the following year.

by Bucer's gift, but the King then turned at considerable length to a remarkable treatise on the social and economic ills of the period, clearly reflecting not only in the thrust of the argument but in his language the thought and aspirations of the Commonwealth Party of which Latimer, Lever, and Hales were the principal exponents. Many months before, Somerset had adopted certain of these views and recommendations, and his stubborn efforts to find and enforce remedies had been amongst the principal causes of his fall from power in late 1549. But the King had evidently absorbed with considerable conviction these startling and, in terms of the interests of the dominant classes, most unpopular views in his extended and eloquently expressed document. His language and sentiments are, of course, decidedly reminiscent of Latimer's famous Lenten Sermons preached before the King and Court in 1549. Though simply written, the essay possesses great clarity of style, vigor of presentation, and an orderly sense of composition. It exhibits as well a persuasive, a nervous, and an occasionally moving eloquence, and above all a warmth of spirit not to be found in the *Chronicle*. It may well be that the paper owes much, more than the young King could have understood, to Somerset's brooding and compassionate conscience.

II. Reasons for Establishing a Mart in England (March 9, 1552)

Also amongst the Cotton MSS. (Nero, C, x, ff. 85 ff.), this memorandum was apparently prepared by the King for discussion in the Council on March 9, 1552.[6] It is an elaborate and detailed blueprint for establishing in England a market designed to replace Antwerp as the entrepôt for European trade. It was inspired, indirectly at least, by the hope that English commerce and finance might thus be strengthened and more directly by the hope that English commerce and finance might

[6] *Chronicle*, p. 115.

thereby be relieved of the recurrent crises in international trade occasioned as the chronic Habsburg-Valois wars swept back and forth across the traditional north-south lines of European commerce. Just such an interruption was at the moment causing considerable distress, for the King notes in his *Chronicle* on March 23, 1552, that the English wool fleet of about sixty sail had at last left England after repeated delays, only to arrive too late to reach the market.

A somewhat similar, if less ambitious, plan had been proposed by Sir Richard Gresham to Cromwell in 1537, when he urged the building in London of a bourse on the Antwerp model. Similar considerations were in the mind of Gresham's greater son, Sir Thomas, when in 1566 he began the building in London of the famous Exchange, principally at his own charge.

But the Edwardian proposal was more far-reaching, contemplating as it did a mart incorporating all the multitudinous commercial activities of Antwerp, whose function as an international trading and financial center it was designed to replace. The plan is set out with great care, and a wholly objective effort is made to assess its weaknesses and strengths. The realities of European trade practices and trade routes are brought under reasonably full and careful examination. Under the most propitious circumstances the plan could hardly have succeeded in 1552, though Antwerp's decline was already setting in. Neither English finance nor commerce was as yet sufficiently strong to provide a necessary base of capital, skill, and tradition, and the center of gravity of European trade was for about a century to move to Amsterdam before shifting to London. But these proposals are nonetheless far from naïve in conception and presentation. The document displays as well the intelligent and sustained interest of the young King in economic affairs and exhibits a certain boldness of vision and spirit which was by this date beginning to characterize his approach to most matters of state.

III. Memorandum as to Ways and Means (Summer, 1552)

These jottings, found in Lansdowne MSS., 1236, f. 21, assess the financial position of the government in the summer of 1552 and may be regarded as preparatory to the detailed consideration lent to fiscal problems by the Council in October of that year.[7] The chief concern is with finding sources of liquid funds wherewith the still heavy current debits in Antwerp could be discharged and English credit restored. Debts, principally arrearages from Crown officers, were to be collected, a parliamentary subsidy was to be applied, and all church plate save that required by the chaste Protestant ritual now enjoined by law was to be expropriated.[8]

It may be noted that Gresham was in fact to be successful in re-establishing the value of sterling on the Antwerp Bourse, as a coinage of restored purity gave him the tool with which to work; at the same time he was whittling down the external debt by a ruthless pre-emption on behalf of the government of the control of the whole of the cloth export. By the end of the reign not more than £100,000 was payable abroad. But the real difficulty—though not so pressing—was that the whole governmental budget was still badly unbalanced, and to this problem the King and Council did not seriously address themselves until the autumn of 1552.

IV. Memorandum for the Council (October 13, 1552)

This interesting and important state paper, again in the King's hand, is preserved in Lansdowne MSS., 1236, ff. 19–20. Though a great variety of topics and problems are only very briefly

[7] See below, document IV.

[8] *Acts of the Privy Council of England*, ed. J. R. Dasent, new ser. III (1550–1552) (London, 1891), 223, 467; new ser. IV (1552–1554) (London, 1892), 219, 265, 270.

sketched, the document reveals the range as well as the direction of the King's thinking. It was almost certainly inspired by the financial crisis then absorbing the attention of both the King and Council but broadens out into a searching set of proposals dealing with financial, religious, economic, and military reforms which the young monarch thought were needed. This on the face of it is a memorandum of aspirations rather than of policy intentions, but many of the points here set down had, we know, engaged Edward's mind earlier, and there was already apparent in his character a stubborn tenacity in securing ends to which he had become intellectually or emotionally committed.

This paper is endorsed in Cecil's hand as the "King's Majesty's Memorial" and was intended for the discussion of the Council at its meeting on October 13, 1552. Twelve members of the Council—an unusually full attendance—were present on that date, including such powerful men as Northumberland, Suffolk, Winchester, Clinton, Cobham, and Cecil. But the record of the meeting is unfortunately even sparser than is usual for this period, and there is no mention of a consideration of this document.[9]

V. Certain Articles Devised and Delivered by the King's Majesty for the Quicker, Better, and More Orderly Dispatch of Causes by His Majesty's Privy Council (January 15, 1553)

The King's growing concern with administrative reform was first maturely displayed when on March 15, 1552, he proposed a Commission to look carefully into the functioning of the several financial courts. Accordingly, on March 23, 1552, commissions were issued to a committee of seven, including the heads of the various financial courts, which sat for eight months before handing in, on December 10, 1552, an impressive and well-

[9] *APC, 1552–1554,* pp. 142–143.

considered report surveying the current fiscal situation and making far-ranging recommendations for reform.[10] Total income was stated as £271,912, of which the Commission regarded £183,998 as certain and the remainder as casual. These revenues flowed in to the government through five financial courts: the Exchequer, the Court of Augmentations, the Duchy of Lancaster, First Fruits, and Wards. Total outlays were reckoned at £235,398 for 1551, but it was pointed out that this total was understated, since very heavy outlays for the navy, for ordnance, and for the defense establishments in Calais and Ireland were not included. The Commission was generally critical of prevailing waste and of needless expense occasioned by the overlapping of various administrative agencies, but dwelt with specific clarity on recommendations to merge all the revenue courts in a single agency (the Exchequer) in order to save duplication of functions, reduce staffing, and eliminate much of waste. These careful and well-argued proposals were taken seriously, the Council drawing up a list of ten specific items of reform to be undertaken so that "faults may be redressed and the superfluous charges diminished." [11] The larger proposals, which would merge the several financial courts, were almost ready for drafting for enactment into law by Parliament when the King's illness and death intervened. But the impetus for reform was by no means wholly lost, the contemplated changes being partially enacted in Queen Mary's first regnal year.[12]

This lively concern with administrative procedures and with the cure of inefficiency and waste is even more substantially demonstrated in the memorandum under notice, which may be found in Cotton MSS., Nero, C, x, ff. 86–89. As early as 1551 the Council had found itself with too heavy an agenda and had be-

[10] Preserved in Harl. MSS., 7382.

[11] S. P. Dom., Edward VI, X, 5, 154.

[12] G. R. Elton, *The Tudor Revolution in Government* (Cambridge, 1962), pp. 230–250, presents the best discussion of this matter.

come chronically, if inexpertly, concerned with financial problems which were often critical in nature. Accordingly, successive committees were constituted, usually with a blending of conciliar and non-conciliar members, to deal with such problems as the royal debts (*Chronicle,* December 30, 1551), with the penal laws (March 3, 1552), to handle requests, and to oversee the revenues. In still another short memorandum, which we have not printed, the King lists thirty-one councillors and nine others, who are "now called into commission," to deal with the range of immediate problems just described, while twenty named councillors, senior in prestige and experience, thereby to some degree relieved, were to meet regularly "to attend the matters of state" and to consult weekly with the King.[13] In November, 1552, the Imperial ambassador reported that the King had begun to attend the Council meetings regularly, was taking the lead in some matters, and was assuming an independent role in its deliberations.[14]

The leadership now being assumed by the King is more formally manifest in the draft proposal under consideration. There also exists a shorter version, or précis, of the *Articles* in Petre's hand which seems almost certainly to have been derivative and probably to have been prepared by the Secretary for use in the Council's discussion of the proposed scheme of reorganization.[15]

As the text of the *Articles* will suggest, the Council was to discuss and determine only the more important matters of state. Fixed days were set for the handling of various classes of business, procedure was to be regularized, and freedom was to be

[13] Cotton MSS., Nero, C, x, f. 79; it may be found in Nichols, *Literary Remains,* II, 498–502, and may probably be dated March, 1552.

[14] *Calendar of . . . State Papers, Relating to . . . Spain, Edward VI, 1550–1552,* ed. by Royall Tyler (London, 1914), 592.

[15] S. P. Dom., Edward VI, X, 1, 15.

left for the consideration of emergency business. The King's version of the proposal is perhaps a little too detailed, and it is slightly verbose, but it nonetheless displays a firm and orderly administrative sense. The plan was to be brought before the Council on a stated date (January 15, 1553), but the minutes for this session carry no record of what could have been no more than a preliminary consideration. The Council minutes are most inadequate for these months and tend to note only actions concluded rather than matters debated. Then, within a few weeks, Edward's fatal illness set in, resulting in a marked and, in the end, a serious, deterioration in the normal functioning of the Council, now almost wholly preoccupied with the problem of succession.

VI. *Notes on the English Occupation of France in the Reign of Henry VI* (late 1552?)

This quite puzzling treatise in the King's hand is found in Cotton MSS., Nero, C, x, ff. 94–97. It has not been certainly dated, though the martial interest here displayed would suggest that it may have been prepared rather late in 1552, when the King was so deeply interested in military affairs on the Continent. It should be said at once that these are working notes, never wholly organized or completed, that deal with the history of a late phase (1427–1434) of the Hundred Years' War. Reflecting the King's own dominant concerns, the interest is principally financial and administrative, with full attention to the taxes and other funds raised in France by the English for the financing of the ambitious operations undertaken in these years and with an analysis of the military resources required. The sources on which the King drew are not fully known, but the principal documentation undoubtedly is derived from the collection of William of Worcester, the chronicler, who in 1436 entered the service of Sir John Fastolf, shortly before that famous and somewhat maligned soldier resigned from active duty in 1440 at the age of sixty-two.

William of Worcester is believed to have written an apologia for Fastolf's policy and achievements in France in manuscript volumes entitled *Acta Domini Johannis Fastolf*, but if so the work is lost—at least under that title. This work may have been available to Edward, though it seems more likely that the materials were in fact included in the important collection of documents compiled by Worcester and now grouped under his name in the Lambeth Palace Library as MS. 506. These interesting papers deal in detail with the period of Bedford's regency in France and are especially concerned with the period to which Edward VI was devoting his researches. The Worcester Collection has been most admirably edited by Joseph Stevenson for the Rolls Series under the title *Letters and Papers Illustrative of the War in France* (2 vols., London, 1869). Edward drew very heavily and directly from these documents, and especially from Fastolf's report on the management of the war in France and his blunt recommendations for a complete revision of tactics if the war were to be continued.[16] There are, however, other sources on which the King seems to have drawn in his studies, notably *Names of the Nobles and Gentry Proceeding into France in 1425* (Harl. MSS., 782, f. 49b) and *List of the Retinue of the Duke of Bedford in the French War* (1545?) (Harl. MSS., 782, f. 52b). But the documents noted do not fully comprehend the sources used by Edward, particularly in his detailed analysis of the revenues gained in France for the prosecution of the war there. We are, then, dealing here with a quite ambitious research undertaking, the pity being that the final drafting of the intended historical account was not to be completed.

There remains the puzzling question of the reasons for the

---

[16] Edward's borrowings are principally from II, 411–412, 529–532, 532–534, 549–550, 559–563, and particularly from II, 575–585.

young monarch's interest in this on the whole inglorious period of the Hundred Years' War. Is it at least possible that the similarity of his own situation to that of the young Henry VI, the Protector-uncle Bedford being in his mind analogous to the Protector-uncle Somerset, was his principal concern? But Fastolf's careful and blunt advice given to an earlier Edward, Duke of Somerset, in 1440 is clearly the central interest of the King, and one wonders if he intended a life or a vindication of that famous soldier whom Shakespeare's dramatic libel was later to damage so unjustly in reputation. At the very least we may be sure that Edward's concern was academic, was historical, in temper and in nature. No passage in the *Chronicle* and no ambitious dream of either Somerset or Northumberland ever contemplated an invasion of France or a revival of an historical claim now dimmed by time and vitiated by English weakness. In point of fact, so low had English power fallen that the fondest hope of the government was for the neutrality and favor of France, for a relation symbolized by the marriage treaty concluded by the young Edward and Elizabeth of France. Edward VI evidently loved the lore of days past and of power long since spent. But he likewise dreamed of a restoration of English strength, at home and abroad, of the building of a state and a church in which his subjects might find more of peace, of well-being, and of dignity. He understood, young though he was, the aspirations and the needs of his people. There was beyond any possible doubt in the boy the potentiality of greatness—and it was the unique greatness of the House of Tudor which was in him. All this was cut short and destroyed in the months when his frail body was ravaged; what he might have been, what he might have done, was left to his great sister to achieve.

THE CHRONICLE
OF EDWARD VI

THE year of Our Lord 1537 was a prince born to King Harry the Eight[h] by Jane Seymour then Queen, who within [a] few days after the birth of her son died and was buried at the castle of Windsor. This child was christened by the Duke of Norfolk, the Duke of Suffolk, and the Archbishop of Canterbury. Afterward [he] was brought up, [un]til he came to six years old, among the women. At the sixth year of his age he was brought up in learning by Mr. Dr. [Richard] Cox, who was after[ward] his Almoner, and John Cheke, (Bachelor of Arts *crossed out*) Master of Arts,[1] two well-learned men, who sought to bring him up in learning of tongues, of the scripture, of philosophy, and all liberal sciences. Also John Belmaine,[2] [a] Frenchman, did teach him the French language. The tenth year not yet (completed *crossed out*) ended, it was appointed he should be created Prince of Wales, Duke of Cornwall, and Count Palatine of Chester. At which time, being the year of Our Lord 1547, the said King died of a dropsy, as it was thought. After whose death in-

[1] Richard Cox (1500–1591), a humanist and reformer much favored by Cranmer, was later in the reign appointed Dean of Christ Church, Oxford, and Vice-Chancellor of the University. John Cheke was the most famous Greek scholar in England and since 1540 had been Professor of Greek at Cambridge.

[2] Jean Belmaine, a French humanist of no great fame, was a rigorous drill-master and an ardent Protestant.

continent [3] came Edward, Earl of Hertford,[4] and Sir Anthony Browne, Master of the Horse, to convey this prince to Enfield, where the Earl of Hertford declared to him and his younger sister Elizabeth the death of their father.

After the death of King Henry the Eighth, his son Edward, Prince of Wales, was come to at Hertford by the Earl of Hertford and Sir Anthony Browne, Master of the Horse, for whom before[hand] was made great preparation that he might [be] created Prince of Wales, and afterward was brought to Enfield, where the death of his father was first showed him, and the same day the death of his father was showed in London, where [there] was great lamentation and weeping; and suddenly he [was] proclaimed King.[5] The next day, being the [31st] of [January] he was brought to the Tower of London, where he tarried the space of three weeks; and in the mean season the Council sat every day for the performance of the will and at length thought best that the Earl of Hertford should be made Duke of Somerset, Sir Thomas Seymour Lord Sudeley, the Earl of Essex Marquis of Northampton, and divers (other *crossed out*) knights should be made barons, as the Lord Sheffield,[6] with divers other[s]. Also they thought best to choose the Duke of Somerset to be Protector of the realm and Governor of the King's person (to which *crossed out*) during his minority, to which all the gentlemen and lords did agree, because he was the King's uncle on his mother's side. Also in this time the late King

[3] "Incontinent": at once.

[4] The reference is to Edward Seymour, the King's uncle, then Earl of Hertford. All members of the Edwardian government are noted, with an indication of the principal offices held, in the *Index*.

[5] This sentence partially repeats that just preceding. The most likely explanation is that the *Chronicle* originally began at this point, the short sketch of his childhood years being added at a later time. The preceding matter is in a somewhat different, an unformed, hand.

[6] Edmund Sheffield was created Baron Sheffield in early 1547. He was killed fighting under Northampton in the streets of Norwich during the Norfolk rising of 1549 (see below, p. 15).

was buried at Windsor with much solemnity, and the officers broke their staves, hurling them into the grave. But they were restored to them again when they came to the Tower. The Lord Lisle was made Earl of Warwick, and the lord great chamberlainship was given to him; and the Lord Sudeley [was] made Admiral of England.

All these (this *in MS.*) things were done, the King being in the Tower. Afterward, all things being prepared for the coronation, the King, being then but nine years old, passed through the City of London (and *crossed out*), as heretofore has been used, and came to the palace of Westminster, and the next day came into Westminster Hall, and it was asked [of] the people (whether they would have him to be their)[7] King, who answered "Yea, yea." Then he was crowned King of England, France, and Ireland by the Archbishop of Canterbury and all the rest of the clergy and nobles, and anointed with all such ceremonies as were accustomed, and took his oath, and gave a general pardon, and so was brought to the hall to dinner, Shrove Sunday, where he sat with the crown on his head, with the Archbishop of Canterbury and the Lord Protector, and all the Lords sat at boards in the hall beneath; and the Lord Marshal's deputy (for my Lord of Somerset was Lord Marshal) rode about the hall to make room. Then came in Sir John Dymoke,[8] Champion, and made his challenge, and so the King drank to him and he had the cup. At night the King returned to his (hall *crossed out*) palace at Westminster, where there were jousts and barriers;[9] and afterward order was taken for all his servants being with his father and [with] him [while] being prince, and the ordinary and unordinary were appointed.

In the mean season Sir Andrew Dudley, brother to my Lord

[7] Probable reading, the MS. being very faint.

[8] Dymoke was the third member of his family in direct descent to serve as King's Champion. His more famous father, of the same name, had served in this role at the coronations of Richard III, Henry VII, and Henry VIII.

[9] "Barriers": lists.

5

of Warwick, being in the "Pauncy," met with the "Lion," a principal ship of Scotland, which thought to take the "Pauncy" without resistance.[10] But the "Pauncy" approached her and she shot, but at length they came very near, and then the "Pauncy," shooting off all one side, burst all the orlop (over love *in MS*.) [11] of the "Lion" and all her tackle, and at length boarded her and took her. But on the return, by negligence, she was lost at Harwich haven with almost all her men.

In the month of May died the French King, called Francis,[12] and his son called Harry was proclaimed King. There came also out of Scotland an ambassador,[13] but [this] brought nothing to pass, and an army was prepared [to go] into Scotland.

Certain injunctions were set forth which took away divers ceremonies; and [a] commission [was] sent to take down images; and certain homilies were set forth to be read in the church.

Dr. Smith of Oxford [14] recanted at [St.] Paul's certain opinions of the mass and that Christ was not according to the order of Melchizedek.

The Lord Seymour of Sudeley married the Queen, whose name was Catherine, with which marriage the Lord Protector was much offended.[15]

There was great preparation made to go into Scotland, and

[10] Dudley, a younger brother of the Duke of Northumberland, was ordered out in the "Pauncy" to patrol the North Sea on February 27, 1547. He had been knighted in 1547 and appointed Admiral of the Northern Seas.

[11] "Orlop": deck.

[12] The King is here in error: Francis I died on March 31, 1547.

[13] David Panter, Bishop of Ross (*Calendar of . . . State Papers, Relating to . . . Spain, IX, Edward VI, 1547–1549,* ed. M. A. S. Hume and Royall Tyler [London, 1912], 127).

[14] Richard Smith, Professor of Divinity at Oxford, whose recantation took place on May 15, 1547.

[15] The marriage of Catherine Parr, the last wife of Henry VIII, with Thomas Seymour took place secretly in *ca.* April, 1547. She died after childbirth on September 7, 1548.

the Lord Protector, the Earl of Warwick, the Lord Dacre,[16] the Lord Grey [of Wilton],[17] and Mr. Bryan [18] went with a great number of nobles and gentlemen to Berwick where, the first day after his coming, he mustered all his company, which were to the number of 13,000 footmen and 5,000 horsemen. The next day he marched on into Scotland and so passed the Path.[19] Then he burned two castles in Scotland and so passed astraight [20] of a bridge where 300 Scottish light horsemen set upon him behind him, who were discomfited. So he passed to Musselburgh, where the first day after he came he went up to the hill and saw the Scots, thinking them—as they were indeed—at the least (23,000 *crossed out*) 36,000 men, and my Lord of Warwick was almost taken, chasing the Earl of Huntly,[21] by an ambush. But he was rescued by one Berteville,[22] with twelve harquebusiers on horseback, and the ambush ran away. The 7th day of September the Lord Protector thought to get the hill, which, the Scots seeing, passed the bridge over the river of Musselburgh,[23] and strove for the higher ground and almost got it. But our horsemen set upon them, who, although they stayed them,

[16] William Dacre, third Baron Dacre "of the North," was a steady and reliable soldier.

[17] Sir William Grey, thirteenth Baron Grey of Wilton, had served in the French war in 1545–1546 and played an important role in the action here described. He was later to command a large force in the repression of the Western Rising. Grey was for some years the commander at Guînes and gained fame for his brilliant defense of that fort after Calais had fallen.

[18] Sir Francis Bryan, commander of horse in the expedition.

[19] Probably the ravine, now known as Cockburnspath, slightly more than a mile inland from the coast.

[20] I.e., parallel with (?).

[21] George Gordon, fourth Earl of Huntly (1514–1562).

[22] Berteville, who was knighted on the field by Warwick, wrote an account of the battle which is preserved in Cotton MSS., Cleopatra, A, xi. A French mercenary and adventurer, he served at Pinkie and was long in the English service, while at the same time supplying news and gossip to the French ambassador in London.

[23] I.e., the river Esk.

yet were put to flight and gathered together again by the Duke of Somerset, Lord Protector, and the Earl of Warwick and were ready to give a new onset. The Scots, being amazed with this, fled their ways, some to Edinburgh, some to the sea[?], and some to Dalkeith, and there were slain 10,000 of them. But of Englishmen 51 horsemen, which were almost all gentlemen, and but one footman [were slain]. Prisoners were taken: the Lord Huntly, Chancellor of Scotland, and divers other gentlemen, and [there were] slain of lords a thousand. And Mr. Bryan, Sadler, and Vane were made bannerets.[24]

After this battle Broughty [Castle] was given to the Englishmen, and Home and Roxburgh and Eyemouth, which were fortified, and captains were put in them; and the Lord of Somerset [was] rewarded with £500 [of] lands.

In the mean season Steph[en] Gardiner,[25] Bishop of Winchester, was, for not receiving the injunctions, committed to ward.

There was also a Parliament called, wherein all chantries were granted to the King and an extreme law made for vagabonds, and divers other things.

Also the Scots besieged Broughty Castle, which was defended against them all by Sir Andrew Dudley, knight, and oftentimes their ordnance was taken and marred.

[24] Sir Francis Bryan, Sir Ralph Sadler, Sir Ralph Vane. The King's account of the battle is remarkably accurate, save for the casualty estimates.

[25] The moderately Catholic and conservative Henrician minister who had by Henry VIII's will been excluded from any share in the government established on the accession of Edward VI. His tribulations in this reign figure prominently in the later pages of the *Chronicle* (see below, pp. 10, 34, 36, 39, 40, 53.

A triumph was, where six gentlemen did challenge all comers at barriers, jousts, and tourney; and also that they would keep a fortress with thirty with them, against a hundred or under, which was done at Greenwich.

Sir Edward Bellingham [1] being sent into Ireland [as] Deputy, and Sir Anthony St. Leger [2] revoked, he took O'Connor and O'More, bringing the lords that rebelled into subjection; and O'Connor and O'More, leaving their lordships, had apiece a hundred pound pension.[3]

The Scots besieged the town of Haddington, where the captain Mr. Wilford every day made issues upon them and slew divers of them.[4] The thing was very weak but for the men, who did very manfully. Oftentimes Mr. Holcroft and Mr. Palmer did victual it by force, passing through the enemies.[5] And at the last the Rhinegrave [6] unaware set upon Mr. Palmer, who (which *in MS.*) was there with near[ly] a thousand and 500 horsemen, and discomfited him, taking him, Mr. Bowes,[7] Warden of the

[1] Bellingham was an experienced soldier who had served in the French war.

[2] St. Leger (1496?–1559) had gained administrative experience as an agent of Thomas Cromwell. He had been appointed Lord Deputy in Ireland in 1540 and was sent out again in 1550 and in 1553.

[3] Brian O'Connor and Patrick O'More, described in the *Acts of the Privy Council* as "wild Irishmen," in February, 1549, were pardoned and granted modest annuities (new ser., II, 1547–1550, ed. J. R. Dasent [London, 1890], 244).

[4] Sir James Wilford, who brilliantly defended Haddington for eighteen months against very heavy odds.

[5] Sir Thomas Holcroft and Sir Thomas Palmer were professional soldiers of considerable ability. Holcroft was rewarded in 1550 for his military services in Scotland. See also pp. 89 (Holcroft) and 86 (Palmer).

[6] Philip Francis, Rhinegrave, who was in the service of France, commanded German mercenary troops to the number of about 3,000 who had formerly served the French before Boulogne.

[7] Sir Robert Bowes (1495?–1554), a soldier and lawyer who became a trusted expert on Scottish and Border affairs.

West Marches, and divers other[s] to the number of 400, and slew a few.

(Upon St. Peter's day the Bishop of Winchester was committed to the Tower *inserted.*)

Then they made divers bragges,[8] and they had [the] like made to them. Then went the Earl of Shrewsbury, General of the Army, with a [force of] 22,000 men and burned divers towns and fortresses, which, the Frenchmen and Scots hearing, levied their siege in the month of September; in the levying of which there came [some] to Tiberio,[9] who as then was in Haddington and, setting forth the weakness of the town, told him that all honor was due to the defenders and none to the assailers; so the siege being levied, the Earl of Shrewsbury entered it and victualed and reinforced it. After his departing by night there came in to the outer court at Haddington 2,000 men, armed, taking the townsmen in their shirts, which yet defended them with the help of the watch, and at length with ordnance issued out upon them and slew a marvelous number, bearing divers hot assaults, and at length driving[?] them home and kept the town safe.

A Parliament was called,[10] where a uniform order of prayer was instituted, before made by a number of bishops and learned men gathered together in Windsor. There was granted a subsidy, and there was a notable disputation of the sacrament in the Parliament House.[11]

Also the Lord Sudeley, Admiral of England, was condemned

---

[8] "Brack" may be meant, which is synonymous with "breach."

[9] Captain Francisco Tiberio, commander of an Italian mercenary troop, was for some years in the English service.

[10] Being the second session of Edward's first Parliament, and sitting from November 24, 1548, until prorogued for Easter on March 14, 1549.

[11] Here the King refers to the famous debate in the House of Lords on the bill for uniformity. It was in these debates that Archbishop Cranmer first fully revealed his now Protestant sentiments on the doctrine of the Eucharist. The reading of the last six words of the sentence is uncertain, the MS. being nearly illegible.

to death and died the March ensuing.[12] Sir Thomas Sharington was also condemned for making false coin, which he himself confessed; [13] divers also were put in the Tower.

[12] So cool is the tone that one finds it difficult to remember that Sudeley was the King's maternal uncle and that much of Sudeley's guilt arose from his efforts to win the confidence and affection of the young monarch.

[13] As Master of the Bristol Mint; as pertinently, Sharington was deeply involved in Sudeley's machinations. The trials of Sudeley and Sharington, it should perhaps be mentioned, took place in early 1549.

Home Castle was taken by night and treason by the Scots. Mr. Wilford in a skirmish was left of his men sore hurt and taken. There was a skirmish at Broughty Castle, wherein Mr. Luttrell,[1] captain after Mr. Dudley, did burn certain villages and took Monsieur de Toge prisoner.[2]

The Frenchmen by night (besieged *crossed out*) assaulted Bolemberg[3] and were manfully repulsed. After[ward] they had made faggots with pitch, tar, tallow, rosin, powder, and wild-fire,[4] to burn the ships in the haven of Boulogne. But they were driven away by the Boulognois and their faggots taken.[5]

In Mr. Bowes's place, who was Warden of the West Marches, was put the Lord Dacre; and in the Lord Grey's place the Earl of Rutland,[6] who after his coming entered Scotland and burned divers villages and took much prey.

The people began to rise in Wiltshire, where Sir William Herbert did put them down, overrun, and slay them. Then they rose in Sussex, Hampshire, Kent, Gloucestershire, Suffolk, Warwickshire, Essex, Hertfordshire, a piece of Leicestershire, Worcestershire, and Rutlandshire, where by fair persuasions, partly of honest men[?] among themselves and partly by gentlemen, they were often appeased, and again, because certain

---

[1] Sir John Luttrell.

[2] A French officer, whose ransom was purchased by the Crown and who was being kept a prisoner in the Tower as late as April, 1550.

[3] An English fort comprising part of the defenses of Boulogne.

[4] "Wildfire": "a composition of highly inflammable substances, readily ignited, and very difficult to extinguish" (*NED*).

[5] The *Chronicle* displays a constant concern with the defense of Boulogne and its outworks. The town and its precincts had fallen to Henry VIII in 1544 and remained a heavy drain on English financial and military resources until it was returned under the terms of the ignominious peace treaty concluded with France in March, 1550.

[6] Henry Manners, second Earl of Rutland.

commissions were sent down to pluck down enclosures, then [they] did arise again.

The French King, perceiving this, caused war to be proclaimed and, hearing that our ships lay at Jersey, sent a great number of his galleys and certain ships to surprise our ships; but they, lying at anchor, beat the French [so] that they were fain to retire with a loss of a thousand of their men. At the same time the French King passed by Boulogne to Newhaven [7] with his army and took Blackness [8] by treason and the Almain camp; [9] which done, Newhaven surrendered. There were also, in a skirmish between 300 English footmen and 700 French horsemen, six noblemen slain. Then the French King came with his army to Boulogne, which, they seeing, raised Bolemberg. But because of the plague he was compelled to retire, and Châtillon was left behind as governor of the army.[10]

In the mean season, because there was a rumor that I was dead, I passed through London.[11]

After that they rose in Oxfordshire, Devonshire, Norfolk, and Yorkshire.

To Oxfordshire the Lord Grey of Wilton was sent with 1,500 horsemen and footmen; whose coming, with the assembling of the gentlemen of the country, did so abash the rebels that more than half of them ran their ways, and [of the] other[s] that tarried were some slain, some taken, and some hanged.

To Devonshire the Lord Privy Seal was sent,[12] who with his band, being but small, lay at Honiton while the rebels besieged

---

[7] The name commonly given by the English to the fortifications at Ambleteuse.

[8] An outwork of Boulogne, near Cape Gris-Nez.

[9] "Almain": German.

[10] Gaspard de Coligny, Seigneur of Châtillon (1517–1572), who later came to England on a special diplomatic mission.

[11] This date may be fixed as July 23, 1549.

[12] I.e., Lord John Russell, later Earl of Bedford.

Exeter, who did r[a]ise divers pretty feats of war. For after divers skirmishes, when the gates were burned, they in the city did continue the fire till they had made a rampart within. Also afterward, when they were undermined and powder was laid in the mine, they within drowned the powder and the mine with water they cast in; which the Lord Privy Seal hearing, thought to have gone to reinforce them [by] a by-way; of which the rebels having spial [13] [they] cut all the trees betwixt Ottery St. Mary and Exeter. For which cause the Lord Privy Seal burned that town and thought to return home. The rebels kept a bridge behind his back and so compelled him with his small band to set upon them, which he did and overcame them, killing 600 of them, and returning home without any loss of men. Then the Lord Grey and Spinola [14] with their bands came to him, and afterward Grey with 200 of Reading, with which bands he, being reinforced, came to raise the siege at Exeter, forbecause they had scarcity of victuals; and as he passed from Honiton he came to a little town of his own, whither came but only two ways, which they had reinforced with two bulwarks made of earth and had put to the defense of the same about 2,000 men, and the rest they had laid: some at a bridge called Honiton bridge, partly at a certain hedge in a highway, and the most part at the siege of Exeter. The rearward of the horsemen, of which Travers was captain, set upon the one bulwark, the vanguard and battle on the other. Spinola's band kept them occupied at their wall. At length Travers drove them into town [Clyst St. Mary], which the Lord Privy Seal burned. Then they ran to a bridge nearby, from whence being driven, there were in a plain about 900 of them slain. The next day there were met about [an]other 2,000 of them at the entry of a highway, who first desired to talk and in the mean season fortified themselves,

---

[13] "Spial": "by spying, observation, watch" (*NED*).

[14] Captain Paolo Baptista Spinola, who commanded about 150 mercenary Italian harquebusiers.

which being perceived, they ran their ways, and that same night the city of Exeter was delivered of the siege.[15]

After that they gathered at Launceston, to whom the Lord Privy Seal and Sir William Herbert went, and overthrew them, taking their chief heads and executing them. Nevertheless, some sailed to Bridgwater and went about sedition but were quickly repressed. Hitherto of Devonshire.

At this time the "Black Galley" taken.[16]

Now to Norfolk. The people suddenly gathered together in Norfolk and increased to a great number, against whom was the Lord Marquis [of] Northampton sent with the number of 1,060 horsemen, who, winning the town of Norwich, kept it one day and one night, and the next day in the morning with loss of 100 men departed out of the town, among whom the Lord Sheffield was slain (taken prisoner *crossed out*). There were taken divers gentlemen and servingmen to the number of thirty, with which victory the rebels were very glad. But afterward, hearing that the Earl of Warwick came against them, they began to stay upon a strong plot of ground upon a hill near to the town of Norwich, having the town confederate with them. The Earl of Warwick came with the number of 6,000 men and 1,500 horsemen and entered into the town of Norwich, which having won, it was so weak that he could scarcely defend it, and oftentimes the rebels came into the streets killing divers of his men and were repulsed again, yea, and the townsmen were given to mischief themselves. So, having endured their assaults

[15] This excellent account covers the final thrust of Russell for the relief of Exeter, from the first action at or near Fenny Bridges through the dreadful final carnage at Clyst Heath. The action described occurred between August 3 and 7, 1549.

[16] This obscure statement probably refers to a naval vessel taken by the French shortly before or after the declaration of war on August 8, 1549. No reference to a ship of this name has been found, though one known as the "Red Galley" (Captain Richard Brook, commanding) was on active service in May, 1549 (*APC, 1547–1550*, p. 284).

three days and stopped their victuals, the rebels were constrained for lack of meat to remove, whom the Earl of Warwick followed with 1,000 Almains and all his horsemen, leaving the English footmen in the town, and overcame them in plain battle, killing 2,000 of them and taking Kett their captain,[17] who in January following was hanged at Norwich and his head hanged out. Kett's brother [William] was taken also and punished alike.

In the mean season Châtillon besieged the pier of Boulogne, [which had been] made in the haven, and after long battery of 20,000 shot or more gave assault to it and were manfully repulsed. Nevertheless they continued the siege still and made often skirmishes and false assaults in which they won not much. Therefore, seeing they profited little that way, they planted ordnance against the mouth of the haven, that no victuals might come to it, which our men seeing, [they] set upon them by night and slew divers Frenchmen and dismounted many of their pieces. Nevertheless, the French came another time and planted their ordnance toward the sand side on the sand hills and beat divers ships of victualers at the entry of the haven; but yet the Englishmen at the King's adventure came into the haven and refreshed divers times the town. The Frenchmen, seeing they could not that way prevail, continued their battery but smally [*sic*], on which before they had spent 1,500 shot in a day, but loaded a galley with stones and gravel which they let go in the stream to sink it, but or ere [18] it sank it came near to one bank, where the Boulognois took it out and brought the stones to reinforce the pier.

Also at Guînes was a certain skirmish in which there was

---

[17] The events here described are compassed by the dates July 9 to August 27, 1549. Robert Kett, of the lesser gentry of Norfolk, was the leader of the rising which commonly bears his name.

[18] "Or ere": before ever.

about a hundred Frenchmen slain, of which some were gentlemen and noblemen.

In the mean season in England rose great stirs, likely to increase much if it had not been well foreseen.[19] The Council, about nineteen of them, were gathered in London, thinking to meet with the Lord Protector and to make him amend some of his disorders. He, fearing his state, caused the Secretary in my name to be sent to the Lords to know for what cause they gathered their powers together and, if they meant to talk with him, [to say] that they should come in peaceable manner.[20] The next morning, being the 6th of October, and Saturday, he commanded the armor to be brought down out of the armory of Hampton Court, about 500 harnesses, to arm both his and my men withal, the gates of the house to be rempared,[21] [and] people to be raised. People came abundantly to the house. That night, with all the people, at nine or ten o'clock at night, I went to Windsor, and there was watch and ward kept every night. The Lords sat in [the] open places of London, calling for gentlemen before them and declaring the causes of accusation of the Lord Protector, and caused the same to be proclaimed. After which time few came to Windsor but only mine own men of the guard, whom the Lords willed, fearing the rage of the people so lately quieted. Then began the Protector to treat by letters, sending Sir Philip Hoby,[22] lately come from his embassy

---

[19] The sense of the personal involvement of the young King seems to begin at this point. His detailed description of Somerset's overthrow remains the most reliable and authoritative record of the event.

[20] It was Sir William Petre who was sent; he remained with the London Lords until the coup had been accomplished.

[21] "Rempared": fortified.

[22] Sir Philip Hoby (1505–1558) had served Henry VIII in numerous diplomatic, military, and administrative capacities. He succeeded Thirlby as ambassador to the Emperor in April, 1548, and was in England on holiday when the opportunity came to serve as negotiator between the Lords of the Council and Somerset. During the remainder of the reign he

17

in Flanders to see to his family, who brought on his return a letter to the Protector very gentle, which he delivered to him, another to me, another to my house, to declare his faults, ambition, vainglory, entering into rash wars in mine youth, negligent looking on Newhaven, enriching of himself of my treasure, following his own opinion, and doing all by his own authority, etc.; which letters were openly read, and immediately the Lords came to Windsor, took him, and brought him through Holborn to the Tower. Afterward I came to Hampton Court, where they appointed by my consent six Lords of the Council to be attendant on me, at least two, and four knights; Lords: the Marquis [of] Northampton, the Earls of Warwick and Arundel, Lords Russell, St. John, and Wentworth; [23] knights: Sir Andrew Dudley, Sir Edward Rogers,[24] Sir Thomas Darcy, Sir Thomas Wroth. After[ward] I came through London to Westminster. The Lord of Warwick [was] made Admiral of England. Sir Thomas Cheyney [was] sent to the Emperor for relief, which he could not obtain.[25] Mr. [Nicholas] Wotton [was] made Secretary.[26]

---

served in diplomatic capacities in France, Flanders, and Germany. By no means stalwart in his religious views, Hoby retained favor in the reign of Queen Mary.

[23] Thomas Wentworth, first Baron Wentworth, was the cousin of Jane Seymour, the King's mother, and of Somerset as well.

[24] Sir Edward Rogers (1498?–1567), a native of Devon, was of a family which profited substantially from the dissolution of the monasteries. He had established himself as a Crown official, skillful in various capacities, in the late years of Henry VIII. In 1549 he was made one of the four gentlemen of the Privy Chamber, but in the next year found himself briefly in prison because of suspected connections with the Earl of Arundel. By June, 1550, he was so far restored in favor that he had gained a pension of £50 per annum. A devout Protestant, Rogers sought refuge abroad under Queen Mary and on his return gained important preferment under Elizabeth.

[25] The Emperor reported that Cheyney had been sent to him to justify the course of action taken against Somerset. Cheyney also "begged us to allow them to raise 4,000 foot and 2,000 horse" with the necessary supplies. The Emperor, for fear of breaking his treaty obligations to France, would do no more than permit England to raise 800 German horse and such

The Lord Protector, by his own agreement and submission, lost his protectorship, treasurership, marshalship, all his moveables, and near[ly] £2,000 [of] lands, by act of Parliament.

The Earl of Arundel committed to his house for certain crimes of suspicion against him, as plucking down of bolts and locks at Westminster, giving of my stuff away, etc., and put to fine of £12,000, to be paid £1,000 yearly; of which he was after[ward] released.

PART OF THE CHRONICLE 3 ANNO REG. REGIS
E. SEXT. IN CHARTA 1549

Also Mr. Southwell committed to the Tower for certain bills of sedition written with his hand and put to [a] fine of £500.[27]

Likewise Sir Thomas Arundel and Sir John committed to the Tower for conspiracies in the west[ern] parts.[28]

A parliament, where was made a manner to consecrate priests, bishops, and deacons.

Mr. Paget, surrendering his comptrollership, was made Lord

---

infantry as they might be able to recruit before the French could protest (*Cal. S. P. Span., 1547–1549*, pp. 478–479).

[26] Nicholas Wotton, Dean of Canterbury and York, appointed in the place of Sir Thomas Smith on October 15, 1549 (*APC, 1547–1550*, p. 345).

[27] Sir Richard Southwell, a Roman Catholic adherent who had gained temporary favor by his support of Northumberland.

[28] These brothers were members of a large, rich, and prolific Cornish family. Both men had lent faithful military and administrative services, principally in the West, to Henry VIII. They were distantly related to Humphrey Arundel, the most effective leader of the Western Rising. Sir John was counted by Lord Russell as not reliable in the crisis of the insurrection. While neither was directly involved, both men were repeatedly examined by the Council and were kept either in prison or under surveillance for about two years. Sir Thomas was released in October, 1551, but almost at once formed a connection with the Duke of Somerset which was to cost him his life in February, 1552. Sir John won his release in June, 1552, but remained under bond not to leave London without official leave. A. L. Rowse, *Tudor Cornwall* (London, 1941), is the best source, especially for the role of the brothers in Cornwall.

Paget of Beaudesert and cited into the higher house by a writ of Parliament.

Sir Anthony Wingfield, before Vice-Chamberlain, made Comptroller. Sir Thomas Darcy made Vice-Chamberlain.

I passed through London the 15th of October. At Hampton Court the Lord of Warwick made Lord Admiral.[29]

Guidotti[30] made divers errands from the Constable of France[31] to make peace with us, upon which were appointed four commissioners to treat, and they after long debatement made a treaty as followeth: [The rest of the page, at the least, is missing.]

[29] As written, but out of place chronologically, and partly crossed out; repeats from p. 18, above.

[30] Sir Anthony Guidotti was a Florentine merchant, long settled in London and much trusted by the Council. He was frequently used in informal but important diplomatic negotiations.

[31] Anne de Montmorency (1492–1567).

24. Peace concluded between England, France, and Scotland by, on the English side, John Earl of Bedford, Lord Privy Seal; Lord Paget de Beaudesert; Sir William Petre, Secretary; and Sir John Mason;[1] on the French side, Monsieur de Rochepot,[2] Mons. Châtillon, Guillart de Mortier,[3] and Bochetel de Sassy,[4] upon condition that all titles, tributes, and defenses should remain; that the fault of one man, except he be unpunished, should not break the league; that the ships of merchandise shall pass to and fro, that pirates shall be called back, and ships of war; that prisoners shall be delivered of both sides; that we shall not war with Scotland, except new occasion be given; that Boulogne, with the pieces of new conquest, and two basilisks,[5] two demicannon, three culverins,[6] two demiculverins, three sakers,[7] six[?teen] falcons,[8] ninety-four harquebuses à

[1] Sir John Mason (1503–1566) was educated at Oxford despite an obscure and humble parentage. He was one of the carefully selected royal pensioners sent abroad (1534–1536) to complete a humanistic education before entering the royal service. Mason aided Wyatt in diplomatic missions in Spain and the Netherlands before being appointed Clerk of the Privy Council in 1544. Knighted early in Edward's reign, Mason was in April, 1550, appointed English ambassador to France. His dispatches display considerable professional competence, but he was obliged, because of health, to request withdrawal in July, 1551. He was employed in various domestic posts during the remaining months of the reign. Though a signatory to Edward's will, Mason lent no loyalty to Northumberland in the dynastic crisis and had soon established himself in Mary's favor. A cold, competent, and imaginative man, Mason was one of the ablest of the group of humanistic officers of state that emerged in the late Henrician years.

[2] François de Montmorency, Seigneur de la Rochepot, a younger brother of the Constable Montmorency.

[3] André Guillart, Seigneur de Mortier, a French privy councillor.

[4] Guillaume Bochetel, Seigneur de Sassy, French Secretary of State.

[5] A large brass cannon, throwing a shot of about 200 pounds.

[6] A heavy cannon, with a very long barrel in relation to its bore.

[7] An old form of cannon, employed in the late fifteenth century in sieges and for ship armament.

[8] A light cannon, obsolete by this date.

croc [9] with wooden tails, twenty-one iron pieces; and Lauder and Dunglass,[10] with all the ordnance, save that that came from Haddington, shall within six months after this peace [is] proclaimed be delivered; and for the French: to pay 200,000 scutes [11] within three days after the delivery of Boulogne, and 200,000 scutes on Our Lady's Day in [the] harvest next ensuing, and that if the Scots razed Lauder, etc., we should raze Roxburgh and Eyemouth. For the performance of which on the 7th of April should be delivered at Guînes and Ardres these hostages:

Marquis de Mayenne	My Lord of Suffolk
Mons. Trémoille	My Lord of Hertford
Mons. d'Enghien	My Lord Talbot
Mons. de Montmorency	My Lord FitzWarren
Mons. de la Hunaudaye	My Lord Maltravers
Vidame de Chartres [12]	My Lord Strange [13]

Also that at the delivery of the town ours should come home, and at the first payment three of theirs; and that if the Scots

[9] An "arquebus supported on a rest by a hook of iron fastened to the barrel. From the size of its calibre it was used to fire through loopholes" (*NED*).

[10] Fortified places in Scotland still held by the English.

[11] Though used to describe several coins of small value, properly the English name for the French *écu*.

[12] The French hostages were: François de Lorraine, Marquis de Mayenne, eldest son of Claude (d. 1550), first Duc de Guise; Louis Trémoille, Seigneur de la Trémoille; Jean de Bourbon, Comte de Soissons and d'Enghien; François de Montmorency, eldest son of the Constable of France; Jean d'Annebaut, son of Claude d'Annebaut, Baron de la Hunaudaye and Admiral of France; François de Vendôme, Vidame of Chartres.

[13] The English hostages were: Henry Brandon, brother to the young Duke of Suffolk; Edward Seymour, Earl of Hertford (Somerset's eldest son by his second wife); George Talbot, only son of the Earl of Shrewsbury; John Bourchier, son and heir apparent to the Earl of Bath; Henry FitzAlan, only son of the twelfth Earl of Arundel; Henry Stanley, son and heir apparent of the third Earl of Derby. It might be noted that most of the English hostages were approximately of the King's age.

raze Lauder and Dunglass we must raze Eyemouth and Roxburgh, and no one[?] after[ward] fortify there. With comprehension [14] of the Emperor.

AN. D'NI 1550

25. This peace proclaimed at Calais and Boulogne.

29. In London. Bonfires.

30. A sermon in thanksgiving for peace, and *Te Deum* sung.

31. My Lord Somerset was (delivered [of] his bonds) and
came to court.[15]

1550—APRIL

2. The Parliament [in] April prorogued to the second day of
the term in October next ensuing.

3. Nicholas Ridley, before of Rochester, made Bishop of London and received his oath.

Thomas Thirlby, before of Westminster, made Bishop of Norwich and received his oath.

5. The Bishop of Chichester,[16] before a vehement affirmer of
transubstantiation, did preach against [it] at Westminster in the
preaching place.

Removing to Greenwich from Westminster.

6. Our hostages passed the Narrow Seas between Dover and
Calais.

7. Mons. de F[umel],[17] gentleman of the King's Privy Chamber, passed from the French King by England to the Scottish
Queen [18] to tell her of the peace.

---

[14] The Emperor had been kept informed of the negotiations.

[15] Not wholly clear in MS., which is frayed and torn.

[16] George Day, later to be deprived of his see.

[17] Thus in *Cal. S. P. Span., 1550–1552*, pp. 59, 62, 108; "M. de Funette"
in *APC, 1547–1550*, p. 424.

[18] Queen Mary of Scotland, the daughter of Claude, Duc de Guise.

An ambassador came from Gustavus the Sweden King,[19] called Andre, for a surer amity touching merchandises.

9. The hostages [were] delivered on both the sides for the ratification of the league with France and Scotland, forbecause some[one] said to Mons. Rochepot, lieutenant, that Mons. de Guise, father to the Marquis de Mayenne, was dead,[20] and therefore the delivery was put over a day.

8. My Lord Warwick made general Warden of the North, and Mr. Herbert President of Wales; and the one had granted to him a thousand marks [worth] of land, the other five hundred, and Lord Warwick 100 horsemen at my (*altered to* King) charge.

9. Licenses signed for the whole Council and certain of the Privy Chamber to keep among them (2,290 *changed to*) 2,340 retainers.

10. My Lord Somerset taken into the Council. Guidotti, the beginner of the talk for peace, recompensed with knightdom, a thousand crowns (pound *crossed out*) reward, a thousand crowns pension, and his son with 250 crowns (pound *crossed out*) pension. Certain prisoners for light matters dismissed. Agreed for delivery of French prisoners taken in the wars. Peter Vannes sent [as] ambassador to Venice.[21] Letters directed to certain nobles to take a blind legate (bishop *crossed out*) coming from the Pope calling himself Bishop of Armagh.[22] Commissions for the delivery of Boulogne, Lauder, and Dunglass.

6. Three Flemish men-of-war would have passed our ships without vailing bonnet, which they seeing shot at them and drove them at length to vail bonnet and so depart.

[19] Gustavus I (Gustavus Vasa); see below, April 24, 1550.

[20] Claude, first Duc de Guise; the date of his death was actually April 12.

[21] Peter Vannes, a native of Lucca, served Henry VIII in numerous diplomatic capacities and was Latin Secretary to both Henry VIII and Edward VI. He represented England in Venice from 1550 to 1556.

[22] Robert Waucop, a Scottish priest, was so named by the Pope; he died in Paris in 1551.

11. Mons. Trémoille, Mons. Vidame de Chartres, and Mons. Hunaudaye came to Dover; the rest tarried at Calais till they had leave.

12. Order taken that whosoever had benefices given them should preach before the King in or out of Lent, and [that] every Sunday there should be a sermon.

16. The three hostages aforesaid came to London, being met at Deptford by the Lord Grey of Wilton, Lord Braye, with divers other gentlemen to the number of twenty, and servingmen one hundred, and so brought into the City and lodged there and kept [in] houses—every man by himself.

18. Mr. Sidney [23] and Mr. Neville [24] made gentlemen of the Privy Chamber. Commission given to the Lord Cobham,[25] Deputy of Calais; Sir William Petre, Chief Secretary; and Sir John Mason, French Secretary, to see the French King take his oath, with certain instructions; and that Sir John Mason should be ambassador ledger.[26]

Commission to Sir John [Maurice] Dennis [27] and Sir William Sharington to receive the first payment and deliver the quittance.[28]

10. Sir John Mason taken into the Privy Council and William Thomas [29] made clerk of the same.

Whereas the Emperor's ambassador [30] desired leave by letters

---

[23] Later Sir Henry Sidney (1529–1586), who under Queen Elizabeth was to have a long career in governmental service in Ireland.

[24] Later Sir Henry Neville.

[25] George Brooke, Deputy of Calais from 1544 to 1549.

[26] I.e., resident ambassador.

[27] Sir Maurice Dennis (or Denys) served as Treasurer of Calais.

[28] Of the amount promised by France for the return of Boulogne (*APC, 1550–1552*, p. 5).

[29] Thomas, who had lived for some years in Italy, became an informal advisor to and confidant of the King (see above, Introduction, pp. xx–xxi).

[30] Francis van der Delft, replaced in May, 1550, by Jean Scheyve (*Cal. S. P. Span., 1550–1552*, p. 90).

patent that my Lady Mary might have (leave to say *crossed out*) mass, it was denied him; and when[?] he said we broke the league with him by making peace with Scotland, it was answered that the French King and not I did comprehend them, saving that I might not invade them without occasion.

10. Lauder being besieged of the Scots, the captain, hearing that the peace was proclaimed in England, delivered it, as the peace did will him, taking sureties that all the bargains of the peace should be kept.

18. Monsieur de Guise died.[31]

20. Order taken for the Chamber that three of the outer Privy Chamber gentlemen should always be here, and two lie in the palat [32] and fill the room of one of the four knights; that the esquires should be diligent in their office, and five grooms should be always present, of which one to watch in the bedchamber.[33]

21. The Marquis de Mayenne, the Duc d'Enghien, and the Constable's son arrrived at Dover.

23. Mons. de la Trémoille and the Vidame of Chartres and Mons. Hunaudaye came to the court and saw the Order of the Garter and the knights with the sovereign receive the communion.

24. Certain articles touching a straiter amity in merchandise sent to the King of Sweden, being these: First, if the King of Sweden sends bullion, he should have our commodities and pay no toll. Secondly, he should bring bullion to no other prince.

---

[31] See the King's entry for April 9, above.

[32] "Palat": presumably meaning "pallet": a mean couch or small bed, usually laid directly on the floor (still so used in Southern U.S.A.); "pallet-chamber" often used for room in which are placed couches for those who lie in guard of the King at night.

[33] These arrangements were designed to lend greater protection to the King in his private quarters.

Thirdly, if he brought osmunds [34] and steel and copper, etc., he should have our commodities and pay custom as an Englishman. Fourthly, if he brought any other he should have free intercourse, paying custom as a stranger, etc.[35]

It was answered to the Duke of Brunswick [Brandenburg] that whereas he offered service with 10,000 men of his band, that the war was ended; and [as] for the marriage of my Lady Mary to him,[36] there was talk for her marriage with the Infante of Portugal, which being determined, he should have answer.[37]

25. The Lord Clinton, captain of Boulogne, having sent away before[hand] all his men saving 1,800 and all his ordnance saving that [which] the treaty did reserve, issued out of the town with these 1,800, delivering it to Mons. Châtillon, receiving of him the six hostages English, a quittance for delivery of the town, and safe-conduct to come to Calais, whither when he came he placed 1,800 on the Emperor's frontiers.

27. The Marquis de Mayenne, Count d'Enghien, and the Constable's son were received at Blackheath by my Lord of Rutland, my Lord Grey of Wilton, my Lord Braye, my Lord Lisle, and

[34] "Osmunds": bars of "a superior quality of iron formerly imported from the Baltic regions, for the manufacture of arrow-heads, fish-hooks, etc." (*NED*).

[35] This summarizes accurately, though briefly, articles proposed by the Privy Council to the Swedish ambassador for a commercial treaty (*APC*, *1550–1552*, pp. 12–14). It is evident that from about this date the young monarch began to take a more direct and personal interest in the affairs of state.

[36] Edward was in error in stating that the suit was advanced by the Duke of Brunswick. The Privy Council minutes describe the proposal as from the Margrave of Brandenburg, as do later references in the Council records. Further, a misfiled dispatch (as of October, 1550, but properly October, 1549) from Albert, Margrave of Brandenburg, transmitted by Dr. Bruno, refers clearly to a proposed match between the Margrave and the Princess Mary (*Calendar of State Papers, Foreign Series, of the Reign of Edward VI, 1547–1553*, ed. W. B. Turnbull [London, 1861], p. 60).

[37] Don Luis, second son of Emmanuel I, King of Portugal.

divers gentlemen, with all the pensioners to the number of 100, beside a great number of servingmen.

It was granted that my Lord of Somerset should have all his moveable goods and leases except those that be already given.

The King of Sweden's ambassador departed home to his master.

29. The Count d'Enghien, brother to the Duke of Vendôme [38] and next heir to the crown after the King's children, the Marquis de Mayenne, brother to the Scottish Queen, and Mons. Montmorency, the Constable's son, came to the court, where they were received with much music at dinner.

26. Certain [ones] were taken that went about to have an insurrection in Kent upon May Day following, and the priest who was the chief worker ran away into Essex, where he was laid for.

30. Dunglass was delivered, as the treaty did require.

MAY

2. Joan Bocher, otherwise called Joan of Kent, was burned for holding that Christ was not incarnate of the Virgin Mary, being condemned the year before but kept in hope of conversion; and the 30th of April the Bishop of London and the Bishop of Ely [39] were to persuade her. But she withstood them and reviled the preacher that preached at her death.[40]

---

[38] Anthony Bourbon, Duke of Vendôme (d. 1562), father of Henry IV.

[39] Thomas Goodrich, since 1534 Bishop of Ely.

[40] Joan Bocher (or Boucher) held radical Anabaptist views mixed with a strain of anti-Trinitarianism. About a year later (April 25, 1551) a Unitarian, George van Parris, was also executed at Smithfield for heresy (see below, p. 58). These were the first executions for heresy in this reign. Somerset had refused to permit Joan's execution, and Cranmer had declined to conduct any active persecution. But in the spring of 1550 the government,

lemen, appareled in yellow; on the other, the Lord Strange,
s. Hunaudaye, and eight others, in blue.

The ambassadors saw the baiting of the bears and bulls.

The ambassadors, after they had hunted, sat with me at
per.

The same went to see Hampton Court, where they did hunt
d the same night return to Durham Place.

One that, by way of (have *in the MS.*) marriage,[54] had
ught to assemble the people and so to make an insurrection
Kent, was taken by the gentlemen of the shire and afterward
nished.

The ambassadors had a fair supper made them by the Duke
Somerset and afterward went into the Thames and saw both
e bear hunted in the river and also wildfire[?] cast out of
ats, and many pretty conceits.

. The ambassadors took their leave and the next day de-
arted.

JUNE

. The King came to Sheen, where was a marriage made be-
ween the Lord Lisle, the Earl of Warwick's son, and the Lady
nne, daughter to the Duke of Somerset, which done and a fair
inner made and dancing finished, the King and the ladies went
nto two chambers made of boughs, where first he [the King]
aw six gentlemen of one side and six of another run the course
f the field, twice over. Their names here do follow:

[54] The meaning is not wholly clear. On May 23 the Privy Council took
note of urgent letters from the Sheriff of Kent warning of a threatened
disturbance to be raised in Kent and Sussex "on Whitson Mondaye next."
Letters were dispatched to various persons in both counties to raise the
gentry to prevent the rising, which was supposed to begin in Heathfield,
Kent (*APC, 1550–1552,* p. 35). It is possible that a wedding there was to
be the occasion for the rising.

The first payment was paid at Calais and received by Sir
Thomas [Maurice] Dennis and Mr. Sharington.

4. The Lord Clinton, before captain of Boulogne, came to the
court, where, after thanks, he was made Admiral of England,
upon the surrender of the Earl of Warwick's patent. He was also
taken into the Privy Council and promised further reward. The
captains also and officers of the town were promised rewards.
Mons. de Brézé [41] also passed by the court [en route] to Scotland, where at Greenwich he came to the King, telling him that
the French King would see that if he lacked any commodity
that he had, he would give it [to] him and likewise would the
Constable of France, who then bore all the suing.

5. The Marquis de Mayenne departed into Scotland with Mons.
de Brézé to comfort the Queen of the death of the Duke of
Guise.

The Master of Erskine [42] and Mons. Morette's [43] brother came
out of Scotland for the acceptance of the peace, who after-
[ward] had passport to go into France.

7. The Council drew [up] a book for every shire, who should
be lieutenants in them and who should tarry with me; [44] but the
lieutenants were appointed to tarry till Châtillon's, Sassy's,[45]
and Bochetel's coming and then to depart.

9. Proclamation was made that the soldiers should return to

as well as most of the bishops, had grown alarmed at the appearance of
active Anabaptism in Kent, Essex, Suffolk, and London.

[41] Artus de Maillé, Seigneur de Brézé and de Maillé.

[42] Thomas Erskine (d. 1551), heir apparent of John, Lord Erskine, pre-
deceased his father.

[43] Charles de Soliers, Seigneur de Morette, envoy extraordinary to England.

[44] Most of the Lords of the Council who possessed military experience
were thus named in order to prevent agrarian risings such as those of the
preceding year.

[45] André Guillart, Seigneur de Mortier, is presumably meant (see below,
May 23, 1550).

their mansions,[46] and the Mayor of London had charge to look through all the wards, to take them and send them to their countries.

The debt of £30,000 and odd money was put over a year,[47] and there was bought 2,500 quintals of powder.[48]

11. Proclamation was made that all wool-winders should take (have *crossed out*) an oath that they would make good cloth there as the Lord Chancellor would appoint them according to an act of Parliament made by Edward the Third.

7. The Lord Cobham, the Secretary Petre, and Sir John Mason came to the French King to Amiens, going on his journey, where they were received of all the nobles and so brought to their lodgings, which were well dressed.

10. The French King took the oath for the acceptance of the treaty.

12. Our ambassadors departed from the French court, leaving Sir John Mason as ledger.

14. The Duke of Somerset was taken into the Privy Chamber, and likewise was the Lord Admiral [Clinton].

15. It was appointed that all the light horsemen of Boulogne and the men of arms should be paid their wages and be led by the Lord Marquis of Northampton, captain of the pensionaries, and all the guard of Boulogne under the Lord Admiral. Also that the chiefest captains should be sent with 600 with them to the strengthening of the frontiers of Scotland.

The (making *crossed out*) comprehension of peace with Scotland was accepted so far as the league went and sealed with the [*unfinished*].[49]

[46] "Mansions": houses or tents (*NED*).

[47] The debt was external, mostly held in Antwerp. A considerable proportion, due in August, was held by the Fuggers.

[48] A "quintal" = 110 or 112 pounds.

[49] The sentence may be concluded: "great seal of Scotland." I.e., comprehending Scotland within the recently concluded treaty with France.

---

16. The Master of Erskine departed into

(17. The French King came to Boul Greenwich *crossed out*.)

17. Removing to Westminster from Green

18. The French King came to Boulogne to delivered to him and to appoint an ord there, which done, he departed.

19. Peter Vannes went as ambassador to from the court with his instructions.

20. The Lord Cobham and Sir William Pe their journey, delivering both the oath, th oath witnessed by divers noblemen of F treaty, sealed with the great seal of France; confessed that I was Supreme Head of the and Ireland, and also King of Ireland.

23. Mons. Châtillon and Mortier and Boch with the Rhinegrave, d'Andelot,[50] the Consta and Chemault[52] the ledger, came to Durha their journey they were met by Mr. Treasur threescore gentlemen at Woolwich and also peals both at Woolwich, Deptford, and the To

24. The ambassadors came to me, presenting also delivering letters of credence from the Fre

25. The ambassadors came to the court, whe take the oath for the acceptance of the treaty dined with me; and after dinner saw a pastime at the ring, whereof on the one side were the l the Vidame [of Chartres], the Lord Lisle,[53] a

[50] François de Coligny, Seigneur d'Andelot, younger br

[51] Henry de Montmorency.

[52] Jean Pot de Rhodes, Seigneur de Chemault, ambas until July, 1551.

[53] John Dudley, son of the Duke of Northumberland.

The Lord Edward [Seymour].   Sir John Appleby.

[The rest omitted in the MS., though space was left.]

And afterward came three masquers of one side and two of another, which ran four courses apiece. Their names be *[left blank]*.

Last of all came the Count of Rangone,[55] with three Italians, who ran with all the gentlemen four courses and afterward fought at tourney. And so after supper he (the King) returned to Westminster.[56]

4. Sir Robert Dudley, third [*sic:* fifth] son to the Earl of Warwick, married Sir John Robsart's daughter,[57] after which marriage there were certain gentlemen that did strive who should first take away a goose's head which was hanged alive on two cross posts.

5. There was tilt and tourney on foot with as great staves as they [could] run withal on horseback.

6. Removing to Greenwich.

8. The gests [58] of my progress were set forth, which were these: from Greenwich to Westminster, from Westminster to Hampton Court, from Hampton Court to Windsor, from Windsor to Guildford,[59] from Guildford to Oatlands, from Oatlands to Richmond, etc.

Also the Vidame [60] made a great supper to the Duke of

---

[55] Pallavicino Rangone was a young Italian nobleman who was for some time in Edward's personal service on a most liberal pension. When his young cousin was killed in 1551, he became the heir of his uncle, Count Guido Rangone.

[56] Manuscript badly frayed: there may have been another word or two following "to."

[57] Amy Robsart, whose mysterious death in 1560 cast some doubt on the relations of Queen Elizabeth and Robert Dudley.

[58] "Gest": "the various stages of a journey, especially of a royal progress; the route planned and followed," first cited by the *NED* in 1550.

[59] There was a royal manor house at Guildford.

[60] The Vidame de Chartres, who among all the French hostages was particularly popular in England.

Somerset and the Marquis of Northampton, with divers masques and other conceits.

9. The Duke of Somerset, Marquis [of] Northampton, Lord Treasurer, [the Earl of] Bedford, and the Secretary Petre went to the Bishop of Winchester to know to what he would stick. He made answer that he would obey and set forth all things set forth by me and my Parliament; and if he were troubled in conscience he would reveal it to the Council and not reason openly against it.[61] (Also . . . *crossed out.*)

The first payment of the French men was laid up in the Tower for all chances.

10. The books of my proceedings was sent to the Bishop of Winchester to see whether he would set his hand to it or promise to set it forth to the people.

11. Order was given for fortifying and victualing Calais for four months; and also Sir Harry Palmer [62] and Sir [Richard] Lee [63] were sent to the frontiers of Scotland to take a view of all the forts there and to report to the Council where they thought best to fortify. There was also sent to Alderney [John] Rogers and [Thomas] Atwood to make fortifications there.[64]

12. The Marquis de Mayenne came from Scotland in post and went his way into France.

13. Commissions were signed to Sir William Herbert and thirty

[61] The beginning of the long proceedings, quite fully noted in the *Chronicle*, which were to result in Gardiner's deposition in February, 1551.

[62] The King means Sir Thomas, whose younger brother, Sir Henry, was at this date still in Calais.

[63] Sir Richard Lee was a professional soldier and a military engineer, much employed on the Border defenses.

[64] John Rogers had served at Boulogne as a military engineer. After strengthening the fortifications on Alderney and Guernsey, he was dispatched to Ireland in early 1551 (*APC, 1550–1552*, pp. 213, 227). Atwood was employed at Alderney, Guernsey, and Scilly in a similar capacity (*ibid.*, p. 46).

others to entreat of certain matters in Wales, and also instructions to the same how to behave himself in the presidentship.

14. The surveyor of Calais was sent to Calais,[65] first to raise the walls of Risebank [66] toward the sand hills and after[ward] to make the wall massy [67] again, and the round bulwark to [be] change[d] to a pointed one which should run 26 feet into the sea to beat [68] the sand hills, and to raise the mount. Secondly, to Newnhambridge [69] to make a high bulwark in the midst, with flankers [70] to beat through all the strait and also four sluices to make Calais haven better. Afterward he was bid to go to Guînes, where first he should take away the four-cornered bulwark to make the outward wall of the keep, and to fill the space between the keep and the said outward wall with the aforesaid bulwark, and to raise the old keep that it might beat[?] the town[?]. Also he was bid to make Purton's bulwark where it is now round without flankers both pointed, and also with six flankers to beat hard to the keep.

Atwood and [Thomas] Lambert were sent to take view of Alderney, Scilly, Jersey, Guernsey, and the Isle of Jethou.

The Duke of Somerset, with five others of the Council, went

[65] Thomas Petitt was the military engineer principally in charge of the elaborate Calais defenses throughout the reign.

This account of the refurbishing of the Calais fortifications is clearer and more comprehensive than that agreed on by the Council on June 13 for transmission to Petitt (*APC, 1550–1552*, p. 47).

[66] The English made a place-name out of the French word "risban," meaning a fortress defending a port.

[67] "Massy" is an earlier use than that first mentioned (1587) by the *NED;* "massive" is synonymous.

[68] The meaning would seem to be "to flank." It is so used several times in this brief passage. No notice of the word in this sense is cited by the *NED.* It might be added that "massy," "beat," and "flankers" are not used in the Privy Council's memorandum from which the King's entry is evidently derived. The King enjoyed words and already possessed his own style.

[69] An outwork of Calais.   [70] Also a first usage (*NED*).

to the Bishop of Winchester, to whom he made this answer: "I, having deliberately seen the Book of Common Prayer, although I would not have made it so myself, yet I find such things in it as satisfy my conscience and therefore both I will execute it myself and also see other my parishioners to do it." This was subscribed by the aforesaid Councillors, that they heard him saying these words.

16. The Lord Marquis [of Northampton], Mr. Herbert, the Vidame, Hunaudaye, and divers other gentlemen went to the Earl of Warwick's, where they were honorably received, and the next day there ran at the ring a great number of gentlemen.

19. I went to Deptford, being bidden to supper by the Lord Clinton, where before supper I saw certain [men] stand upon the end of a boat without hold of anything and ran one at another until one was cast into the water. At supper Mons. Vidame and Hunaudaye supped with me. After supper was there a fort made upon a great lighter on the Thames, which had three walls and a watchtower in the midst, of which Mr. Winter was captain,[71] with forty or fifty other soldiers in yellow and black. To the fort also appertained a galley of yellow color with men and munition in it for defense of the castle. Wherefore there came four pinnaces with their men in white handsomely dressed, which, intending to give assault to the castle, first drove away the yellow pinnace, and after[ward] with clods, squibs, canes of fire, darts made for the nonce, and bombards [they] assaulted the castle; and at length [they] came with their pieces and burst the outer walls of the castle, beating them of the castle into the second ward, who after[ward] issued out and drove away the pinnaces, sinking one of them, out of which all the men in it, being more than twenty, leaped out and swam in the Thames. Then came the Admiral of the Navy with three other pinnaces and won the castle by assault and burst the top of it down and took the captain and under-captain. Then the

[71] William Winter, the King's Surveyor of Ships.

Admiral went forth to take the yellow ship and at length clasped with her, took her, and assaulted also her top, and won it by composition [72] and so returned home.

20. The Mayor of London caused the watches to be increased every night because of the great frays, and also one alderman to see good rule kept every night.

22. There was a privy search made through all Sussex for all vagabonds, gypsies, conspirators, prophets, ill players, and such-like.

24. There were certain [men who] in Essex about Romford went about a conspiracy, which were taken and the matter stayed.[73]

25. Removing to Greenwich.

23. Sir John Gates,[74] Sheriff of Essex, went down with letters to see the Bishop of London's injunctions performed, which touched plucking down of superaltars,[75] altars, and suchlike ceremonies and abuses.

29. It was appointed that the Germans should have the Austin Friars for their church to have their service in, for avoiding of all sects of Anabaptists and suchlike.[76]

17. The French Queen was delivered of a third son, called Mons. d'Angoulême.[77]

---

[72] I.e., by treaty, or agreement.

[73] This is the principal authority for the incident, one of a number which the nervous government was putting down with harsh vigilance as the dreaded summer months approached.

[74] Gates, a courtier and servant of the Crown, had enjoyed Henry VIII's favor and confidence. A strong partisan of Northumberland, he was executed with the Duke.

[75] I.e., reredos.

[76] Under the supervision of the noted Polish reformer, John à Lasco, who had arrived in England about a month earlier. The congregation consisted principally of Flemish, Dutch, German, Italian, and French denizens in London.

[77] Afterward to succeed to the French throne as Charles IX. The King's

13. The Emperor departed from Argentina [Strassburg] to Augusta [Augsburg].

30. John Ponet made Bishop of Rochester and received his oath.

JULY

5. There was money provided to be sent into Ireland for payment of the soldiers there, and also order taken for the dispatch of the strangers in London.

7. The Master of Erskine passed into Scotland, coming from France. Also the French ambassador [78] did come before me, first, after showing the birth of Mons. d'Angoulême, afterward declaring that, whereas the French King had for my sake let go the prisoners at St. Andrew's, who before they were taken had shamefully murdered the Cardinal,[79] he desired that all Scots that were prisoners [should be released]; it was answered that all were delivered. Then he moved for one called the Archbishop of Glasgow, who since the peace came disguised without passport and so was taken; it was answered that we had no peace with Scotland such that they might pass [through] our country, and the Master of Erskine affirmed the same.[80]

---

entry is dated, quite out of sequence, as June 17; but the birth is dated June 27, and Mason's dispatch informing the Council of the event was dated June 29 (*Cal. S. P. For., 1547–1553*, p. 49). This suggests that the King occasionally added entries after a month had passed and that in this instance he simply misdated the event. So too in the next (and added) entry, which appears to have been drawn from a dispatch from Mason dated Paris, June 14 (*ibid.*, pp. 48–49). In this instance the dating of the Emperor's departure from Strassburg is correct.

[78] Seigneur de Chemault.

[79] Those taken in 1547 on the capture of St. Andrews, shortly after the assassination of Beaton in 1546. Among those in this group who were condemned to the galleys was John Knox.

[80] Alexander Gordon, brother to the Earl of Huntly, was in 1547 elected Archbishop of Glasgow, though, the election being disputed, the Pope instead appointed James Beaton to the see. Gordon, who was later to

8. It was agreed that the two hundred that were with me, and two hundred with Mr. Herbert, should be sent into Ireland.[81] Also that the mint should be set awork that it might win £24,000 a year and so bear all my charges and [82] Ireland for this year, and [add] £10,000 to my coffers.[83]

9. The Earl of Warwick, the Lord Treasurer, Sir William Herbert, and the Secretary Petre went to the Bishop of Winchester with certain articles signed by me and the Council, containing the confessing of his fault: the supremacy, the establishing of holy days, the abolishing of [the] six articles, and divers other, whereof the copy is in the Council chest, whereunto he put his hand, save (saving *in MS.*) to the confession.

10. Sir William Herbert and the Secretary Petre were sent unto him to tell him I marveled that he would not put his hand to the confession; to whom he made answer that he would not put his hand to the confession forbecause he was innocent; and also the confession was but the preface of the articles.

11. The Bishop of London, the Secretary Petre, Mr. Cecil,[84] and Goodrich were commanded to make certain articles according to the laws and to put them in the submission.[85]

---

embrace Protestantism, was, as stated, detained in England while trying to pass from France to Scotland. The Council, not wishing to offend France, was uncertain of its position until "the treaties being examined it appeared plaine that he rested good prisoner" (*APC, 1550–1552*, p. 62; Alexandre Teulet, *Relations politiques de la France et de l'Espagne avec l'Écosse au XVIe Siècle* [Paris, 1862], I, 240–242).

[81] I.e., from the bands of semi-professional horse now attached to the King and to the principal Lords.

[82] Thus in the MS.; "and" is probably a slip for "in."

[83] From this decision was to result the ruinous debasement of the Irish coinage.

[84] Sir William Cecil, Principal Secretary to Edward VI; afterward Lord Burghley, the great Elizabethan minister.

[85] The submission, that is, of the Bishop of Winchester.

12. It was appointed that under the shadow of preparing for the same[?] (ea *in MS.*) matters there should be sent £5,000 to the Protestants to get their good will.[86]

14. The Bishop of Winchester did deny the articles that the Bishop of London and the other had made.

13. Sir John Gates sent into Essex to stop the going away of the Lady Mary, because it was credibly informed that Scepperus should steal her away to Antwerp, divers of her gentlemen were there, and Scepperus a little before came to see the landing places.[87]

16. It was appointed that the two hundred with the Duke of Somerset and two hundred with the Lord Privy Seal and four hundred with Mr. St. Leger should be sent to the seacoast.

17. It was agreed that on Wednesday next we should go in one day to Windsor and dine at Sion.

18. It was thought best that the Lord Bowes should tarry in his wardenship still, and the Earl of Warwick should tarry here and be recompensed.

19. The Bishop of Winchester was sequestered from his fruits for three months.

20. Hooper was made Bishop of Gloucester.[88] The merchants

[86] The reference is at once intriguing and very obscure. In the Privy Council minutes for July 4 it is indicated that the progress of the King's affairs in Scotland, among other places, was being hindered for want of ready cash. On the next day the officers of the mint were called in and asked to name funds that could be made available (*APC, 1550–1552,* pp. 62–63). It seems probable that the King here refers to money being moved into Scotland in these months, which was being employed with considerable success in enlarging the English interest and in advancing Protestantism.

[87] Corneille Scepperus (M. d'Eecke) was in command of the Emperor's naval reconnaissance in this ill-conceived venture of which the Privy Council was fully informed.

[88] John Hooper, the great preacher and Marian martyr.

were commanded to stay as much as they could their vent [89]
into Flanders because the Emperor had made many strait laws
against them that professed the Gospel.

21. A muster was made of the Boulognois, who were wholly
paid for all past and a month to come.

Sir John Wallop, Francis Hall, and Doctor Cook were appointed commissioners to appoint the limits between me and the
French King.[90]

23. Removing to Windsor.

22. The Secretary Petre and [the] Lord Chancellor were appointed to go to the Lady Mary to cause her to come to Woking
or to the court.

25. It was appointed that half the French King's first payment
should be bestowed on paying £10,000 at Calais, £9,000 in Ireland, £16,000 in the North, 2,000 in the Admiralty, so that every
crown might go for one of our nobles.[91]

27. Because the rumor came so much of Scepperus' coming, it
was appointed that they of the Admiralty should set my ships in
readiness.[92]

26. The Duke of Somerset went to set order in Oxfordshire,
Sussex, Wiltshire, and Hampshire.

28. The Lady Mary after long communication was content to

[89] "Vent": "market or outlet for commodities"; the *NED* gives 1548
as the first use.

[90] Sir John Wallop, commander at Guînes, Francis Hall, comptroller at
Calais, Sir Richard Reed, a master of chancery, and William Cook, a
master of requests, were appointed to arbitrate the boundaries of the
King's possessions remaining in France (*APC, 1550–1552*, p. 82: July 17).

[91] I.e., was to be given the exchange value of 6s.8d. for each crown;
but by proclamation on December 6 the crown was declared to have
the value of 6s.4d., unless presented forthwith to the mint, where it
would be exchanged at the rate of 7s. There are numerous entries in the
Acts of the Privy Council on this matter.

[92] To safeguard against the attempt to carry Mary out of the country.

come to Leighs [93] to the Lord Chancellor and then to Hunsdon,[94] but she utterly denied to come to the court or Woking at that time.

31. The Earl of Southampton died.[95]

14. Andrea Doria took the city of Africa [Mehedia] from the pirate Dragut, who in the mean season burned the country of Genoa.[96]

8. The Emperor came to Augsburg.[97]

[AUGUST]

4. Mr. St. Leger was appointed by my letters patent to be deputy there [in Ireland] and had his commission, instructions, and letters to the nobles of Ireland for the same purpose.[98]

5. The same deputy departed from the castle of Windsor.

6. The Duke of Somerset departed to Reading to take an order there.

7. It was appointed that of the money delivered to me by the French King there should be taken 100,000 crowns: to pay

[93] Leighs Priory, the country seat which Rich had established near Braintree in Essex.

[94] The residence of George Carey, later Baron Hunsdon, in Hertfordshire.

[95] Wriothesley, the former Lord Chancellor, died in London but was buried at his seat in Titchfield, Hampshire.

[96] Edward was much interested in this ambitious operation led by Andrea Doria against Arraiz Dragut, who had heavily fortified Mehedia. The Sultan intervened on the grounds that Dragut was in his service and that the city was his property. The King is in error in stating that Doria had carried the city on July 14. In point of fact the first assault was not made until July 25 in what was to prove a long and difficult operation (*Venetianische Depeschen vom Kaiserhofe,* ed. Gustav Turba, II [Vienna, 1892], 443–445, 483, 484).

[97] Once more, the final entries for the month are evidently *post scripta,* inserted after the diplomatic dispatches had been received.

[98] St. Leger, going out for a second tour of duty in Ireland, replaced the very competent and successful Sir Edward Bellingham, who had recently died.

10,000 pounds at Calais, [15],000 in the North and 2,000 in the Admiralty and 8,000 in Ireland.[99]

8. Mons. Hunaudaye took his leave to depart to Calais and so upon the payment to be delivered home; and Trémoille, being sick, went in a horse-litter to Dover.

9. The French ambassador came to Windsor to sue for a passport for the Dowager of Scotland, which being granted, so she came like a friend, he required 300 horse to pass with 200 keepers, which was not wholly granted, but only that 200 horse with 150 keepers in one company, coming into this realm as should be appointed, should without let pass into France and not return this way.[100]

11. The Vidame of Chartres showed his license to tarry here and a letter written to the same purpose.[101]

10. The ambassador of France departed, not a little contented with his gentle answers.

12. Removing to Guildford.

13. The Parliament was prorogued to the 20th of February next following.[102] Mr. Cook, Master of Requests, and certain

[99] See July 25, above, for a somewhat different account.

[100] The Queen Mother (Mary) wished to visit her daughter, Mary Queen of Scots, then in France. The journey was not made as here arranged; rather Mary passed by sea (September 7, 1550) from Edinburgh to Dieppe, returning to Scotland by way of England in November, 1551 (see below, pp. 89–94). For details of the proposed passage through England, see *APC, 1550–1552*, pp. 95–96, 101.

[101] François de Vendôme, the last of the French "hostages," did not leave England until shortly after September 8, 1550, when the Council granted a passport to him and his entourage of thirty persons to proceed through Scotland on his journey to France. Henry Dudley was appointed to accompany him, and a groom of the chamber was instructed to proceed ahead of the party in order to arrange for lodgings (*ibid.*, p. 121).

[102] To be prorogued again until October 13. The proposed date for the new session is stated as January 20 in *APC, 1550–1552*, p. 104. The Privy Council minutes, incidentally, contain no reference to the declared intention to review the statutes.

other lawyers were appointed to make a short table of the laws and acts that were not wholly unprofitable and to present it to the board.[103]

1[3?]. The Lord Chancellor fell sore sick, with forty more of his house, so that the Lady Mary came not thither at that time.

14. There came divers advertisements from [Sir Thomas] Chamberlain,[104] ambassador with the Queen of Hungary,[105] that their very intent was to take away the Lady Mary and so to begin an outward war and an inward conspiracy, insomuch that the Queen said Scepperus was but a coward and, for fear of one gentleman that came down, durst not go forth with his enterprise to my Lady Mary.[106]

16. The Earl of Maxwell came down to the north borders with a good power to overthrow the Grahams, who were a certain family that were yielded[107] to me. But the Lord Dacre stood before his face with a good band of men and so put him from his purpose, and the gentlemen called Grahams skirmished with the said Earl, slaying certain of his men.[108]

17. The Council appointed among themselves that none of them

[103] This is an earlier instance of the use of the convenient word "board" in this sense than that noted (1575) in the *NED*.

[104] Chamberlain was for some time president of the guild of English merchants trading in Flanders, a post resembling that of a modern consul (*Cal. S. P. Span.*, *1547–1549*, p. 246). He was accredited, with Sir Thomas Smith, to try to smooth out Anglo-Flemish relations in January, 1548. Though never popular in Flanders, he was later appointed ambassador to the Queen Regent in Brussels.

[105] The Emperor's sister, Mary, who served as Queen Regent in the Netherlands from 1530 until 1550, was Queen Dowager of Hungary.

[106] The Queen Dowager and the Emperor were blandly denying that the incident had ever occurred or been planned.

[107] I.e., submissive.

[108] This marauding force of Scots and French was led by Sir John Maxwell, the brother of the then Earl of Maxwell. Sir John was in March, 1552, appointed Warden of the Western Marches but was too deeply involved in clan feuds to be effective. He was later to become an ardent partisan in Scotland for Mary Queen of Scots.

should speak in any man's behalf for land to be given, reversion of offices, leases of manors, or extraordinary annuities, except for certain captains who served at Boulogne, their answer being deferred to Michaelmas next.[109]

18. A proclamation that until Michaelmas all strangers that sued for pensions should go their way.

20. Removing to Woking.

15. The second payment of the French was paid and Hunaudaye and Trémoille delivered.

21. Eight thousand pounds of the last payment was appointed to be paid to the dispatch [110] of Calais, and 5,000 to (at *in MS.*) the North.

24. Ten thousand [pounds] was appointed to be occupied to win money to pay the next year [for] the outward pay[?], and it was promised that the money should double every month.[111]

20. Removing to Oatlands.

27. Andrea Doria gave a hot assault to the town of Africa, kept by the pirate called Dragut Arraiz, but was repulsed by the townsmen.

[109] This self-denying ordinance was induced by the financial crisis which had by this date overtaken the government.

[110] "Dispatch" seems to antedate the earliest use (1581) of the word in this sense to be cited by the *NED.*

[111] The matter here discussed remains most obscure. The word "paise" is clearly written in the MS., but I am supposing that "pay" is meant. It was decided, in other words, to use £10,000, presumably in exchange manipulations in Antwerp (later rather successfully managed by Gresham) in order to gain larger resources wherewith to pay down English debits there. But the astonishing rate of gain "promised" is hardly credible, even to the always sanguine Northumberland. This passage, so casually and vaguely set down, is the earliest indication of the King's rapidly maturing interest in the financial position of the government. Reforms and measures of considerable merit and importance were to be advanced in the next year.

29. The pirate gave a hot assault to Andrea Doria by night and slew the captain of Tunis, with divers other notable men.

31. The Duke Maurice [of Saxony] made answer to the Emperor that if the Council were not free he would not come to (at *in MS.*) it.

SEPTEMBER

2. Maclamore in Ireland, before a rebel, by the means of Mr. Brabazon surrendered himself and gave pledges.[112]

6. Mr. Wotton gave up his secretaryship, and Mr. Cecil (took it.)[113]

SEPTEMBER A° D'NI 1550, 2ª CHARTA

8. Removing to Nonesuch.

15. Removing to Oatlands.

22. A proclamation was set forth by the which it was commanded, first, that no kind of victual, no wax, tallow candles, nor no such thing should be carried over except to Calais, putting in sureties to go thither. Secondarily, that no man should buy or sell the selfsame things again, except brokers, who should not have more than ten quarters of grain at once. Thirdly, that all justices should divide themselves into hundreds, rapes, and wapentakes, to look in their quarters [to see] what superfluous corn were in every barn and appoint it to be sold at a reasonable price. Also that one of them must be in every market to see the corn brought. Furthermore, whosoever shipped over anything aforesaid to the parties of beyond sea or [to] Scotland after eight days following the publication of the proclamation

[112] Sir William Brabazon had served since 1534 as Vice-Treasurer and General Receiver for Ireland. I have found no notice of Maclamore (could M'Callum More be meant?). This probably refers to the pacification of Mac-Art-Cavenagh, who in August, 1550, was subdued by Brabazon, being forced to renounce his name and sue for pardon.

[113] Probable reading; MS. frayed.

should forfeit his ship and the ware[s] therein, half to the lord of the franchise and half to the finder thereof. Whoso bought to sell again after the day aforesaid should forfeit all his goods, farms, and leases to the use one half of the finder, the other of the King. Whoso brought not in corn to the market as he was appointed should forfeit ten pounds, except the purveyors took it up or it was sold to his neighbors.[114]

25. Letters sent out to the justices of [the] peace for the due execution thereof.

18. Andrea Doria had a repulse from the town of Africa and lost many of his men and the captain of Tunis and nevertheless left not yet the siege.

24. Order was given for the victualing of Calais.

26. The Lord Willoughby,[115] Deputy of Calais, departed and took his journey thitherward.

28. The Lord Treasurer [Paulet] sent to London to give order for the preservation of the City with the help of the Mayor.

15. Whereas the Emperor required a Council, they were content to receive it so it were free and ordinary, requiring also that every man might be restored to his right and a general peace proclaimed. They desired also that in the mean season no man might be restrained to use his [the Emperor's] fashion of religion.

18. The Emperor made answer that the Council should be to the glory of God and maintenance of the empire, at Trent. He knew no title to any of his territories. Peace he desired and in the mean season would have them observe the Interim and

[114] The proclamation (*STC* 7832) was dated September 24, 1550; text in *Tudor Royal Proclamations*, ed. P. L. Hughes and J. F. Larkin, I (New Haven, 1964), 499–503.

[115] William Willoughby, first Baron Willoughby of Parham, apparently appointed in place of Cobham, who since May had been engaged in arbitration with the French King. See above, pp. 30, 31, and *APC, 1550–1552*, p. 128 (Sept. 22).

[the] last Council of Trent; he would also that they of Bremen and Hamburg, with their associates, should leave their seditions and obey his decrees.[116]

21. George, Duke of Mecklenburg, came with 8,000 men of war to the city of Magdeburg, being Protestant, against whom went forth the Count of Mansfeld and his brother with 6,000 men and eight guns, to drive him from pillage. But the other, abiding the battle, put the Count to flight, took his brother prisoner, and slew 3,000 men, as it is reported.[117]

OCTOBER

4. Removing to Richmond.

5. The Parliament prorogued to the twentieth of January.

6. The French King made his entry into Rouen.[118]

10. It was agreed that [Sir John] York, master of one of the mints at the Tower, should make this bargain with me, viz.: To make the profit of (my *crossed out*) silver rising of the bullion that he himself brought, [he] should pay all my debts, to the sum of £120,000 [119] or above, and remain accountable for the overplus, paying no more but 6*s.* and 6*d.* the ounce, till the ex-

[116] This and the preceding entry reflect fairly accurate and immediate knowledge of the attitude of the German Protestant princes toward the Emperor's demand that the Council of Trent be reconvened. The foreign papers, in so far as they relate to German affairs, are singularly sparse for the autumn of 1550, and it is not clear from what source the King derived his information. The "Interim" is the religious settlement imposed by the Emperor on Germany by decree at the Diet of Augsburg in 1548.

[117] This action occurred on September 22, 1550. Full and formal diplomatic information on the sortie, so far as can be determined, did not reach London until December. The siege of Magdeburg was shortly to become a matter of keen interest in London.

[118] This event was described in glowing detail by Sir John Mason, who was with the French King, in a dispatch dated October 6 from Rouen. The entrance was in fact made on October 1 (*Cal. S. P. For.*, *1547–1553*, pp. 56–57).

[119] Stated as 1,200,000, in error, in the MS.

change were equal in Flanders, and after[ward] 6s. and 2d. Also that he should declare all his bargains to any [who] should be appointed for to oversee him and leave off when I would. For which I should give him £15,000 in prest-[money] [120] and leave to carry £8,000 overseas to abase the exchange.[121]

16. Removing to Westminster.

19. Prices were set on (of *in* MS.) all kind of grains, butter, cheese, and poultry ware by a proclamation.

20. The Frenchmen came to Sandingfield and Fiennes-wood to the number of 800 and there on my ground did spoil my subjects that were relieved by the wood.[122]

26. The French ambassador came to excuse the aforesaid men, saying they thought it not meet that that wood should be spoiled of us, being thought and claimed as theirs, and therefore they lay there.

24. There were 1,000 men embarked to go to Calais, and so to Guînes and Hammes, Risebank, Newnhambridge, the Cause-[wa]y, and the bulwarks, with victuals for the same.[123]

NOVEMBER

19. There were letters sent to every bishop to pluck down the altars.

20. There were letters sent down to the gentlemen of every shire for the observation of the last proclamation touching corn,

[120] I.e., in advance.

[121] Further light on this scheme is to be found in S. P. Dom., Edw. VI, X, 45 (Oct. 8, 1550), when Peckham, Treasurer of the Mint, was instructed to pay in to York all coin and bullion brought into the mint. This strange scheme resulted in further debasement of the coinage and in large profits for York, who in 1552 was pardoned for various offenses in the mint and required to pay the large sum of £9,532 6s.2d. to amend his accounts (*Calendar of the Patent Rolls Preserved in the Public Record Office, Edward VI*, IV, *1550–1553* [London, 1926], 301).

[122] In the marches of Calais.

[123] For strengthening Calais and its outworks.

because there came none to the markets—commanding them to punish the offenders.[124]

29. Upon the letters written back by the same, the proclamation was abolished.[125]

[DECEMBER]

15. There were (was *in MS.*) letters sent for the taking of certain chaplains of the Lady Mary for saying mass, which she denied.

19. Borthwick was sent to the King of Denmark with privy instructions for marriage of the Lady Elizabeth to his son.[126]

20. There was appointed a band of horsemen divided amongst the nobles, a hundred to the Duke of Somerset. Fifty [each] to my Lord Marquis North[ampton], to the Earl of Warwick, Lord Privy Seal, Mr. Herbert, Mr. Treasurer (To the Lord Treasurer *crossed out*), Lord Ma[rquis] Dorset, Earl of Wilt-[shire], Lord Wentworth, Lord Admiral, Lord Paget, Mr. Sadler, Mr. Darcy.

21. Removing to Greenwich.

26. Peace concluded between the Emperor and the Scots.

---

[124] S. P. Dom., Edw. VI, XI, 5, 6 (Nov. 17, 1550).

[125] Grain was simply withheld from the markets. Upon most strenuous complaints from responsible persons in leading market towns, the order requiring the sale of grain at fixed prices was rescinded (*ibid.*, XI, 10, 11, 15).

[126] Sir John Borthwick had for more than a year past been serving as English agent to the Baltic countries. A Danish envoy was in London in late November, 1550, and these negotiations probably followed. Borthwick was instructed by the Council to stress the commercial and religious bonds between the two countries. This done, he was to open the marriage proposals, stressing the learning, religion, and appearance of the princess. Further, he was to disclaim all official powers and even the Council's knowledge of his representations (Harl. MSS., 353, ff. 38–39). A full discussion of this proposal may be found in Nichols, *Literary Remains*, II, 297–299. The prince in question was the future Frederick III of Denmark.

6. The Earl of Arundel remitted of £8,000 which he ought to have paid for certain faults he had committed within twelve years.[1]

7. There was appointed, forbecause the Frenchmen did go about practice [2] in Ireland, that there should be prepared four ships, four barks, four pinnaces, and twelve victualers to take three havens, of which two were on the south side toward France and one in James Carr's the Scot's country,[3] and also to send and break the aforesaid conspiracies.

10. Three ships, being sent forth into the Narrow Seas, took certain pirates and brought them into England, where the most part [of them] was hanged.

27. Mons. de Lansac [4] came from the French King by way of request to ask that Cawe Mills, the fishing of the Tweed, Edrington,[5] the Ground [De]batable,[6] and the Scottish hostages that were put here in the King's my father's days should be delivered to the Scots; that they might be suffered to traffic as though they were in peace, and that all interest of the aforesaid houses [hostages?] should be delivered to the Scots. Also that those pris-

---

[1] Arundel enjoyed no power in the period of Somerset's dominance. He was one of several Roman Catholic adherents who lent support to Warwick at the moment of crisis when Somerset was deposed. Then, and very quickly, Warwick turned on Arundel with dubious charges, including the looting of the King's stores at Westminster, which were never fully revealed. He was fined £12,000, of which the larger part is here remitted.

[2] "Practice": conspiracy or treachery (NED).

[3] The vessels came into the Firth of Forth on January 25, 1551, under the command of William Winter, capturing, grounding, or scattering the small French naval force lying there. "The Homes and the Carrs" were on reflection disposed to lend their aid and support.

[4] Louis de Saint-Gelais, Seigneur de Lansac, later ambassador to Rome.

[5] Edrington Castle (near Berwick-on-Tweed) and the adjacent Cawe Mills.

[6] In Northumberland, between the Esk and the Sark.

oners which were bound to pay their ransoms before the peace (their departure *crossed out*) last concluded should not enjoy the benefit of the peace.[7]

18. The Lord Cobham was appointed to be general lieutenant of Ireland.[8]

30. Letters written to Mr. St. Leger to repair to the south[ern] parts of Ireland with his force.

FEBRUARY

3. Mr. Croft appointed to go into Ireland and there with [John] Rogers and certain artificers to take the havens aforesaid and begin some fortifications.[9]

5. Divers merchants of London were spoken withal for provision of corn out of Denmark, about 40,000 quarters.

10. Mountford [10] was commanded to go to provide for certain preparations of victuals for the ships that should go into Ireland.

11. Also for provision to be sent to Berwick and the north parts.

16. Whalley was examined for persuading divers nobles of the realm to make the Duke of Somerset Protector at the next Par-

---

[7] The entry antedates a similar entry of February 1, 1551, in *APC, 1550–1552*, pp. 204–205. The Council determined "to take deliberacion, praying the Frenche to have pacience for a fewe daies and they shulde be aunswered accordingly." On February 14 the Council returned a conciliatory and on the whole yielding answer to the points reasonably advanced by the French in relation to the recent treaty of peace.

[8] Cobham, sometime Deputy of Calais (see above, pp. 30, 31, 47), was appointed to take charge of military preparations against a feared invasion by the French (*APC, 1550–1552*, p. 195: January 19, 1551).

[9] Sir James Croft was one of the most experienced of the professional soldiers available, suggesting the serious concern of the Council for the safety of Ireland.

[10] Osbert Mountford (or Munford) was a great dealer in bread grains, often officially engaged by the government as victualer.

liament and stood to the denial, the Earl of Rutland affirming it manifestly.[11]

13. The Bishop of Winchester, after a long trial, was deposed of his bishopric.

20. Sir William Pickering,[12] knight, was dispatched to the French King for answer to Mons. de Lansac, to declare that, although I had [the] right in the aforesaid places yet I was content to forbear them under conditions to be agreed on by commissioners on both sides, and [that] for the last article I agreed without condition.

25. The Lord Marquis Dorset appointed to be Warden of the North Borders, having three sub-wardens, the Lord Ogle [in the Middle March], and Sir [Nicholas Strelley] in the East, and the Lord [John] Conyers in the West.[13]

Also Mr. Aucher had the charge for victualing of Calais.[14]

28. The learned man Bucer died at Cambridge, who was two days after[ward] buried in St. Mary's Church at Cambridge, all the whole university with the whole town bringing him to the grave, to the number [of] 3,000 persons; also there was an oration of Mr. Haddon made very eloquently at his death and a

[11] Richard Whalley, Receiver of Yorkshire, was a loyal friend to the Duke of Somerset. He was first denounced by Rutland to the Council on February 16 for "evil words" and was committed to the Fleet. He and Rutland were heard again by the Council on February 18. Whalley was discharged under bond in early April but was one of the first of Somerset's known supporters to be arrested in October (*APC, 1550–1552*, pp. 215, 217, 248, 295, 391).

[12] Sir William Pickering (1516–1575), courtier and diplomatist, was in late June, 1551, appointed resident ambassador to France, serving until his recall some time after Mary's accession.

[13] The Council, in appointing Henry Grey, third Marquis of Dorset, recorded its wish to have a "man of honor" and experience in the North (*APC, 1550–1552*, p. 223). The three subordinate wardens were all experienced soldiers or administrators. Strelley, long an officer in the royal service, was captain of Berwick.

[14] Sir Anthony Aucher was killed in the siege of Calais (1558).

sermon of [Dr. Matthew Parker]. After that Mr. Redman made a third sermon. Which three sermons made the people wonderfully to lament his death. Last of all, all the learned men of the university made their epitaphs in his praise, laying them on his grave.[15]

MARCH

3. The Lord Wentworth, Lord Chamberlain, died about ten of the clock at night, leaving behind him sixteen children.[16]

8. Sir John York had great loss, about £2,000 worth[?] of silver, by treason of Englishmen, which he brought for provision of the mints. Also [Sir Andrew] Judd 1,500; also Tresham [Sir John Gresham] 500; so the whole came to £4,000.[17]

FEBRUARY

20. The Frenchmen came with a navy of 160 sails into Scotland, laden with provision of grain, powder, and ordnance, of which sixteen great ships perished on Ireland['s] coast, two laden with

[15] This moving passage on the death of Martin Bucer suggests the genuinely religious interests of the King. He left space for the name of Matthew Parker, Elizabeth's first Archbishop of Canterbury.

[16] Lord Wentworth had succeeded Arundel as Lord Chamberlain of the Household. He was aged fifty at his death.

[17] The incident is very obscure, particularly in English official sources. Evidently these three prominent Englishmen, acting with governmental knowledge, were betrayed to the Flemish authorities when on the point of smuggling out bullion. Jean Scheyve, the imperial ambassador, reported on April 9, 1551, that "for the last few days no one has talked about anything here except the confiscation of metal and ammunition made a short time ago at Antwerp, and the Council have been much exercised about it" (*Cal. S. P. Span., 1550–1552,* p. 264). Scheyve suggested that at first restitution was to be demanded on the grounds that the property belonged to the King, but that since the total worth involved was not more than £4,000 to £5,000 it had been decided not to press the matter. He indicated further that York and his friends had been recompensed by profitable licenses for the export of leather and other goods.

artillery and fourteen with corn. Also in this month the Deputy there set at one certain of the west lords that were at variance.

MARCH

10. Certain new fortifications were devised to be made at Calais, [so] that at Gravelines the water should be let in in my ground and so should fett [18] a compass by the six bulwarks to Guînes, Hammes, and Newnhambridge, and that there should be a wall of 8 foot high and 6 broad of earth to keep out the water, and to make a great marsh about the territory of Calais 37 miles long. Also for flankers at the keep of Guînes [are] willed to be made, a three-cornered bulwark at the keep, to keep it. Furthermore, at Newnhambridge a massy wall to the French side there as was agreed. Besides, at the west jetty there should be another jetty which should defend the victualers of the town always from shot from the sandhills.

5. Mr. Aucher had £2,000 in money, wherewith he provided out of Flanders for Calais 2,000 quarters of barley [and] 500 of wheat.

18. The Lady Mary, my sister, came to me to Westminster, where after salutations she was called with my Council into a chamber where was declared how long I had suffered her mass (against my will *crossed out*) in hope of her reconciliation and how now, being no hope, which I perceived by her letters, except I saw some short amendment, I could not bear it. She answered that her soul was God['s] and her faith she would not change, nor dissemble her opinion with contrary doings. It was said I constrained not her faith but willed her (not as a king to rule *inserted*) but as a subject to obey. And that her example might breed too much inconvenience.

[18] "Fetch a compass" is probably meant, i.e., take a circuitous course (*NED*).

19. The Emperor's ambassador came with [a] short message from his master of [threatened] war, [to know] if I would not suffer his cousin the princess to use her mass. To this was no answer given at this time (but at the next *crossed out*).[19]

20. The Bis[hops] of Canterbury, London, [and] Rochester did conclude [that] to give license to sin was sin; to suffer and wink at it for a time might be borne, so all haste possible might be used.[20]

23. The Council, having the Bishops' answers, seeing [that] my subjects, lacking their vent in Flanders, might put the whole realm in danger; [that] the Flemings had cloth enough for a year in their hand and were kept far under; the danger of the Papists, the 1,500 quintals of powder I had in Flanders, the harness they had for preparation for the gendarmery, the goods my merchants had there at the wool fleet, [they] decreed to send an ambassador to the Emperor, Mr. [Nicholas] Wotton, to deny the matter wholly and persuade the Emperor in it, thinking by his going to win some time for a preparation of a mart, conveyance of powder, harness, etc., and for the surety of the realm. In the mean season to punish the offenders, first, of my servants that heard mass, next, of hers.[21]

22. Sir Anthony Browne [22] sent to the Fleet for hearing mass, with Sergeant Morgan.[23] Sir Clement Smith,[24] which a year before heard mass, chided.

[19] Jean Scheyve's account of his Council audience and later negotiations, dated April 6, is in *Cal. S. P. Span.*, *1550–1552*, pp. 251–261.

[20] I.e., in the matter of continuing the toleration of the Princess Mary's private masses.

[21] The Council minutes, interestingly, reveal nothing of this embarrassing decision.

[22] The eldest son of the Henrician favorite of the same name, later (1554) created Viscount Montague.

[23] Sir Richard Morgan, sergeant-at-law, Chief Justice of Common Pleas, 1556.

[24] Sir Clement Smith was an uncle by marriage to the King, having married Dorothy Seymour.

25. The ambassador of the Emperor came to have his answer but had none save that [some]one should go to the Emperor within a month or two to declare this matter.

22. Sir William Pickering came with great thanks from the French King.

27. Removing to Greenwich.

31. A challenge made by me that I, with sixteen of my chamber, should run at base, shoot, and run at ring with any seventeen of my servants, gentlemen in the court.

Mr. Croft arrived in Ireland and came to Waterford to the Deputy consulting for fortification of the town.

APRIL

1. The first day of the challenge at base, or running, the King won.

3. Mons. de Lansac came again from the French King to go to Scotland for appointing of his commissioners on the Scottish side, who were: the French ambassador in Scotland, the Bishop [of Orkney or of Ross], the Master of Erskine, and [*unfinished*].[25]

5. Sir Thomas Darcy made Lord Darcy of Chiche and Lord Chamberlain, for maintenance whereof he had given him 100 marks to his heirs general and 300 to his heirs male.

6. I lost the challenge of shooting at rounds and won at rovers.[26]

7. There were appointed commissioners on my side: either the Bishop of Lichfield,[27] if he had no impediment, or [of] Nor-

---

[25] The French commissioners were: Henry Clutin d'Oisel, Seigneur de Villeparisis, the French ambassador to Scotland; the Bishops of Orkney (Robert Reid) and of Ross (David Panter); the Masters of Ruthven and of Erskine (Teulet, *Relations politiques*, I, 258).

[26] "Rovers": in archery, shooting at a target selected at random and not at a fixed distance from the archer.

[27] Richard Sampson.

wich, Mr. Bowes, Mr. Beckwith, and Sir Thomas Chaloner.[28]

8. Sir John Gates made Vice-Chamberlain and captain of the guard, and had 120 pound[s worth of] land.

9. Ponet, Bishop of Rochester, received his oath for the bishopric of Winchester, having 2,000 marks [worth of] land appointed to him for his maintenance.

7. A certain Aryan of the Strangers, a Dutchman, being excommunicated by the congregation of his countrymen, was after long disputation condemned to the fire.[29]

9. The Earl of Wiltshire had fifty more [men-at-arms] in my Lord Marquis Dorset's place, [now become] Warden of the North, and my Lord of Rutland in my Lord Wentworth's place [an]other fifty.

10. Mr. Wotton had his instructions made to go withal to the Emperor to be as ambassador ledger in Mr. Morison's place and to declare this resolution: that if the Emperor would suffer my ambassador with him to use his service,[30] then I would his; if he would not suffer mine, I would not suffer his. Likewise that my sister was my subject and should use my service appointed by act of Parliament.

Also it was appointed to make twenty thousand pound weight for necessity somewhat baser, [in order] to get gains [of] £160,000 clear, by which the debt of the realm might be paid, the country defended from any sudden attempt, and the coin amended.

[28] The English commissioners were Thomas Thirlby, Bishop of Norwich, Sir Robert Bowes, Sir Leonard Beckwith, and Sir Thomas Chaloner.

[29] I.e., George van Parris, who held Unitarian as well as Anabaptist views; see above, p. 28, n. 40; dated April 24 in Charles Wriothesley, *Chronicle of England*, ed. W. D. Hamilton, Camden Society, new ser. XX, (London, 1877), II, 47.

[30] I.e., his religious worship within the embassy precincts. Sir Richard Morison, a humanist, had earlier been ambassador to the Hanse towns; he served as ambassador credited to the Emperor until 1553. Roger Ascham accompanied him abroad as secretary.

11. Mr. Pickering had his instructions and dispatch to go into France as ambassador ledger there in Mr. Mason's place, who desired very much to come home, and Mr. Pickering had instructions to tell the French King of the appointing of my commissioners in Scotland aforesaid.

12. They of Magdeburg, having in January last past taken in a conflict the Duke of Mecklenburg and three other earls, did give an onset on Duke Maurice by boats on the river when it overflowed the country, and slew divers of his men and came home safe, receiving a great portion of victuals into the town.[31]

15. A conspiracy opened of the Essex men who within three days after minded to declare the coming of strangers and so to bring people together to Chelmsford and then to spoil the rich men's houses if they could.[32] Woodcock! [33]

16. Also [a conspiracy] of Londoners who thought to rise on May Day against the strangers of the City; and both the parties committed to ward.[34]

23. This day the French King and the Lord Clinton chosen into the Order of the Garter, and appointed that the Duke of Somerset, the Marquis of Northampton, the Earl of Wiltshire, and the Earl of Warwick should peruse and amend the Order.

[31] The progress of the siege of Magdeburg was followed with close, if inexact, attention by the English government. The King's information seems to be derived from a news account dated December 29, 1550, which had originated in Hamburg and had been passed on to England, probably through Antwerp (*Cal. S. P. For., 1547–1553*, p. 64).

[32] The Council took no special note of the Essex disturbances, though on this date it did issue a general order to all justices strictly to enforce the laws against vagabondage, unlawful games, seditions, and rumors (*APC, 1550–1552*, p. 260).

[33] "Woodcock": here evidently used in an exclamatory sense with reference to capture by some trickery, or as a consequence of gullibility or folly (*NED*).

[34] The Recorder and certain other "substantial men of London" on April 19 warned the Council that slanderous books and bills were being circulated in the City which might provoke a rising (*APC, 1550–1552*, p. 262).

PART OF APRIL, A° 1551°, 3ᵃ CHARTA,
5° REGNI E. 6ⁱ

24. The Lords sat at London and banqueted one another this day and [for] three days after, for to show agreement amongst them whereas discord was bruited, and somewhat to look to the punishment of talebearers and apprehending of evil persons.

25. A bargain made with the Fuggers [35] for about £60,000 that in May and August should be paid, for the deferring of it. First, that the Fuggers should put it off for ten in the hundred. Secondly, that I should buy 12,000 mark weight at six shillings the ounce, to be delivered at Antwerp and so conveyed over. Thirdly, I should pay 100,000 crowns for a very fair jewel of his, four rubies marvelous big, one orient and great diamond, and one great pearl.[36]

27. Mallett,[37] the Lady Mary's chaplain, apprehended and sent to the Tower of London.

30. The Lord Marquis [of] Northampton appointed to go with the Order and further commission of treaty and that in post, having joined with him in commission the Bishop of Ely, Sir Philip Hoby, Sir William Pickering, and Sir John Mason, knights, and two other lawyers: Smith that was Secretary and [Dr. John Oliver].[38]

[35] The well-known banking house which held much of the English debt in Antwerp.

[36] Suggesting the low state of English credit in the Antwerp money market. It was not until 1552 that Gresham's effort to restore English credit placed him in a sufficiently strong position to reject humiliating conditions of this sort.

[37] Francis Mallett, later (1554–1560) Prebendary of Westminster and Dean of Lincoln.

[38] Sir Thomas Smith had been replaced by Nicholas Wotton as Secretary (see above, p. 19, n. 26); Oliver was a master of requests.

MAY

2. There was appointed to go with my Lord Marquis the Earls of Rutland, Worcester, and Ormonde, the Lords Lisle, Fitzwalter, and Braye, Abergavenny, and Evre,[39] and divers other gentlemen to the number of (twenty *altered to*) 30 in all.

3. The challenge at running at ring performed, at the which first came the King, sixteen footmen, and ten horsemen, in black silk coats pulled out with white silk taffeta; then all lords having three[?] men likewise appareled, and all gentlemen, their footmen in white fustian pulled out with black taffeta. The other side came all in yellow taffeta. At length the yellow band took it twice in 120 courses, and my band tainted [40] often—which was counted as nothing—and took never—which seemed very strange—and so the prize was of my side lost. After that, tourney followed between six of my band and six of theirs.[41]

4. It was appointed that there should be but four men to wait on every earl that went with my Lord Marquis [of] Northampton, three on every lord, two on every knight or gentleman; also that my Lord Marquis should in his diet be allowed for the loss in his exchange.

5. The muster of the gendarmery appointed to be the first of June if it were possible; if not, the 8th.

[39] The full list of the embassy to France may be found in *Cal. S. P. For.*, *1547–1553*, p. 123. The mission thus accredited, counting servants, numbered over two hundred. Only the following need still to be identified: William Somerset, third Earl of Worcester; Thomas Butler, tenth Earl of Ormonde; Thomas Radcliffe, third Earl of Sussex, Lord Fitzwalter; Henry Neville, Lord Abergavenny; William Evre, Baron of Wilton, mistakenly listed as "Rivers."

[40] "Tainted": hit.

[41] This tournament, held at Greenwich, is also described in *The Diary of Henry Machyn . . . 1550 to 1563*, ed. J. G. Nichols, Camden Soc., XLII (London, 1848), p. 5.

6. The teston cried down[42] from 12*d*. to 10*d*. and the groat from 4*d*. to 3*d*.

9. One [Robert] Stuart, a Scotsman, meaning to poison the young Queen of Scotland, thinking thereby to get favor here, was, after he had been a while in the Tower and Newgate, delivered on my frontiers at Calais to the French, for to have him punished there according to his deserts.[43]

10. Divers lords and knights sent for to furnish the court at the coming of the French ambassador that brought hither the Order of St. Michael.

12. A proclamation proclaimed to give warning to all those that keep many farms, multitudes of sheep above the number limited in the law, viz., 2,000, decay[ed] tenements and towns, regraters, forestallers, men that sell dear, having plenty enough, and put plow ground to pasture, and carriers over sea of victuals, that if they leave not these enormities they shall be straitly punished very shortly, so that they should feel the smart of it; and to command execution of laws made for these purposes before.[44]

(14. The Earl of Warwick made—, *uncompleted entry crossed out.*)

14. There mustered before me 100 archers, two arrows apiece, all of the guard, [who] afterward shot together, and they shot at an inch board, which some pierced quite and stuck in the

[42] I.e., devalued. The consequence was a sharp and immediate price rise which further unsettled the economy. On May 10 the Lord Mayor and other merchant leaders of London were upbraided before the Council for having "suddenly raised the prices of all things to a marvelous reckoning" (*APC, 1550–1552,* p. 272).

[43] See Teulet, *Relations politiques,* I, 260, 269; "Papiers des Pot de Rhodes, 1529–1648," ed. by Hiver de Beauvoir, in *Mémoires de la Commission Historique du Cher,* II (Bourges and Paris, 1864), 75–283: Stuart's confession, pp. 132–133.

[44] Text of proclamation "ordering reform of coinage, engrossing, enclosures" in *Tudor Royal Proclamations,* I, 520–522.

other board; divers pierced it quite through with the heads of their arrows, the boards being very well seasoned timber. So it was appointed there should be ordinary 100 archers and 100 halberdiers, either good wrestlers or casters of the bar, or leapers, runners, or tall men of personage.

15. Sir Philip Hoby departed toward France with ten gentlemen of his own, in velvet coats and chains of gold.[45]

16. Likewise did the Bishop of Ely depart with a band of men well-furnished.

20. A proclamation made that whosoever found a seditious bill and did not tear and deface it should be partaker of the bill and punished as the maker.[46]

21. My Lord Marquis [of] Northampton had commission to deliver the Order [of the Garter] and to treat of all things, and chiefly of marriage for me to the Lady Elizabeth, his daughter: first, to have the dot 12,000 marks a year and the dowry at least 800,000 crowns. The forfeiture 100,000 crowns at the most, if I performed not; and paying that to be delivered. And that this should not impeach the former covenants with Scotland; with many other branches.

22. He departed himself in post.

24. An earthquake was at Croydon and Bletchingley and in the most part of Surrey, but no harm was done.

30. Whereas before commandment was given that £160,000 should be coined of 3 ounces in the pound fine for discharge of debts, and to get some treasure to be able to alter all, now was it stopped, saving only £80,000 to discharge my debts and 10,000

[45] On the diplomatic mission being sent to France to negotiate, among other matters, a marriage treaty with Elizabeth, the eldest daughter of Henry II, then six years of age. She later (1559) married Philip II of Spain.

[46] *STC* 7838 (May 20, 1551); text in *Tudor Royal Proclamations*, I, 522–523.

mark weight that the Fuggers delivered in the last exchange at 4 ounces in the pound.[47]

31. The musters deferred till after midsummer.

JUNE

2. It was appointed that I should receive the Frenchmen that came hither at Westminster, where was made preparation for the purpose, and four garnish of new vessels prepared, taken out of church stuff, [such] as miters and golden missals and primers and crosses and relics of Plessay.[48]

4. Provision made in Flanders for silver and gold plate and chains to be given to these strangers.[49]

7. A proclamation set forth that exchanging or rechanging should be made under the punishment set forth in King Henry the 7.['s] time, duly to be executed.[50]

10. Mons. Maréchal [51] departed (out of Fra—*crossed out*) from

[47] In successive alterations of the bullion value of gold and silver coinage the government reaped a profit of £537,000 from the mints from the beginning of the reign to this date. The dislocating effects on the economy were so great, however, that in April, 1551, the Council had accepted the fact that the coinage must be restored to a better standard, but first resolved on one further debasement, the profits to be applied to Crown debts. Coinage began at the debased standard mentioned in the above entry until July, 1551, when £114,500 had been gained in mint profits. Then in September the Council ordered a restoration of the standard of silver coinage at 11 oz. 1 pennyweight of silver and 19 pennyweights of alloy. But the heavy profits gained in the debasement were wholly consumed by outlays in Ireland, Calais, and on the Scottish border.

[48] Nichols (*Literary Remains*, II, 320) suggests that Plessay may refer to church plate earlier confiscated from the College of Pleshey in Essex.

[49] Presumably the King here refers to a consignment of church plate to be shipped abroad to meet obligations in Antwerp. On June 1 the Council had ordered such plate to the value of £3,700 to be drawn from the Jewel House and that it should be passed through customs without "any let" (*APC, 1550–1552*, p. 288).

[50] *STC* 7839 (June 10, 1551); text in *Tudor Royal Proclamations*, I, 523–524.

[51] Jacques d'Albon, Marquis de Fronsac, Seigneur de St. André, was

the [French] court to Boulogne in post and so hither by water in his galleys and foists.[52]

In this month and the month before was great business for the city of Parma, which Duke Horatio [Ottavio] had delivered to the French King. For the Pope accited [53] him as holding it *in capite* of him, whereby he could not alienate it without the Pope's will; but he came not at his day, for which cause the Pope and [the] Imperials raised 3,000 men and took a castle on the same river side. Also the French King sent Mons. de Thermes,[54] who had been his general in Scotland, with a great piece of his gendarmery into Italy to help Duke Horatio [Ottavio].[55] Furthermore, the Turk made great preparations for war, which some feared would at length burst out.

3. I was elected of the company of St. Michael in France, by the French King and his Order.

13. Agreement made with the Scots for the borders, between the commissioners aforesaid for both the parties.

In this month [Arraiz] Dragut, a pirate, escaped Andrea Doria, who had closed him in a creek, by force of his galley

---

reported by Sir John Mason as having left Chateaubriant on June 11 on his mission to England, with a great train of from 400 to 500 horse, including the best musicians at the French Court (*Cal. S. P. For.*, *1547–1553*, p. 128).

[52] "Foist": a light galley propelled by oars and sail.

[53] "Accite" or "ascite": to cite or to summons.

[54] Paul de la Barthe, Seigneur de Thermes (1482–1562), later (1557) designated Marshal of France, was appointed ambassador to Rome in 1550 and shortly afterward was named commander of the French forces in Italy.

[55] Parma was in bitter dispute between the papacy and the Emperor. The Spanish had occupied the city in 1547, with the consequence that the papacy sought the aid of France, it being then agreed that Parma and Piacenza were to be given to Orazio Farnese rather than to Ottavio Farnese, the Emperor's son-in-law. On the death of Julius III (Feb. 7, 1550), Parma was restored to Ottavio, who could not regain the city without once more calling in a French army. After inconclusive fighting, of which the action here described is part, an uneasy truce was at last concluded in April, 1552, which permitted Ottavio to hold Parma unmolested for two years.

slaves that digged another way into the sea and took two of Andrea's galleys that lay far into the sea.

14. Pardon given to those Irish lords that would come in before a certain day, limited by the Deputy, with advertisement to the Deputy to make sharp war with those that would resist, and also should minister my laws everywhere.

18. Because of my charges in fortifications at Calais and Berwick [that] should be paid, it was agreed that, besides the debt of the realm, £80,000 [*could be read* £60,000], there should be £40,000 coined, three ounces fine [and] nine of alloy, and 5,000 pound weight should be coined in a standard of seven ounces fine, at the least.[56]

17. Superantio [Giacomo Soranzo] came as ambassador from Venice in Daniel Barbaro's place.[57]

16. I accepted the Order of St. Michael by promise to the French ambassador.

17. My Lord Marquis [of] North[ampton] came to Nantes with the commissioners and all the noblemen and gentlemen that came over sea with him.

20. Upon advertisement of Scepperus' coming and rigging of certain ships in Holland, also for to show the Frenchmen pleasure at their coming, all the navy that lay in Gillingham water was appointed to be rigged and furnished with ordnance and lie in the river of Thames, to the intent that if Scepperus came

[56] *APC, 1550–1552*, p. 305 (June 15, 1551), places a rather different construction on the decision.

[57] Barbaro had been a most popular and effective ambassador in England. His "Report . . . of his Legation in England" (*Calendar of State Papers . . . Relating to . . . Venice, etc.*, V, *1534–1554*, ed. Rawdon Brown [London, 1873], 338–373), delivered to the Venetian Senate in May, 1551, is a valuable source for the reign of Edward VI. Soranzo's report (August, 1554, *ibid.*, pp. 532–563) likewise contains much pertinent information on various aspects of the reign: debasement of coinage and consequent rise of prices (pp. 551–552), the "sweating sickness" (pp. 541–542), the character of London (pp. 543–544), etc.

afterward he might be met with, and [that] at least the Frenchmen should see the force of my navy.[58]

22. The Lady Mary sent letters to the Council, marveling at the imprisonment of Doctor Mallett, her chaplain, for saying of the mass before her household, seeing it was promised the Emperor's ambassador she should not be molested in religion, but that she and her household should have the mass said before them continually.

24. They [the Council] answered that because of their duties to their king, country, and friends, they were compelled to give her answer that they would see not only him but also all other mass-sayers and breakers of order straitly punished, and that as for promise they had nor would give none to make her free from the punishment of the law in that behalf.

18. Châtillon came to my Lord Marquis [of Northampton] and there banqueted him by the way, at two times, between Nantes and Chateaubriant, where the King lay.

15. Mandosse,[59] a gentleman of the King's chamber, was sent to him to conduct him to the court.

19. My Lord Marquis came to Chateaubriant, where half a mile from the castle there met him [the Comte d'Enghien and the Duc de Montpensier [60]] with one hundred gentlemen, and brought him to the court, and so, booted and spurred,[61] to the French King.

20. The French King was invested with the Order of the Garter in his bedchamber, where he gave a chain to Garter worth £200 and his gown dressed with aglets [62] worth £25. The Bishop of

---

[58] *Cal. S. P. For.*, *1547–1553*, p. 122 (June 7, 1551).

[59] Possibly to be identified as Bernardino de Mendoza, a Spanish officer sometime in the employ of the French King.

[60] Louis de Bourbon, Duke of Montpensier.

[61] "Booted and spurred" first cited in 1552 by *NED*.

[62] "Aglet": a metallic spangle worn as an ornament of dress.

Ely making an oration and the Cardinal of Lorraine [63] making him answer.[64]

At afternoon the Lord Marquis moved the French King to the marriage of the Scottish Queen to be consummated, whose hearing he appointed to the commissioners.

21. The Cardinal[s] of Lorraine and of Châtillon,[65] the Constable, [and] the Duke of Guise were appointed commissioners on the part of France, who absolutely denied the first motion for the Scottish Queen,[66] saying both they had taken too much pain and spent too many lives for her, also a conclusion was made for her marriage to the Dauphin. Then was proposed the marriage of the Lady Elizabeth, the French King's eldest daughter, to which they did most cheerfully assent. So after they agreed neither party to be bound in conscience nor honor until she was twelve years of age and upwards. Then they came to the dot, which was first asked 1,500,000 scutes of France, at which they made a mock. After, for *donatio propter nuptias*, the[y] agreed that it should be as great as hath been given by the King my father to any wife he had.

22. Our commissioners came to 1,400,000 of crowns, which they refused; then to a million, which they denied; then to 800,000 crowns, which they said they would not agree to.[67]

23. Then our commissioners asked what they would offer. First

[63] Charles de Guise, Cardinal of Lorraine, brother of the Dowager Queen of Scotland.

[64] The King's entries for June 15, 18, 19, 20, and 23 are derived principally from Northampton's reports to the Council (*Cal. S. P. For., 1547–1553,* pp. 129, 133)

[65] Odet de Coligny, Cardinal of Châtillon.

[66] I.e., for the honoring of the long disputed and earlier marriage treaty with Edward VI.

[67] The commissioners were here following their instructions, later amended, however, to permit them to drop, if need be, to 600,000 crowns (*Cal. S. P. For., 1547–1553,* p. 139).

they offered 100,000 crowns, then 200,000, which they said was the most and more than ever was given. Then followed great reasonings and showings of precedent, but no nearer they could come.⁶⁸

24. They went forward to the penalty if the parties misliked [one another] after that the King's daughter was twelve and upwards, which the French offered 100,000, 50,000 crowns, or promise. Then, that she should be brought at her father's charge three months before she was twelve, sufficiently jeweled and stuffed.⁶⁹ Then bonds to be delivered alternatively at London and Paris, and so forth.

26. The Frenchmen delivered the aforesaid answers written to my commissioners.

JULY

1. Whereas certain Flemish ships, twelve sail in all, six tall men-of-war, looking for eighteen more of men-of-war, went to Dieppe, as it was thought, to take Mons. le Maréchal [St. André] by the way, order was given that six ships, being before prepared, with four pinnaces and a brigantine, should go both to conduct him and also to defend if anything should be attempted against England by carrying over the Lady Mary.

2. A brigantine sent (ship sent *crossed out*) to Dieppe to give knowledge to Mons. le Maréchal of the Flemings' coming, to whom all the Flemings vailed their bonnet. Also the French

⁶⁸ *Ibid.*, p. 133 (June 23, 1551). The commissioners then asked for further and amended instructions from the Council for the resolution of the impasse. They were on July 2 authorized to accept a dot of 200,000 crowns provided the princess be fully furnished and transported to England at French expense (Harl. MSS., 353, f. 112; *Cal. S. P. For., 1547–1553*, p. 140).

⁶⁹ An odd usage; the meaning is that, in view of the small dowry being accepted, the princess was to be set down in England at French charge and was to be fully outfitted and furnished.

ambassador was advertised; who answered that he thought him sure enough when he came into our streams [70]—terming it so.

2. There was a proclamation signed for shortening of the fall of the money to that day in which it should be proclaimed, and [it was] devised that it should be in all places of the realm within one day proclaimed.[71]

3. The Lords Clinton (and Cobham *crossed out*) were appointed to meet the French[man] at (Woolwich *altered to*) Gravesend and so to convey him to Durham Place, where he should lie.

4. I was banqueted by the Lord Clinton at Deptford, where I saw the "Primrose" and the "Mary Willoughby" launched.

The Frenchmen landed at Rye, as some thought for fear of the Flemings lying at the land's end,[72] chiefly because they saw our ships were let by the wind [so] that they could not come out.

6. Sir Pe[ter] Meutas [73] at Dover was commanded to come to Rye to meet Mons. le Maréchal, who so did, and after he had delivered his letters, written with mine own hand, and made my recommendations, he took order for horses and carts for Mons. le Maréchal, in which he made such provision as was possible (meet *crossed out*) to be for the sudden.[74]

7. Mons. le Maréchal set forth from Rye, and in his journey Mr.

[70] The meaning seems to be that the French ambassador thought himself safe when he entered English waters; and see the July 4 entry following.

[71] I.e., to devalue the coinage by reducing the value of the shilling to 9d. and then to restore the standard of the coinage. The proclamation was dated July 9 and was delivered to the sheriffs sealed, with strict instructions that the seals be not broken before July 8. For the proclamation, see STC 7840; text in *Tudor Royal Proclamations*, I, 525.

[72] Presumably off South Foreland. The original French intention had been to land at Dover.

[73] Sir Peter Meutas, the commanding officer in Guernsey.

[74] I.e., under conditions of sudden need.

Culpepper,[75] [*a blank*], and divers other gentlemen, and their men, to the number of 1,000 horse well-furnished, met him and so brought him to Maidstone that night.

Removing to Westminster.

8. Mons. le Maréchal came to Mr. Baker's,[76] where he was very well feasted and banqueted.

9. The same came to my Lord Cobham's to dinner and at night to Gravesend.

Proclamation made that a teston should go at 9*d*. and a groat at 3*d*. in all places of the realm at once.

At this time came the sweat into London, which was more vehement than the old sweat.[77] For if one took cold, he died within three hours, and if he escaped, it held him but nine hours, or ten at the most. Also, if he slept the first six hours, as he should be very desirous to do, then he raved and should die raving.

11. It grew so much—for in London the tenth day there died seventy in the liberties, and this day 120, (that I did remove *crossed out*) and also one of my gentlemen, another of my grooms, fell sick and died—that I removed to Hampton Court with very few with me.

The same night came the Maréchal, who was saluted with all my ships being in the Thames, fifty and odd, all with shot well furnished and so with the ordnance of the Tower. He was met by the Lord Clinton, Lord Admiral, with forty gentlemen at Gravesend, and so brought to Durham Place.

[75] Alexander Culpepper, who had just succeeded his father as Sheriff of Kent.

[76] Sir John Baker, a Privy Councillor and the Speaker of the House of Commons.

[77] The last serious epidemic of sweating sickness had occurred in 1528. The King's graphic description of the epidemic differs very little from that of contemporary chroniclers (also Soranzo in *Cal. S. P. Ven., 1534–1554*, pp. 541–542)

13. Because of the infection at London, he came this day to Richmond, where he lay with a great band of gentlemen, at least 400, as it was by divers esteemed, where that night he hunted.[78]

14. He came to me at Hampton Court at nine of the clock, being met by the Duke of Somerset at the wall end and so conveyed first to me, where, after his master's recommendations and letters, he went to his chamber on the Queen's side, all hanged with cloth of arras, and so was the hall and all my lodging. He dined with me also. After dinner, being brought into an inner chamber, he told me he was come not only for delivery of the Order but also for to declare the great friendship the King his master bore me, which he desired I would think to be such to me as a father beareth to his son, or brother to brother. And although there were divers persuasions, as he thought, to dissuade me from the King his master's friendship, and witless men made divers rumors, yet he trusted I would not believe them. Furthermore [he declared] that, as good ministers on the frontiers do great good, so do ill [ministers] much harm. For which cause he desired no innovation should be made on things [which] had been so long in controversy by handstrokes,[79] but rather by commissioners' talk. I answered him that I thanked him for his Order and also his love, etc., and I would show like love in all points. For rumors, they were not always to be believed; and that I did sometime provide for the worst but never did any harm upon their hearing. For ministers, I said I would rather appease these controversies with words than do anything by force. So after[ward] he was conveyed to Richmond again.

16. He came to present the Order of [St.] Michael; where, after

---

[78] There is evident admiration and boyish affection in the King's rather extended comments on the visit of the Maréchal St. André. These passages are among the few in which the tight self-discipline of the young King is relaxed, when evident enjoyment and enthusiasm are expressed, and when a boy seems somehow to be precisely his proper age.

[79] I.e., by violence.

with ceremonies accustomed he had put on the garments, he and Mons. Gyé,[80] likewise of the Order, came—one at my right hand, the other at my left—to the chapel where, after the communion [was] celebrated, each of them kissed my cheek. After[ward] they dined with me and talked after dinner and saw some pastime and so went home again.[81]

18. A proclamation made against regraters and forestallers, and the words of the statute recited, with the punishment for the offenders. Also letters were sent to all officers and sheriffs for the executing thereof.[82]

19. Another proclamation made for punishment of them that would blow rumors of abasing and enhancing of the coin to make things dear withal.[83]

The same night Mons. le Maréchal St. André supped with me; after supper saw a dozen courses, and after[ward] came and made me ready.

20. The next morning he came to see mine arraying and saw my bedchamber and went a-hunting with hounds and saw me shoot and saw all my guard shoot together. He dined with me, heard me play on the lute, ride [rode?], came to me in my study, supped with me, and so departed to Richmond.

19. The Scots sent an ambassador hither for receiving the treaty, sealed with the Great Seal of England, which was delivered [to] him. Also I sent Sir Thomas Chaloner, Clerk of my

[80] François de Rohan, Seigneur de Gyé, a professional diplomatist, formerly accredited to Rome, "deputed . . . to assist" St. André, whose "reputation and experience in such matters are not yet very great" in the opinion of Simon Renard, Imperial ambassador in France (*Cal. S. P. Span., 1550–1552*, p. 307)

[81] For a full description of the ceremony, see "Papiers des Pot de Rhodes," pp. 146–148, and *Mémoires de . . . Vieilleville*, I (vol. XXVI of Petitot, *Collection complète des mémoires . . . de France* [Paris, 1822]), 339 ff.

[82] STC 7841 (July 17, 1551); text in *Tudor Royal Proclamations*, I, 526–527.

[83] STC 7842 (July 18, 1551); text in *Tudor Royal Proclamations*, I, 528–529.

Council, to have the seal of them for confirmation of the last treaty at Norham.[84]

This day my Lord Marquis [of Northampton] and the commissioners, coming to treat of the marriage, offered by later instructions 600,000 crowns, after[ward] 400,000 s[cutes], and so departed for an hour. Then, seeing they could get no better, [they] came to the French offer of 200,000 s[cutes], half to be paid at the marriage, half six months after that. Then the French agreed that her dot should be but 10,000 marks of lawful money of England. Thirdly, it was agreed that if I died she[?] should[?] not have the dot, saying they did that for friendship's sake without precedent.[85]

19. The Lord Marquis, having received and delivered again the treaty sealed, took his leave, and so did all the rest.

At this time was there a bickering at Parma between the French and the Papists. For Mons. de Thermes, Pietro Strozzi, and Fontanello, with divers other gentlemen to the number of thirty, with 1,500 soldiers, entered Parma. Gonzaga [86] with the Emperor's and Pope's band lay near the town. The French made sallies and overcame [them], slaying the Prince of Macedonia [87] and il signor Battista,[88] the Pope's nephew.

[84] Norham Castle (Northumberland). The treaty, comprehending Scotland within the amity of the Anglo-French treaty, was concluded on June 10, 1551.

[85] Thus the French had at last driven the English commissioners down to the amount which the Council, by further amendment of instructions, had fixed as the minimum. The treaty was concluded on July 19, 1551 (*Cal. S. P. For., 1547–1553*, p. 150).

[86] Fernando di Gonzaga, the Emperor's commander in the area.

[87] Vannes reported on November 24, 1551, that the "Prince of Macedonia," master of the Pope's camp, had been slain "a few days ago" (*Cal. S. P. For., 1547–1553*, p. 198). The son of Constantine Arianiti, who had also been in the papal service, this officer, rather grandly styled "Prince of Macedonia and Duke of Acaia," was killed on November 16, 1551, in a skirmish near Parma. He had visited England in 1540 (Franz Babinger, "Das Ende der Arianiten," in *Sitzungsberichte der bayerischen Akademie der Wissenschaften, "phil. hist. Klasse,"* 1960, no. 4, p. 86).

[88] The report was in error: Giovanni Battista del Monte was actively

22. Mr. Sidney made one of the four chief gentlemen.

23. Mons. le Maréchal came to me, declaring the King his master's well-taking [of] my readiness to this treaty, and also how much his master was bent that way. He presented Mons. Boisdauphin [89] to be ambassador here, as my Lord Marquis the 19th day did present Mr. Pickering.

26. Mons. le Maréchal dined with me; after dinner saw the strength of the English archers. After he had so done, at his departure I gave him a diamond from my finger worth by estimation £150 both for [his] pains and also for my memory. Then he took his leave.

27. He came to me a-hunting to tell me the news and show the letter his master had sent him, and doubles [90] of Mons. Thermes' letter and Marillac's letters, [he] being ambassador with the Emperor.[91]

28. Mons. le Maréchal came to dinner to Hyde Park, where there was a fair house made for him, and he saw the coursing there.

30. He came to the Earl of Warwick's,[92] lay there one night, and was well received.

29. He had his reward, being worth three thousand pounds in gold of current money, Mons. de Gyé £1,000, Mons. Chemault £1,000, Mons. Morvilliers 500, the secretary 500, and the Bishop [of] Périgueux 500.[93]

---

engaged on October 3, 1551, at Mirandola (*Cal. S. P. For.*, *1547–1553*, pp. 176, 184); he died April 14, 1552 (*Venetianische Depeschen vom Kaiserhofe*, ed. Gustav Turba, II [Vienna, 1892], 566, n. 6).

[89] René de Laval, Seigneur de Boisdauphin et de Téligny, formerly Maître d'Hôtel to the French King, who remained ambassador to England until 1553.

[90] "Doubles": a duplicate of a writing.

[91] Charles de Marillac, a professional diplomatist who had served France as ambassador in England from 1539 to 1543.

[92] At Sheen.

[93] Jean Morvilliers, Bishop of Orleans; Jacques Bourdin, Seigneur de Villaines, secretary of state; Jean de Lustrac, Bishop of Périgueux (Lucien

AUGUST

3. Mons. le Maréchal departed to Boulogne and had certain of my ships to conduct him thither.

9. Twenty-four Lords of the Council met at Richmond to commune of my sister Mary's matter—who at length agreed that it was not meet to be suffered any longer, making thereof an instrument signed with their hands and sealed, to be of record.[94]

11. The Lord Marquis with the most part of his band came home and delivered the treaty, sealed.

12. Letters sent for Rochester, Englefield, Waldegrave, etc., to come the seventeenth day, but they came not until another letter was sent to them the thirteenth day.[95]

14. My Lord Marquis' reward was delivered at Paris, worth £500, my Lord of Ely's 200, Mr. Hoby's 150, the rest all about one scantling.[96]

14. Rochester, etc., had commandment neither to hear nor to suffer any kind of service but the communion and orders set forth alar [at large?] by Parliament, and had one[?] letter to my Lady's house from my Council for their credit, another to her self from me. Also appointed that I should come to, and sit at, Council, when great matters were in debating, or when[?] I would.

This last month M. de Thermes with 500 Frenchmen came to

Romier, *La carrière d'un favori. Jacques d'Albon de Saint-André* [Paris, 1909], p. 73).

[94] There were twenty-two Councillors who subscribed to the minute of this important meeting. Members absent from London a week earlier had been summoned to attend (*APC, 1550–1552*, pp. 328–330).

[95] The Princess Mary's servants here mentioned were: Robert Rochester, Comptroller of her Household; Sir Francis Englefield, later to be outlawed by Elizabeth for high treason; and Sir Edward Waldegrave, a Privy Councillor in the reign of Queen Mary.

[96] "Scantling": a small portion or amount (*NED*).

Parma and entered safely. Afterward certain issued out of the town and were overthrown, as M. Sipier, d'Andelot, Petro Corso, and others were taken and some slain. After they gave a skirmish, [they] entered the camp of Gonzaga and spoiled a few tents and returned.[97]

15. Sir Robert Dudley and Barnaby [Fitzpatrick] [98] sworn two of the six ordinary gentlemen.

The last month the Turks' navy won a little castle in Sicily.

17. Instructions sent to Sir James Croft [as Lord Deputy in Ireland] for divers purposes, whose copy is in the Secretary's hands.

18. The teston cried down from ninepence to sixpence, the groat from threepence to twopence, the twopence to a penny, the penny to an halfpenny, the halfpenny to a farthing, etc.[99]

M. de Thermes and [M.] Sipier overthrew three ensigns of horsemen at three times, took one dispatch sent from Don Fernando [di Gonzaga] to the Pope concerning this war, and another from the Pope to Don Fernando, discomfited four en-

[97] The account is based principally on the dispatch from Wotton and Morison to the Council dated from Augsburg July 28 (*Cal. S. P. For., 1547–1553*, pp. 154–155). The MS., being faded and worn, is very difficult to read with certainty from the August 9 through the August 14 entry.

[98] Fitzpatrick, the son of an Irish peer, was sent as a child to England as a pledge for his father's loyalty. Educated with Edward, he became the companion and closest personal friend of the young King. In this same year Edward sent him abroad to complete his education at the court of Henry II and for rather more than a year was to maintain a close, though singularly avuncular, correspondence with him (Nichols, *Literary Remains*, I, 65 ff.). Fitzpatrick returned from France in December, 1552. His life, after Edward's death, was spent mostly in Ireland, where he was regarded as a loyal subject of the English Crown. He died in 1581.

[99] The final stage of devaluation and restoration of the standard of coinage. The draft copy is dated from Hampton Court on August 11, while on August 12 instructions for issuing the proclamation were forwarded to the sheriffs, the seals not to be broken until August 16 (S. P. Dom., Edw. VI, XIII, 33, 34, 47; text in *Tudor Royal Proclamations*, I, 529–530).

signs of footmen, and took the Count Camillo [di Gonzaga] of Castiglione, and slew a captain of the Spaniards.[100]

22. Removing to Windsor.

23. Rochester, etc., returned, denying to do openly the charge of the Lady Mary's house for displeasing her (here *in MS.*).[101]

26. The Lord Chancellor, Mr. Comptroller, and the Secretary Petre sent to do the same commission.

27. Mr. Coverdale made Bishop of Exeter.[102]

28. Rochester, etc., sent to the Fleet.

The Lord Chancellor, etc., did that they were commanded to do to my sister and her house.[103]

31. Rochester, etc., committed to the Tower.

The Duke of Somerset, taking certain that [there] began a new conspiracy for destruction of the gentlemen at Wokingham two days past, executed them with death for their offense.[104]

29. Certain pinnaces were prepared to see that there should be no conveyance overseas of the Lady Mary secretly done. Also appointed that the Lord Chancellor, the Lord Chamberlain, the Vice-Chamberlain, and the Secretary Petre should see by all means they could whether she used the mass, and if she did that the laws should be executed on her chaplains. Also that when I came from this progress to Hampton Court, or Westminster, both my sisters should be with me till further order were taken for this purpose.

---

[100] *Cal. S. P. For., 1547–1553*, p. 168 (Pickering to Council, Sept. 4, 1551).

[101] I.e., declining to deliver the Council's orders with respect to Mary's household (see above, p. 76, August 14).

[102] Miles Coverdale, one of the most eminent of the first generation of reformers.

[103] See S. P. Dom., Edw. VI, XIII, 35 (August 29, 1551), for the full account.

[104] Somerset had been appointed Lord Lieutenant of Berkshire and Buckinghamshire on his return to the Council. The incident mentioned is obscure.

SEPTEMBER A° D'NI 1551, 4 CHARTA, 5° REGNI E. 6[i]

3. The French ambassador came to declare, first, who [how] the Emperor wronged divers of his master's subjects and vassals, arrested also his merchants, and did cloakedly [105] begin war. For he besieged Mirandola round about with forts he had made in the French King's country. Also he stayed certain ships (of war *crossed out*) French going a-fishing to the Newfoundland. Furthermore, he sent a dozen ships which bragged they would take the Dowager of Scotland, which thing stayed her so long at Dieppe. Whereupon his master had taken the hool [wool] fleet of Antwerp, conveying it to his country into his ports by a ten ships he had sent forth under Baron de la Garde.[106] Also minded to send more help to Piedmont and Mirandola. For this cause he desired that on my coasts the Dowager might have safe passage and might be succored with my servants at the seacoast if any chance [107] should happen. He was willed to put it in writing. He showed how the Turks' navy, having spoiled a piece of Sicily, went to Malta and there took an isle adjacent called Gozo; from thence they went to Tripoli. In Transylvania, Rusta Bassa [108] was leader of the army and had spoiled it wholly. In Hungary the Turks had made a fort by the mines to get them. Magdeburg was freshly victualed, and Duke Maurice came his way, [it] being suspected he had conspired with them there.[109]

[105] "Cloakedly": an early, but not the first use of the word in this sense.

[106] Antoine Escalin des Aimars, Baron de la Garde, ambassador extraordinary from France to England.

[107] I.e., mischance(?).

[108] Rusta(n) Bassa, a Turkish general who in 1552 was given command of the Turkish army in Syria.

[109] Maurice of Saxony had been entrusted, with the reluctant consent of the Emperor, with the siege of Magdeburg. Maurice, already conspiring against Charles V, in November, 1551, secured the surrender of the city, having secretly given to the burghers assurances that the city's privileges would be preserved and that the free exercise of conscience would be ensured.

4. It was answered to the French ambass[ador] that the Dowager should[?] in all my ports be defended from enemies [and] tempest, and likewise[?] also thanks were given for the news.

5. The Emperor's ambassador came to require that my sister[?] Mary's[?] officers should be restored to their liberty and [that] she should have[?] her[?] mass till the Emperor was certified thereof.[110] It was answered, first, that I needed not to answer except I list, because he spoke without commission, which was seen by the shortness of the time since the committing of her officers, of which the Emperor could not be advertised. He was willed no more to move these piques, in which he had been often answered, without commission. He was answered that the Emperor was by this time advertised, although the matter pertained not to him. Also, that I had done nothing but according to a king's office herein, in observing the laws that were so godly and in punishing the offenders. The promise to the Emperor was not so made as he pretended, [as is] affirmed by Sir Philip Hoby, being at that [time] there [the] ambassador.[111]

6. Deliberation touching the coin. Memor. that there were divers standards—9 ounces fine a few; 8 ounces fine as ill as four, because although that that [sic] was fine, yet a shilling was reckoned for two shillings; 6 ounces, very many; 4 ounces, many also; 3 ounces £130,000 now of late. Whereupon agreed that the teston being called to sixpence, 4 with help of 6 should make ten fine, 8 fine with help of nine, being fewer than those of eight, should make ten ounces fine; the two ounces of alloy should quit the charges of minting; and those of threepence, being but few, should be turned to [the stan]dard of 4, of farthings and halfpence and pence for to serve for the poor people, because [the mer]chants made no exchange of it and the

[110] Corner of MS. torn.

[111] For Scheyve's report to the Emperor on these conversations, see Cal. S. P. Span., 1550–1552, pp. 356–364 (Sept. 12, 1551).

sum was not great; also to [bear the] charges,[112] forbecause it was thought that few or none were left of 9 ounces fine, 8 ounces were nought, and 6 ounces were two ways devised, one without any craft, the other was not fully six—of which kind was not a few.[113]

9. A proclamation set forth touching the prices of cattle, of hogs, pigs, beefs, oxen, mutton, butter, and cheese, after a reasonable price, not fully so good cheap as it was when the coin was at the perfectest, but within a fifth part of it or thereabouts.[114]

10. I removed to Farnham.

12. A proclamation set forth touching the coin: that whereas it was so that men for gain melted down the 9*d.* teston continually, and the 6*d.* also, there should be no person in any wise melt it down, upon pain to incur the penalty of the laws.[115]

13. A letter directed to the Lord Treasurer, the Lord Great Master, and the Master of the Horse, to meet at London for the ordering of my coin and the payment of my debts; which done, to return and make report of their proceedings.

11. War proclaimed in Britain between the Emperor and the

---

[112] Corner of MS. torn; [. . .] words supplied.

[113] The restoration of the coinage and ways of dealing with rumors of further debasements were discussed in the Council on August 29 and again on September 7, but not in this context. These remarks of the King seem to be private, and rather obscure, speculations on a matter which had come to concern him deeply. He seems here to be regarding the existing and, in varying degrees, debased coinage as the bullion from which coinage of a new standard would now be minted. The Council's instructions (September 25) to Sir Edmund Peckham with respect to the new minting indicate that the matter had been submitted personally to the King, and only then were directions being issued respecting the standard and the impression of the new coinage (S. P. Dom., Edw. VI, XIII, 47).

[114] *STC* 7843 (September 9, 1551); text in *Tudor Royal Proclamations*, I, 530–533.

[115] *STC* 7844 (September 11, 1551); text in *Tudor Royal Proclamations*, I, 534–535.

French, by these terms: "Charles Roi d'Espagne et Duc de Milan," leaving out Emperor.

10. Four towns taken by the French soldiers that were the Emperor's in Piedmont, Chieri, and Amiens [St. Damian]. Also the Emperor's country there was spoiled, and 120 (130 *crossed out*) castles or fortresses taken.

Proclamation made in Paris touching the bulls, that no man should go for them to Rome.

Other ships also taken by [the] Prior de Capua: merchants, to the number of a dozen. Prior [of] Capua had thirty-two galleys.[116]

19. The French ambassador sent this news also, that the Turk had taken Tripoli.

20. The Secretary Cecil and Sir Philip Hoby sent to London to help the Lord Treasurer, etc., in the matters of the Bishops of Chichester, Worcester, and Durham,[117] and examination of my sister's men.

18. Removing to Windsor.

20. The Lords at London, having tried all kinds of stamping, both of the fineness of nine, eight, six, four, and three, proved that without any loss but sufferable the coin might be brought to eleven (nine *crossed out*) ounces fine. For whereas it was thought before that the teston was through ill officers and ministers corrupted, it was tried that it had the valuation just, by eight sundry kinds of melting; and four hundred pounds of sterling money, a teston being but sixpence, made four hundred pounds 11 ounces fine of money sterling.

22. Whereupon they reported the same, and then it was con-

[116] Leo Strozzi, Prior of Capua and a brother to Pietro, was shortly to desert the French service (*Cal. S. P. For., 1547–1553*, p. 177). He served France as an admiral and general until his death in 1558 from wounds received in an assault on Sarlino.

[117] Day, Heath, and Tunstall, who were shortly to be deprived of their sees.

cluded that the teston should be eleven ounces fine, the proportion of the pieces according to the gold, so that five shillings of silver should be worth five of gold.[118]

23. Removing to Oatlands.

24. Agreed that the stamp of the shilling and sixpence should be: of [on] one side a king painted to the shoulders, in Parliament robes, and with a chain of the Order; [119] five shillings, of silver, and half-five shillings, should be a king on horseback armed, with a naked sword hard to his breast. Also that York's mint,[120] and Throckmorton's mint in the Tower, should go and work the fine standard. In the city of York and Canterbury should the small money be wrought of a baser state. Officers for the same were appointed.

A piece of Berwick wall fell because the foundation was shaken by working of a bulwark.

28. The Lord Marquis Dorset, grieved much with the disorder of the Marches toward Scotland, surrendered the wardenship thereof to bestow where I would.

27. The wardenship of the North given to the Earl of Warwick.[121]

Removing to Hampton Court.

28. Commissioners appointed for sitting on the Bishop of Chichester and Worcester—three lawyers and three civilians.[122]

10. The Imperials took the suburbs of Heding and burned them.[123]

[118] S. P. Dom., Edw. VI, XIII, 47 (September 25, 1551).

[119] I.e., portrayed with the Order of the Garter.

[120] York was Master of the Mint at Southwark prior to succeeding Sir Nicholas Throckmorton as Master of the Tower Mint.

[121] A few days later (October 4) it was announced to the Council that Warwick was to be advanced to a duchy, as was Dorset (*APC, 1550–1552*, p. 379).

[122] *Ibid.*, pp. 368–369 (September 28, 1551).

[123] The King probably meant Hesdin, which had been surrendered to

26. The passport of the Dowager of Scotland was made for a longer time, until Christmas, and also, if she were driven, to pass by land quietly into Scotland.[124]

20. Mons. d'Angoulême was born,[125] and the Duke of Vendôme had a son [126] by the Princess of Navarre, his wife.

30. The feast of Michaelmas was kept by me in the robes of the Order.[127]

OCTOBER

1. The commission for the making of five shillings, half-five shillings, groats,[128] and sixpences 11 ounces fine, and pence with halfpennies and farthings four ounces fine, was followed and signed.

1. There was Rich, Lord Chancellor of England, did send back a letter for the execution of the commission for certain [ones] to sit on the Bishops of Chichester and Worcester because there were but eight hands [signed] to it.[129]

2. I wrote a letter that I marveled that he would refuse to sign that bill or deliver that letter that I had willed any one about me to write. Also that it should be a great impediment for me to send to all my Council and I should seem to be in bondage. But

---

France in 1537 and which was recaptured and destroyed by Imperial forces in 1553. In December, 1552, the French were preparing to give the place a strong garrison.

[124] *APC, 1550–1552*, p. 364 (September 24, 1551).

[125] The future Henry III.

[126] Henry de Bourbon, who died in 1553 shortly before the birth of his brother, the future Henry IV.

[127] The King was most proud of his membership in the Order of St. Michael. The Council transmitted to the French government the full details of this expression of amity (*Cal. S. P. For., 1547–1553*, p. 175).

[128] Nichols (*Literary Remains*, II, 346) has pointed out that "groat" here means shilling.

[129] There were in fact only eight subscribed as present at the meeting of the Council when the commission was approved (*APC, 1550–1552*, p. 369).

by oversight it chanced and [not] thinking the more the better.[130]

5. Jarnac [131] came in post for declaration of two things: the one that the Queen had a third son of which she was delivered, called le duc d'Angoulême, of which the King prayed me to be godfather. I answered I was glad of the news and that I thanked him for that I should be godfather, which was a token of [the] good will he bore me. Also that I would dispatch for the accomplishment thereof the Lord Clinton, Lord Admiral of England.

He said he came also to tell me a second point of the good success of his master's wars. He told how the last month in Champagne beside Sedan, 1,000 horse Imperial with divers Hungarians, Martin van Rossem [132] being their captain and leader, entered the country and the alarum[?] came. The skirmish began so hot that the French horse, about two or three hundred men of arms, came out and took van Rossem's brother and slew divers. Also how in Piedmont, since the taking of the last four towns, three others were taken: Monteglio [Montechiaro], Saluzzo, and the town of Borgo. The Turks had come to Naples and spoiled the country and taken Ostia in the mouth of [the] Tiber. Also in Sicily he had taken a good haven and a town.

6. Jarnac departed, having been in the court under my lodging

---

[130] This important and lengthy letter, the gist of which is accurately set out here, is preserved in S. P. Dom., Edw. VI, XIII, 55 (October 1, 1551). The King maintained that his express direction on advice of the Council was quite sufficient in this and all similar instances. Rich resigned his post shortly afterward (December 21, 1551); see below, p. 101. This and the preceding paragraph have been crossed off but are presented because of the importance of the matter.

[131] Gui de Chabot, Baron de Jarnac, Governor of La Rochelle.

[132] An experienced professional soldier, who in 1543 had defeated the Imperial forces at Sittard with a Danish-Clevish army. Now a commander in the Imperial army, he was in March, 1553, made Governor of Luxemburg.

the night before. The Bishops of Worcester and Chichester were deposed for contempts.

7. There was appointed to go with the Lord Admiral, Mr. [Henry] Neville, Mr. Barnaby, gentlemen of the chamber, Sir William Stafford, Sir Adrian Poynings, Sir John Norton, Sir John Tyrrell, knights, and Mr. Brooke.[133]

8. Letters directed to the captains of the gendarmery that they should muster the 8th of November, being the Sunday after All Hallows Day.

11. Harry, Marquis of Dorset, created Duke of Suffolk; John, Earl of Warwick, created Duke of Northumberland; William, Earl of Wiltshire, created Marquis of Winchester; Sir William Herbert created Earl of Pembroke and Lord of Cardiff.[134] Mr. Sidney, Mr. Neville, Mr. Cheke, all three of the Privy Chamber, made knights.[135] Also Mr. Cecil, one of the two chief Secretaries.

13. Proclamation signed touching the calling in of testons and groats, that they that list might come[?] to the mint and have fine silver of twelvepence for two testons.

3. Prior de Capua departed the French King's service and went to his order of knights in Malta, partly for displeasure to the Count Villiers,[136] the Constable's brother-in-law, partly for that Malta was assailed often by the Turks.

7. Sir Thomas Palmer[137] came to the Earl of Warwick, since

---

[133] "Mr. Barnaby" was Barnaby Fitzpatrick, the King's friend; Poynings was a soldier who gained a considerable military reputation under Elizabeth; Norton was also a professional soldier who had served in Scotland and in France; Tyrrell had served the Crown in minor diplomatic capacities; "Mr. Brooke" was possibly a son of Lord Cobham.

[134] For details of the ceremony, see S. P. Dom., Edw. VI, XIII, 56.

[135] I.e., Sir Henry Sidney, Sir Henry Neville, and Sir John Cheke.

[136] Honorat de Savoie, Marquis de Villars, Comte de Tende (1509–1580), was for most of his long life a professional soldier in the French army and was made a marshal of France and Admiral after the death of Coligny.

[137] Palmer was a skillful and courageous soldier who had recently returned

that time Duke of Northumberland, to deliver him his chain, being a very fair one, for every link weighed one ounce, to be delivered to Jarnac and so to receive as much. Whereupon in my Lord's garden he declared a conspiracy. How at St. George's Day last, my Lord of Somerset (who then was going to the North if the Master of the Horse, Sir William Herbert, had not assured him on his honor that he should have no hurt) went to raise the people, and the Lord Grey before, to know who were his friends. Afterward a device was made to call the Earl of Warwick to a banquet with the Marquis of Northampton and divers other[s] and to cut off their heads. Also, if he found a bare company about them by the way, to set upon them.[138]

11. He declared also that Mr. Vane had 2,000 men in readiness. Sir Thomas Arundel [139] had assured my Lord that the Tower was safe. Mr. Partridge [140] should raise London and take the

---

from an assignment to survey the defenses along the Scottish border (see above, p. 34). His hatred of Somerset, which was returned, had been well known since late 1548 and may possibly have been connected with a military failure of Palmer's in Scotland. Since early 1551 he had been regarded as a partisan of Northumberland and was one of those executed with him in 1553.

[138] The King's account of the alleged conspiracy (under dates October 7, 11, 14, 15, 17, 18, and 19) is an important source for the study of the bizarre and highly controversial evidence produced against Somerset. Other materials are to be found in S. P. Dom., Edw. VI, XIII, 57, 64, 65, 66, 67, and in the Acts of the Privy Council. It is evident that the King entertained no doubts regarding the allegations and that his version of the conspiracy and his later reporting of the trial were derived from what Northumberland, or Northumberland's partisans, had told him. It should be remarked that the more incredible particulars in the charges were not pressed at Somerset's trial.

[139] Sir Thomas Arundel, of Dorset, had been knighted in 1533. He was executed for his share in the alleged conspiracy, upon the slightest of evidence.

[140] Sir Miles Partridge, who had won fame for his skill and valor at Pinkie, was a friend and close follower of Somerset's. He was hanged in 1552.

Great Seal with the [ap]prentice[s] of London. Seymour [141] and Hammond [142] should wait upon him, and all the horse of the gendarmery should be slain.

15. Removing to Westminster, because it was thought this matter might easilier [*sic*] and surelier be dispatched there, and likewise all other [matters].

14. The Duke [of Somerset] sent for the Secretary Cecil to tell him he suspected some ill. Mr. Cecil answered that if he were not guilty he might be of good courage; if he were, he had nothing to say but to lament him. Whereupon the Duke sent him a letter of defiance and called Palmer who, after denial [was] made of his declaration, was let go.

16. This morning none was at Westminster of the conspirators. The first was the Duke, who came, later than he was wont, of himself. After dinner he was apprehended. Sir Thomas Palmer [was taken] on the terrace walking there. Hammond, passing by Mr. Vice-Chamberlain's door, was called in by John Peers [143] to make a match at shooting, and so [was] taken. Newdigate was called for as from my Lord his master and taken.[144] Likewise were John Seymour and Davy Seymour.[145] Arundel also was taken, and the Lord Grey, coming out of the country. Vane, upon two sendings of my Lord in the morning, fled at the first sending; he said my Lord was not stout, and if he could get home he cared for none of them all, he was so strong. But after-

[141] Alexander Seymour, a distant relative of Somerset, had recently been returned as a member of Parliament.

[142] Lawrence Hammond has not been satisfactorily identified. It is probable that he was a Yeoman of the Guard. He was in due course released without punishment.

[143] Peers was an officer in the Yeomen of the Guard.

[144] Francis Newdigate was the Steward of the Duke's household.

[145] John Seymour was Somerset's eldest son by his first marriage; he died in December, 1552, while still a prisoner in the Tower. David Seymour, probably a distant relation of Somerset, was never under straiter imprisonment than house arrest.

[ward] he was found by John Peers in a stable of his man's at Lambeth, under the straw. These went with the Duke to the Tower this night, saving Palmer, Arundel, and Vane, who were kept in chambers here, apart.

17. The Duchess [of Somerset], Crane and his wife,[146] with the chamber keeper, were sent to the Tower for devising these treasons; James Wingfield also, for casting out of bills seditious. Also Mr. Partridge was attached and Sir James [Thomas] Holcroft.[147]

18. Mr. Bannister and Mr. Vaughan were attached and sent to the Tower, and so was Mr. Stanhope.[148]

19. Sir Thomas Palmer confessed that the gendarmery on the muster day should be assaulted by 2,000 footmen of Mr. Vane's, and my Lord's hundred horse, besides his friends which stood by, and the idle people which took his part. If he were overthrown he would (set upon *crossed out*) run through London and cry "Liberty, liberty," to raise the [ap]prentices, and if he could he would go to the Isle of Wight or to Poole.

22. The Dowager of Scotland was by tempest driven to land at Portsmouth, and so she sent word she would take the benefit of the safe-conduct to go by land and to see me.[149]

---

[146] Little is known about William Crane. Under torture he implicated Somerset in the alleged conspiracy, who at the trial demanded that he be permitted to face his accuser. Crane and his wife were in due course both released without penalty.

[147] Holcroft, a friend and close supporter of the Duke of Somerset, was charged particularly with having been privy to the plot to seize Northumberland. See also above, p. 9, n. 5.

[148] John Bannister was a servant to Somerset and the brother of Mrs. James Wingfield, whose husband had been arrested for "casting out of bills seditious." George Vaughan has not been further identified. Sir Michael Stanhope had been favored by Henry VIII and had given able service in the Scottish wars. He had been briefly imprisoned at the time of Somerset's first fall and was executed in 1552.

[149] *APC, 1550–1552,* p. 397 (October 25, 1551); for a full account of the

26. She came from Portsmouth to Mr. White's house.[150]

24. The Lords sat in the Star Chamber and there declared the matters and accusations laid against the Duke, meaning to stay the minds of the people.

25. Certain German princes in the beginning of this month desired aid in [the] cause of religion of 400,000 thalers, if they should be driven to make shift by necessity, and offered the like also if I entered into any war for them.[151] Whereupon I called the Lords and considered, as appears by a scroll in the board at Westminster; and thereupon appointed that the Secretary Petre and Sir William Cecil [and] another Secretary [Wotton] should talk with the messenger to know the matter precisely and the names of those that would enter the confederacy.

28. The Dowager came to Sir Richard Cotton's house.[152]

29. She came from Sir Richard Cotton's to the Earl of Arundel['s] [153] to dinner and [was] brought to Mr. Browne's house,[154] where met her gentlemen of Sussex.

30. She came and was conveyed by the same gentlemen to

---

royal visit, see *Cal. S. P. For., 1547–1553*, pp. 190–191 (Council to Pickering, November 5, 1551).

[150] Southwick Priory, about three miles northeast of Fareham, Hants, had been granted to John White in 1538; he was later Bishop of Winchester under Queen Mary.

[151] The princes were Maurice, Elector of Saxony, the Marquis of Brandenburg, the Duke of Mecklenburg, and the Landgrave of Hesse, preparing for the conspiracy against the Emperor under Maurice's leadership. Similar proposals were at about the same time extended to Henry II, who in January, 1552, ratified an agreement with Maurice already being negotiated at the date of Edward's entry here (*Cal. S. P. For., 1547–1553*, p. 187: October ?, 1551, and p. 197).

[152] At Warblington (near Havant), Hants.

[153] Presumably at Stanstead Park (Stanstead, Sussex), rather than at Arundel.

[154] Sir Anthony Browne's house at Cowdray Castle, near Midhurst, Sussex.

Guildford, where the Lord William Howard [155] and the gentlemen of Surrey met her.

All this month the Frenchmen continued spoiling of the Emperor's frontiers, and in a skirmish at Asti [156] they slew (800 *crossed out*) 100 Spaniards.

31. A letter directed to Sir Arthur Darcy to take the charge of the Tower and to discharge Sir John Markham upon this: that, without making any of the Council privy, he suffered the Duke to walk abroad and certain letters to be sent and answered between Davy Seymour and Mrs.[?] Po[yn]ings, with other divers suspicions.

17. There were letters sent to all emperors, kings, ambassadors, noblemen, men, and chief men in countries, of the late conspiracy.

31. She [the Dowager Queen of Scotland] came to Hampton Court, conveyed by the same Lord and gentlemen aforesaid, and two miles and a half from thence, in a valley, there met her the Lord Marquis of Northampton, accompanied with the Earl of Wiltshire, son and heir to the Lord High Treasurer Marquis of Winchester, the Lord Fitzwalter, son to the Earl of Sussex, the Lord Evre, the Lord Braye, the Lord Robert Dudley, the Lord Garret, [157] Sir Nicholas Throckmorton, Sir Edward Rogers, and divers other gentlemen, besides all the gentlemen pensioners, men of arms, and ushers, sewers, [158] and carvers, to the number of 120 gentlemen, and so she was brought to Hampton

[155] Lord William Howard, first Baron Howard of Effingham; see also below, p. 147, n. 176.

[156] In Piedmont.

[157] Gerald Fitzgerald, whose father, the ninth earl of Kildare, had been executed for treason in 1537, was restored to some of his paternal estates by Edward in 1552; he was the son-in-law of Sir Anthony Browne and (by the latter's second marriage) also his brother-in-law.

[158] "Sewer": an attendant at a meal who supervised the details of the dining.

Court.[159] At the gate thereof met her the Lady Marquis of Northampton, the Countess of Pembroke, and divers other ladies and gentlewomen to the number of threescore, and so she was brought to her lodging on the Queen's side, which was all hanged with arras, and so was the hall and all the other lodgings of mine in the house very finely dressed. And for this night and the next day all was spent in dancing and pastime, as though it were a court, and great presence of gentlemen resorted thither.

26. Letters were written forbecause of this business to defer the musters of the gendarmery till the [*blank*] day of December.

NOVEMBER

1. The Dowager perused [160] the house of Hampton Court and saw some coursing of deer.

2. She came to the Bishop's Palace at London, and there she lay, and all her train lodged about her.

3. The Duke of Suffolk, the Earl of Warwick, [the Earl of] Wiltshire, and many other Lords and gentlemen were sent to her to welcome her and to say on my behalf that if she lacked anything she should have it, for her better furniture, and also [that] I would willingly see her the day following.

The 26th of October Crane confessed the most part, even as Palmer did before, and more also; how that the place where the nobles should have been banqueted and their heads stricken off was the Lord Paget's house, and how the Earl of Arundel knew of the matter as well as he, by Stanhope who was a messenger between them. Also some part [of] how he went to London to get friends once in August last, feigning himself sick.

[159] The Council had on October 25 dispatched letters to the nobility, summoning them and their ladies to attend. At the same time the Princesses Mary and Elizabeth had been apprised of the visit (*APC, 1550–1552*, p. 397).

[160] "Perused": an early use of the word in this sense.

Hammond also confessed the watch he kept in his chamber at night. Brend also confessed much of this matter.[161] The Lord Strange confessed how the Duke willed him to stir me to marry his third daughter, the Lady Jane, and willed him to be his spy in all matters of my doings and sayings and to know when some of my Council spoke secretly with me.[162] This he confessed of himself.

4. The Duke of Suffolk [and] the Lord Fitzwalter, the Lord Braye, and divers other Lords and gentlemen, accompanied with his [Suffolk's] wife, the Lady Frances, the Lady Margaret,[163] the Duchesses of Richmond and of Northumberland, the Lady Jane, daughter to the Duke of Suffolk, the Marchionesses of Northampton and Winchester, the Countesses of Arundel, Bedford, Huntingdon, and Rutland, with 100 other ladies and gentlewomen, went to her and brought her through London to Westminster. At the gate there received her the Duke of Northumberland, Great Master, and the Treasurer and Comptroller and the Earl of Pembroke with all the sewers and carvers and cupbearers, to the number of thirty. In the hall I met her with all the rest of the Lords of my Council, as the Lord Treasurer, the Marquis of Northampton, etc., and from the outer gate up to the presence chamber on both sides stood the guard. The court, the hall, and the stairs were full of serving-

[161] Probably the John Brend who was an officer in the Scottish war and who had since been employed in minor diplomatic capacities in Scotland; in February 1547/1548 he was sent to treat with the Duke of Argyll (*APC, 1547–1550*, p. 170). Under the pseudonym of "William Watson," he had also been employed on a special mission to the cities of Bremen, Hamburg, and Lübeck, in part to enjoin them not to send naval supplies to the Scots (Instructions, December 11, 1547, *Cal. S. P. For.*, *1547–1553*, p. 14; warrant for payment, *APC, 1547–1550*, p. 151).

[162] Lord Strange repeated this charge in Somerset's presence at the trial, though it was peripheral to the charges being pressed. There may be truth in it. Lady Jane Seymour was then about ten years of age.

[163] Margaret Douglas, daughter of Queen Margaret of Scotland by her second marriage to the Earl of Angus; a granddaughter of Henry VII.

men; the presence chamber, great chamber, and her presence chamber, of gentlemen; and so, having brought her to her chamber, I retired to mine. I went to her to dinner. She dined under the same cloth of estate at my left hand. At her reward [rearward?] dined my cousin Frances and my cousin Margaret.[164] At mine sat the French ambassador. We were served by two services: two sewers, cupbearers, carvers, and gentlemen. Her maître d'hôtel came before her service, and mine officers before mine. There were two cupboards,[165] one of gold four stages [in] height, another of massy silver six stages. In her great chamber dined at three boards the ladies only. After dinner, when she had heard some music, I brought her to the hall and so she went away.

5. The Duke of Northumberland, the Lord Treasurer, the Lord Marquis of Northampton, the Lord Privy Seal, and divers other[s] went to see her and to deliver a ring with a diamond and two nags, as a token from me.

6. The Duke of Northumberland with his band of [one] hundred, of which forty were in black velvet with white and black sleeves, sixty in cloth; the Earl of Pembroke with his band and fifty more; the Earl of Wiltshire with fifty-eight of his father's band; all the pensioners, men of arms, and the equerry, with divers ladies, [such] as my cousin Marg[ar]et, the Duchesses of Richmond and Northumberland, brought the Queen to Shoreditch through Cheapside and Cornhill, and there met her gentlemen of Middlesex 100 horse, and so she was conveyed out of the realm, met in every shire with gentlemen.[166]

8. The Earl of Arundel [167] committed to the Tower with Sir

---

[164] I.e., the Lady Frances and the Lady Margaret, as above.

[165] Presumably carried in for the serving of food.

[166] Elaborate arrangements were made to conduct the royal party northward in seventeen stages, with from ten to twenty escorts of the countryside for each stage, to Norham, where the Queen Dowager passed into Scotland (Harl. MSS., 290, f. 7, in Cecil's hand).

[167] Arundel was not at first charged, but, as Crane's suspect confession

[Thomas] Stradley [Stradling] and St. Albin his men,[168] because Crane did more and more confess of him.

7. A Frenchman was sent again into France to be delivered again to the Frenchmen at the borders because of a murder he did at Dieppe, and thereupon he fled hither.

14. Answer was given to the Germans,[169] which did require 400,000 thalers if need so required for maintenance of religion: first, that I was very well inclined to make peace, amity, or bargain with them I knew to be of mine religion (forbecause this messenger was sent only to know my inclination and will to enter, and not with full resolution of any matters). Secondly, I would know whether they could get unto them any such strength of other princes as were able to maintain the war and to do the reciproque [170] to me again if need should so require. And therefore willed those three princes—Duke Maurice of Saxony, the Duke of Mecklenburg, and the Marquis John of Brandenburg, from which he was sent—to open the matter to the Duke of Prussia [171] and to all princes about them and somewhat to get the good will of Hamburg, Lübeck, Bremen, etc., showing them an inkling of the matter. Thirdly, I would have the matter of religion made more plain, lest when war should be made for other quarrels they should say it were religion. Fourthly, he should come with more ample commission from the same states to talk of the sum of money and other appurtenances. This answer was given lest, if I assented wholly at the first, they would declare mine intent to the Steads [172] and whole

---

began to implicate him, was arrested on November 8. Though he was kept a close prisoner for a year, Northumberland never brought the peer to trial. He was released on condition of a confession which he subsequently disavowed.

[168] Sir Thomas Stradling was Sheriff of Glamorganshire. Nothing more is known about St. Albin, who was imprisoned in the Marshalsea.

[169] See above, p. 90 (October 25, 1551).

[170] "Reciproque": "the like" (*NED*).   [171] Albert of Brandenburg.

[172] I.e., the Hanse towns.

senates and so to come abroad, whereby I should run into danger of breaking the league with the Emperor.[173]

16. The Lord Admiral took his leave to go into France for [the] christening of the French King's son.

18. [Mr.] Fossey, secretary to the Duke Maurice, who was here for [the] matter above specified [*unfinished*].[174]

20. A proclamation appointed to go forth for that there went one before this time: that set prices of beef, oxen, and muttons, which was meant to continue but to November, whenas the Parliament should have been—to abrogate that and to appoint certain commissioners to cause the graziers to bring to the market and to sell at prices reasonable. And that certain overseers should be besides to certify of the justices' doings.[175]

23. The Lord Treasurer [Winchester] appointed High Steward for the arraignment of the Duke of Somerset.

At this time Duke Maurice began to show himself friend to the Protestants, who before that time had appeared their enemy.

[173] Westminster, November 19, 1551. Full text of the reply of the English government is in Cecil's hand in Latin draft printed in Nichols, *Literary Remains*, II, 366 n.

[174] "Fossey" may probably be identified as an agent named John Füss who was sent to England by Maurice of Saxony in early September. In *Briefe und Akten zur Geschichte des sechzehnten Jahrhunderts*, ed. A. von Druffel, II (Munich, 1880), 19, he is described as a secretary of the Marquis of Brandenburg. He was introduced at court by Lasco (*Cal. S. P. Span., 1550–1552*, p. 369). The Imperial ambassador was troubled in late September because he could gain no information concerning the mission (*ibid.*, p. 374). But in late December, reporting on Füss's departure, the ambassador correctly guessed that an effort had been made to secure English support for some Protestant German grouping which would offer resistance to the Interim (*ibid.*, p. 425). A letter dated January 8, 1552, reports the arrival of Füss in Germany and his report that England had displayed a mild interest in a defensive league (Druffel, *Briefe und Akten*, II, 18).

[175] The new proclamation was to renew and extend STC 7843 (September 9, 1551). I have found no copy of the intended proclamation. See also *APC, 1550–1552*, p. 420 (November 20, 1551).

27. The [a]foresaid proclamation proclaimed.

17. The Earl of Warwick, Mr. Harry Sidney, Sir Harry Neville, and Sir Harry Gates did challenge all comers at tilt the 3rd of January and at tourney the 6th of January, and this challenge was proclaimed.

28. News came that Maximilian,[176] coming out of Spain, nine of galleys with his stuff, and 120 jennets [177] and his treasure was taken by the French.

24. The Lord Admiral entered France and came to Boulogne.

26. The captain of Portsmouth had word and commandment to bring the model of the castle and plate,[178] to the intent it might be fortified, because Baron de la Garde had seen it,[179] having an engineer with him and, as it was thought, had the plat of it.

30. Twenty-two peers, as nobles, besides the Council, heard Sir Thomas Palmer, Mr. Hammond, Mr. Crane, and Newdigate swear that their confessions were (was *in MS.*) true, and they did say that that was said without any kind of compulsion, force, envy, or displeasure, but as favorably to the Duke as they could swear to with safe conscience.

DECEMBER, A° D'NI 1551°, 5° A° R^i R^s E. 6^i. 5^a CHARTA

1. The Duke of Somerset came to his trial at Westminster Hall. The Lord Treasurer sat as High Steward of England under the cloth of estate on a bench between two posts, three degrees (steps *crossed out*) high: all the Lords, to the number of twenty-six, *videlicet:*

[176] Maximilian of Austria, afterward as Maximilian II, Holy Roman Emperor (1564–1576).

[177] "Jennet": a small (and prized) Spanish horse.

[178] "Plate": earlier form of "plat" or "plot," meaning plan or map.

[179] De la Garde would have had opportunity to observe the Portsmouth fortifications when he had arrived there on October 22 with ten warships as escort of the Queen Dowager of Scotland (*Cal. S. P. For., 1547–1553*, p. 190).

DUKES	BARONS
Suffolk	Abergavenny
Northumberland	Audley
	Wharton
MARQUISES	Evre
Northampton	Latimer
	Burgh
EARLS	Zouche
Derby	Stafford
Bedford	Wentworth
Huntingdon	Darcy
Rutland	Stourton
Bath	Windsor
Sussex	Cromwell
Worcester	Cobham
Pembroke	Braye

VISCOUNTS
Hereford

These sat a degree [180] under and heard the matter debated.[181] First, after the indictments [were] read, five in number[?], the learned counsel laid to my Lord of Somerset Palmer's confession.[182] To which he answered that he never minded to raise the North and declared all ill he could devise of Palmer; but he was afraid for bruits,[183] and that moved him to send to Sir William Herbert. Replied it was again, that the worse Palmer was, the more he served his purpose. For the [planned] banquet: first he swore it was untrue and required more witnesses; when Crane's confession was read, he would

[180] "Degree": i.e., one of a flight, or set, of steps.

[181] The King actually names twenty-eight peers (if Winchester be counted) as being present. It should be remarked that of the forty-seven temporal peers of England only this fraction was present at the trial.

[182] The trial was actually based on three indictments.

[183] "Bruits": rumors.

have had him come face to face. For London: he meant nothing
for hurt of any lord, but for his own defense. For the gendarmery: it were but a mad matter for him to enterprise, with his 100
against 900. For having men in his chamber at Greenwich, confessed by Partridge: it seemed he meant no harm, because,
when he could have done harm, he did it not. My Lord Strange's
confession: he swore it was untrue, and the Lord Strange took
his oath it was true. Newdigate's, Hammond's and Alexander
Seymour's confessions he denied, because they were his men.

The lawyers rehearsed [184] how to raise men at his house for
an ill intent, as to kill the Duke of Northumberland, was treason
by an act 3° (2 *crossed out*) anno of my reign against unlawful
assemblies: for to devise the death of the Lords was felony; [185]
to mind resisting his attachment was felony; to raise London
was treason; and to assault the Lords was felony.[186] He answered he did not intend to raise London, and that swore the
witness[es] [who] were not there.[187] His assembling of men
was but for his own defense. He did not determine to kill the
Duke of Northumberland, the Marquis, etc., but spoke of it and
determined after[ward] the contrary; and yet seemed to confess he went about their death. The Lords went together. The
Duke of Northumberland would not agree that any searching of
his death should be treason. So the Lords acquitted him of
high treason and condemned him of treason felonious, and so he
was adjudged to be hanged. He gave thanks to the Lords for
their open trial and cried mercy of the Duke of Northumberland, the Marquis of Northampton, and the Earl of Pembroke
for his ill meaning against them, and made suit for his (life *inserted*), wife and children, servants and debts, and so departed
without the ax of the Tower. The people, knowing not the matter, shouted half a dozen times so loud that from the hall (pal-

[184] "Rehearsed": cited, quoted.

[185] It was, in fact, treason under the statute.

[186] Somerset was tried under 3 & 4 Edward VI, c. 5.

[187] The meaning is not clear. Burnet may be right in suggesting that the
intended word order was, "swore that the witnesses were not there."

ace *crossed out*) door it was heard at Charing Cross plainly, and rumors went that he was quit of all.[188]

2. The peace concluded by the Lord Marquis was ratified by me before the ambassador and delivered to him signed and sealed.[189]

3. The Duke told certain Lords that were in the Tower that he had hired Berteville to kill them, which thing Berteville, examined on, confessed, and so did Hammond, that he knew of it.[190]

7. I saw the musters of the new band [of] men of arms, 100 of my Lord Treasurer's, 100 of Northumberland, 100 Northampton, 50 Huntingdon, 50 Rutland, 120 of Pembroke, 50 Darcy, 50 Cobham, 100 Sir Thomas Cheyney, and 180 of the pensioners and their bands, with the old men of arms, all well-armed men, some with feathers, staves, and pencels of their colors, some with sleeves and half coats, some with bards [191] and staves, etc. The horses all fair and great, the least would not have been given for less than £20. There was none under 14 handful and a half the most part,[192] and almost all horses. With their guidon [193] going before them, they passed twice about St. James's field and compassed it [a]round and so departed.

15. There were certain devices for laws delivered to my learned Council to pen, as by a schedule appeareth.[194]

---

[188] Seeing the ax turned away from the prisoner, the people outside the hall thought that the verdict had been one of acquittal.

[189] The King here refers to the marriage treaty with France.

[190] Berteville was imprisoned on the charge of having been the assassin hired by Somerset to slay Northumberland, but the evidence was never introduced at the trial. It is significant that he was released on November 1 and that a few weeks later the Council provided him with a house and paid certain of his debts. It is all too clear that prejudiced and almost certainly false information was being fed to the King by sources very close to Northumberland. For Berteville, see also p. 7, n. 22.

[191] "Bards": trappings for the forequarters of a horse.

[192] "Handful": i.e., hand, or hand-breadth; an earlier use of the term than that cited by the *NED*.

[193] "Guidon": pennant.

[194] In preparation for the forthcoming Parliament.

18. It was appointed I should have six chaplains ordinary, of which two [are] ever to be present and four always absent in preaching: one year two in Wales, two in Lancashire and Derby; next year two in the Marches of Scotland, two in Yorkshire; [the] 3rd year two in Devonshire, two in Hampshire; [the] 4th year two in Norfolk, Suffolk, and Essex, and two in Kent, Sussex, etc. These six to be Bill, Harley, (Estcourt *crossed out*), Perne, Grindal, (Bradford *crossed out*).[195]

20. The Bishop of Durham was, for concealment of treason written to him and not disclosed at all till the party did open him, committed to the Tower.[196]

21. Richard Lord Rich, Chancellor of England, considering his sickness, did deliver his seal to the Lord Treasurer, the Lord Great Master, and the Lord Chamberlain, sent to him for that purpose during the time of his sickness, and chiefly of the Parliament.[197]

5. The Lord Admiral came to the French King and after[ward] was sent to the Queen and so conveyed to his chamber.

6. The Lord Admiral christened the French King's child and called him by the King's commandment Edward Alexander [Henry]. All that day there was music, dancing, and playing, with triumph in the court. But the Lord Admiral was sick of a

---

[195] The clergymen mentioned are William Bill, later (1560) Dean of Westminster; John Harley, later (1553) Bishop of Hereford, deprived by Queen Mary; Andrew Perne, later Dean of Ely; Edmund Grindal, later Archbishop of Canterbury. Each chaplain was granted an annuity of £40 for his labors. Estcourt has not been identified; John Bradford was a famous preacher who suffered death under Queen Mary. It seems probable that these two were never appointed.

[196] Cuthbert Tunstall, then in his seventy-seventh year, was almost certainly falsely charged with misprision of treason. His real offense was sympathy for Somerset. Northumberland's attempt to secure his deprivation by act of Parliament failed when the Commons demanded that the Bishop be heard. He was later deprived by commission, the treason charge being dropped.

[197] Rich had been seriously ill and was making a slow recovery; however, his real offense was suspected sympathy for Somerset.

double quartan.[198] Yet he presented Barnaby to the French King, who took him to his chamber.

7. The treaty was delivered to the Lord Admiral; and the French King read it in open audience at mass, with the ratification of it. The Lord Admiral took his leave of the French King and returned to Paris very sick.

The same day the French King showed the Lord Admiral letters that came from Parma, how the Frenchmen had gotten two castles of the Imperials, and in the defense of the one the Prince of Macedonia was slain on the walls and was buried with triumph at Parma.

22. The Great Seal of England [was] delivered to the Bishop of Ely to be keeper thereof during the Lord Rich's sickness.

The band of 100 men of arms, which my Lord of Somerset late had, appointed to the Duke of Suffolk.

23. Removing to Greenwich.

24. I began to keep holy this Christmas and continued till Twelfth Night.[199]

26. Sir Anthony St. Leger, for matters laid against him by the Bishop of Dublin, was banished [from] my chamber till he had made answer, and had the articles delivered him.[200]

28. The Lord Admiral came to Greenwich.

30. Commission was made out to the Bishop of Ely, the Lord Privy Seal, Sir John Gates, Sir William Petre, Sir Robert Bowes, and Sir Walter Mildmay for calling in my debts.[201]

[198] "Double quartan": an ague or fever, periodic in nature.

[199] Northumberland and the Council arranged elaborate entertainments for this Christmas season at court and in London, probably to divert attention from the impending execution of the Duke of Somerset.

[200] St. Leger had reluctantly introduced the English liturgy in Ireland, and Archbishop Browne had in August, 1551, forwarded a bitter complaint to the Council flatly accusing him of Romanist sympathies. St. Leger answered the charges convincingly and was re-admitted to royal favor in April, 1552.

[201] This commission may be regarded as inaugurating the important effort

[JANUARY, 1552]

1. Orders was taken with the chandlers of London for selling there tallow candles, which before some denied [1] to do; and some were punished with imprisonment.

3. The challenge that was made in the last month was fulfilled. The challengers were:

The Earl of Warwick	Sir Harry Neville
Sir Harry Sidney	Sir Harry Gates

Defendants

The Lord William [Howard]	Sir Will. Stafford
The Lord Fitzwalter	Sir John Perrot
The Lord Ambrose [Dudley]	Mr. Norris
The Lord Robert [Dudley]	Mr. Digby
The Lord FitzWarren	Mr. Warcopp
Sir G[eorge] Howard	Mr. Courtney

Mr. Knollys
The Lord Braye
Mr. Paston
Mr. Carey
Sir Anthony Browne
Mr. Drury [2]

---

to reorganize and improve the administration of governmental finance. The ministers here named represented all of the revenue courts, and they were instructed to collect or to re-arrange all debts due to the Crown and to secure the audit of all accounts. A total of £16,667 of delinquent moneys had been paid in by the close of the fiscal year 1552. The effort was persistent, at least a dozen further commissions being appointed in 1552 and 1553. These efforts were organically connected with the ambitious scheme for the reorganization of the entire structure of financial administration on which we have commented in the Introduction.

[1] "Denied": refused.

[2] Further identification of this somewhat incidental list of names seems unnecessary.

These, eighteen in all, ran six courses apiece at tilt against the challengers, and (in the end *crossed out*) accomplished their courses right well, and so departed again.

5. There were sent to Guînes Sir Richard Cotton and Mr. Braye to take view of Calais, Guînes, and the marches, and with advice of the captains and engineers to devise some amendment, and thereupon to make me certificate, and upon mine answer to go further [in]to the matter.[3]

4. It was appointed that if Mr. Stanhope lost Hull, then that I should no more be charged therewith, but that the town should take it and should have £40 a year for the repairing of the castle.[4]

2. I received letters out of Ireland, which appear in the Secretary's hand. And thereupon the earldom of Thomond was by me given from O'Brien's heirs, whose father [Murrough O'Brien] was dead, and had it for term of life, to Donough, Baron of Ibrachan, and his heirs male. Also letters were written of thanks to the Earls of Desmond and Clanricard and to the Baron of Dungannon.[5]

3. The Emperor's ambassador moved me severally that my sister Mary might have mass, which, with no little reasoning with him, was denied him.

---

[3] Sir Edward Braye had for some time past been commander at Calais; Cotton had formerly been Treasurer at Boulogne (*APC, 1550–1552*, p. 454: January 2, 1552).

[4] The meaning is that the municipal government of Hull had undertaken to maintain the defenses of the town, formerly part of the responsibility of Sir Michael Stanhope, who was now in the Tower (see above, p. 89). By indenture (February 20, 6 Edw. VI) Crown lands to the value of £50 per annum were conveyed to the town to help with the responsibilities now undertaken.

[5] Murrough O'Brien had in 1543 been created Earl of Thomond for life; now upon petition of his son and successor the earldom was vested in the son (Donough) and his heirs male (Nichols, *Literary Remains*, II, 386 n.).

6. The [a]foresaid challengers came in to the tourney, and the [a]foresaid defendants entered in after[ward] with two more with them—Mr. [William] Tyrrell and Mr. Robert Hopton—and fought right well, and so the challenge was accomplished. The same night was first a play; after a talk between one that was called Riches, and the other Youth,[6] whether [7] [one] of them was better. After some pretty reasoning there came in six champions of either side:

On Youth's side came:

My Lord Fitzwalter	Sir William Cobham
My Lord Ambrose [Dudley]	Mr. Carey
Sir Anthony Browne	Warcopp

On Riches' side:

My Lord FitzWarren	Digby
Sir Robert Stafford	Hopton
Mr. Courtney	Hungerford [8]

All these fought two to two at barriers in the hall. Then came in two appareled like Almains: the Earl of Ormonde and Jacques Granado; [9] and two came in like friars; but the Almains would not suffer them to pass till they had fought. The friars were Mr. Drury and Thomas Cobham.[10] After this followed two masques: one of men, another of women. Then a banquet of 120 dishes. This was the end of Christmas.

---

[6] This interlude may have been written by Sir Thomas Chaloner; no copy survives.

[7] "Whether": in the ME sense of a pronoun meaning "which of two."

[8] There seems to be no need for detailed identification of this list of courtiers, similar to those on pp. 103 and 106.

[9] Sir Jacques Granado, esquire of the stables, had been sent to Henry II in October, 1551, with a gift of geldings from Edward (*Cal. S. P. For., 1547–1553*, pp. 185, 186, 194, 200, 202, 375).

[10] Probably Thomas Drury, a captain in the royal service; Thomas Cobham has not been identified.

7. I went to Deptford to dine there and break up the hall.[11]

8. Upon a certain contention between Lord Willoughby and Sir Andrew Dudley, captain of Guînes, for their jurisdiction, the Lord Willoughby was sent for to come over to the intent the controversy might cease and order might be taken.[12]

12. There was a commission granted to the Earl of Bedford, and to the Mr. Vice-Chamberlain, and certain other[s], to call in my debts that were owing me, and the days past, and also to call in those that be past when the days be come.[13]

17. There was a match run between six gentlemen of a side at tilt.

Of one side	Of the other side
The Earl of Warwick	The Lord Ambrose
The Lord Robert [Dudley]	The Lord Fitzwalter
Mr. Sidney	Sir Francis Knollys
Mr. Neville	Sir Anthony Browne
Mr. Gates	Sir John Perrot
Anthony Digby	Mr. Courtney.
These won by 4 taints.[14]	

18. The French ambassador moved that we should destroy the Scottish part of the Debatable Ground, as they had done ours. It was answered, first, the Lord Conyers,[15] that made the agreement, made it none otherwise but as it should stand with his superior's pleasure. Whereupon, the same agreement being misliked because the Scottish part was much harder to overcome, word was sent to stay the matter; nevertheless the Lord Maxwell[16] did upon malice to the English Debatables [i.e., De-

[11] I.e., to close the Christmas festival.

[12] Northumberland, Dudley's brother, brought their bitter jurisdictional dispute before the Council in a memorandum addressed to Cecil (S. P. Dom., Edw. VI, XIV, 1).

[13] Another in the series of commissions appointed for this purpose (see above, p. 102, n. 201).

[14] "Taints": broken lances.   [15] Deputy Warden of the West Marches.

[16] Scottish Warden of the West Marches.

batable Grounds] overrun them. Whereupon [it] was [now] concluded that, if the Scots will agree [to] it, the ground shall be divided; if not, then shall the Scots waste their Debatables, and we ours, commanding them by proclamation to depart.[17]

This day the Steelyard [18] put in their answer to a certain complaint that the Merchant Adventurers laid against them.

19. The Bishop of Ely, *custos sigilli*, was made Chancellor because as *custos sigilli* he could execute nothing in the Parliament that should be done but only to seal ordinary things.

21. Removing to Westminster.

22. The Duke of Somerset had his head cut off upon Tower Hill between eight and nine o'clock in the morning.[19]

16. Sir William Pickering delivered a token to the Lady Elizabeth—a fair diamond.[20]

18. The Duke of Northumberland, having under him 100 men of arms and 100 light horse, gave up the keeping of fifty men-at-arms to his son, the Earl of Warwick.

23. The sessions of Parliament began.

24. John Gresham was sent over into Flanders to show to the Fuggers, to whom I owe money, that I would defer it or, if I paid it, pay it in English to make them keep up their French crowns, with which I [was] minded to pay them.[21]

[17] For further details on this thorny frontier issue, see S. P. Scotland, Edw. VI, V, 64 (December 21, 1551), 69, 70, 71 (August?, 1552); *APC, 1550–1552*, pp. 443, 456, 459.

[18] I.e., the Hanseatic merchants, who had long enjoyed special privileges in the Steelyard in London.

[19] As suggested in our introductory comment, this stands as the most puzzling and possibly the most revealing passage in the *Chronicle*.

[20] I.e., to the Princess Elizabeth of France, to whom Edward was now by treaty betrothed. The gem came from the estate of Catherine Parr.

[21] Almost certainly Thomas Gresham, the famous nephew of Sir John, is meant. Gresham was shortly to be appointed the royal financial agent

25. The answer of the Steelyard was delivered to certain of my learned Council to look on and oversee.

27. Sir Ralph Vane was condemned of felony in treason, answering like a ruffian.[22]

Paris [23] arrived with horses and showed how the French King had sent me six curtals,[24] two Turks, a Barbary [horse], two jennets, a stirring horse, and two little mules, and showed them to me.

29. Sir Thomas Arundel was likewise cast [25] of felony in treason, after long controversy; for the matter was brought in trial by seven of the clock in the morning [of the] 28th day; at noon the quest went together; they sat shut up together in a house, without meat or drink, because they could not agree, all that day and all night; this 29th day in the morning they did cast him.[26]

---

in Antwerp and to begin his vigorous and skillful restoration of English credit there.

[22] Sir Ralph Vane (or Fane), a professional soldier, vigorously denied any complicity in Somerset's alleged conspiracy but was nonetheless condemned and executed.

[23] This may well be the George Paris, an Irish rebel, who had been watched by the English ambassador while seeking favor and aid at the French court. On his arrival in England he sought a pardon, granted April 13, 1552, and proceeded shortly to Scotland, where by November he was suspected as an English agent and imprisoned. The English government sought to secure his release by means of the pardon and a permit to restore lands formerly belonging to Paris in Ireland (see p. 151), but this evidently unreliable man was still in prison well after Edward's death (*Cal. S. P. For.*, 1547–1553, pp. 48, 63, 89, 92; *Calendar of the State Papers relating to Ireland*, . . . 1509–1573, ed. H. C. Hamilton [London, 1860], pp. 107, 112, 128, 129; *Cal. S. P. Span.*, 1550–1552, pp. 454, 587–588; *APC*, 1550–1552, p. 471; *APC*, 1552–1554, pp. 12, 138, 202, 244–245; *Cal. Pat. Rolls, IV, 1550–1553*, 335).

[24] "Curtal": a horse with a docked tail.   [25] "Cast": convicted.

[26] Vane, Arundel, Stanhope, and Partridge were found guilty under the same statute invoked against Somerset. They were executed on February 27.

FEBRUARY, A° 6° REGNI EDWARDI 6[i]

2. There was a King of Arms made for Ireland, whose name was Ulster, and his province was all Ireland, and he was the first [to be] fourth King of Arms [27] and the first Herald of Ireland. The Emperor took the last month and this a million of pounds in Flanders.

6. It was appointed that Sir Philip Hoby should go to the Regent [28] upon pretense of ordering of quarrels of merchants, bringing with him £63,000 in French crowns to be paid in Flanders at Antwerp to the Schetz and their family of debts I owe them,[29] to the intent he might dispatch both under one.

8. Sir Miles Partridge was condemned of felony for the Duke of Somerset's matter, for he was one of the conspirators.

8. Fifty men-at-arms appointed to Mr. [Sir Ralph] Sadler.

9. John Beaumont, Master of the Rolls, was put in prison for forging a false deed from Charles Brandon, Duke of Suffolk, to the Lady Anne Powis of certain lands and leases.[30]

[27] I.e., this appointment, the first for Ireland, was the fourth for the realm. The person thus appointed was Bartholomew Butler, who was to serve until 1564.

[28] The Emperor's sister, Mary, Regent of the Netherlands.

[29] This was the first substantial payment made against foreign debts, which a few months earlier had totaled about £250,000. The sum was principally derived from arrearages being paid in, from the further sale of Crown lands, and from early receipts from the sale of surplus church plate. The principal payment was made to the great banking house of Jasper Schetz, with whom Gresham was then lodging. Gresham was at this time engaged in arranging for staggered short-term loans designed to bring the large English floating debt under control. Between March 1 and July 27, 1552, he had arranged refundings totaling slightly more than £106,000.

[30] The offense was particularly outrageous. Beaumont forged the Duke's name to a deed drawn in favor of Lady Powis, the Duke's elder daughter, while having persuaded Lady Powis, who was then suing in his court, to convey the lands thus fraudulently gained to him for an arranged sum of money (see below, p. 128: June 4, 1552).

10. Commission was granted out to thirty-two persons to examine, correct, and set forth the ecclesiastical laws.[31] The persons' names were these:

The Bishops	The Divines
Canterbury	Taylor of Lincoln
Ely	Taylor of Hadleigh
London	Mr. Cox, almoner
Winchester	Sir John Cheke
Exeter	Sir Anthony Cooke
Bath	Petrus Martyr
Gloucester	Johannes à Lasco
Rochester	Parker of Cambridge

Civilians	Lawyers
Mr. Secretary Petre	Justice Bromley
Mr. Secretary Cecil	Justice Hales
Mr. Traheron	Gosnold
Mr. Reed	Goodrich
Mr. Cook	Stamford
May, Dean of [St.]Paul's	Caryll
Skinner	Lucas
[Blank.] [32]	Gawdy [33]

[31] The reform and codification of the canon law had long been urged by Archbishop Cranmer. The work, carried forward principally by Cranmer and Martyr, was completed before the end of the reign but never gained the status of law.

[32] Richard Lyell.

[33] The King's list differs somewhat from that ordered by the Council on October 6, 1551, with instruction that the Lord Chancellor draft the commission, and empowering any eight of the thirty-two "to rough hewe the Cannon Lawe" and then to submit it for the approval of the entire commission (*APC, 1550–1552,* p. 382). Those appointed by the King's list may be briefly identified as follows. The bishops were: Cranmer, Goodrich, Ridley, Ponet, Coverdale, Barlow, Hooper, and Scory. The divines were: John Taylor (later Bishop of Lincoln), Rowland Taylor of Hadleigh, Suffolk (a Marian martyr), Richard Cox, Sir John Cheke (not a

10. Sir Philip Hoby departed with somewhat more crowns than came to 53,500 and odd pounds and had authority to borrow in my name of Lazarus Tucker £10,000 Flemish at 7 in the 100, for six months, to make up the pay, and to employ that that was in bullion to bring over with him.[34] Also, to carry 3,000 mark weight upon a license the Emperor granted the Schetz, which they did give me. After that to depart to Bruges, where the Regent lay, and there to declare to her the griefs [of] my subjects.

11. There was delivered of armor, by John [Thomas] Gresham, merchant, 1,100 pairs of corselets and horsemen harnesses, very fair.[35]

14. It was appointed that the "Jesus of Lübeck," a ship of 800 tons, and the "Mary Gonston" of 600 tons, should be let out for one voyage to merchantmen for £1,000, they at the voyage to Levant end to answer the tackling [of] the ship, the ordnance, munition, and to leave it in that case they took it.[36] Certain

---

clergyman), Sir Anthony Cooke (also not a clergyman), Peter Martyr, John à Lasco, and Matthew Parker (later Archbishop of Canterbury). The civil lawyers were: Petre and Cecil from the Council, Bartholomew Traheron, Sir Richard Reed (Master of Requests), William Cook (later High Judge of the Admiralty), William May, and Anthony Skinner (a chancery clerk). The lawyers were: Sir Thomas Bromley (Justice of the King's Bench), Sir James Hales, John Gosnold, Richard Goodrich, William Stamford, John Caryll, John Lucas (Master of Requests), and Thomas Gawdy. Several of these lawyers were promoted in the numerous judicial appointments made about three months later (see below, p. 122: May 14, 1552).

[34] Lazarus Tucker was one of the great bankers in Antwerp in this period. A friend of Gresham, he secured a loan of £10,000 for the hard-pressed English government in February, 1552, at 14 per cent interest. Tucker's financial relations with the English government continued well into the reign of Mary Tudor

[35] Gresham was buying military stores abroad.

[36] An unusual but not unprecedented undertaking for raising funds by hiring out royal ships for commercial voyages.

other of the worst of my ships were (was *in MS.*) appointed to be sold.

9. Proclamation was made at Paris that the bands of the Dauphin, the Duke of Vendôme, the Count d'Enghien, the Constable of France, the Duke of Guise and of Aumale,[37] the Count of Sancerre,[38] the Maréchal St. André, Mons. de Jarnac's, and Tavannes',[39] should, the 15th day of March, assemble at Troyes in Champagne to resist the Emperor. Also that the French King would go thither in person with 200 gentlemen of his household and 400 archers of his guard.

16. The French King sent his secretary, de l'Aubespine,[40] to declare this voyage to him (Mr. Pickering *inserted*), and to desire him to take pains to go with him and to be a witness of his doings.

19. Whereupon it was appointed that he should have 2,000 crowns for his furnishment besides his diet, and Barnaby 800.[41]

20. The Countess of Pembroke died.[42]

18. The Merchant Adventurers put in their replication to the Steelyard's answer.

23. A decree was made by the board [43] that, upon knowledge and information of their charters, they had found: first, that they [44] were no sufficient corporation. Secondarily, their num-

[37] Claude de Guise, who had commanded the French infantry in Italy.

[38] Louis de Bueil, Count of Sancerre.

[39] Gaspard de Saulx, Seigneur de Tavannes.

[40] Claude de l'Aubespine, Baron de Châteauneuf, Secretary of State to Henry II.

[41] Edward wrote in detail to his friend, Barnaby Fitzpatrick, respecting the role he was to play in the expedition (Nichols, *Literary Remains*, I, 76–77: February 25, 1552). His evident sense of almost personal involvement reflects a kind of vicarious participation with his friend.

[42] She was a sister to the late Queen, Catherine Parr.

[43] I.e., by the Council. Another, and now evidently a casual, use of a new and handy word. See above, p. 44, for what appears to be the first notice of the word, and see below, p. 122.

[44] I.e., the Steelyard merchants.

ber, names, and nation was unknown. Thirdly, that when they had forfeited their liberties King Edward the Fourth did restore them on this condition: [that they] should color [45] no strangers' goods, which they had done. Also that, whereas in the beginning they shipped not past eight cloths, after[ward] 100, after-[ward] 1,000, after that 6,000, now in their names were shipped 14,000 cloths in one year, and but 1,100 of all other strangers. For these considerations, sentence was given that they had forfeited their liberties and were in like case with other strangers.

28. There came ambassadors from Hamburg and Lübeck to speak on the behalf of the Steelyard merchants.

29. A Fleming would have searched the "Falcon" for Frenchmen. The "Falcon" turned, shot off, boarded the Fleming, and took him.

Payment was made of £63,500 Flemish to the Fuggers, all saving £6,000, which he borrowed in French crowns, by Sir Philip Hoby.

MARCH

2. The Lord of Abergavenny was committed to ward for striking the Earl of Oxford in the chamber of presence.

The answer for the ambassadors of the Steelyard was committed to the Lord Chancellor, the two Secretaries, Sir Robert Bowes, Sir John Baker, Judge Montagu, Griffith Solicitor, Gosnold, Goodrich, and Brooke.[46]

3. It was agreed that for better dispatch of things certain of the

---

[45] "Color": the meaning is ambiguous; probably used in the ME sense of "misrepresent," or to represent as one's own; i.e., they are charged with having represented foreign goods as domestic. The full text of the revocation may be found in *APC, 1550–1552*, pp. 487–489 (February 24, 1552).

[46] The five last-named were Sir Edward Montagu, Edward Griffith (or Griffin), John Gosnold (the Solicitor General), Richard Goodrich, and Robert Brooke (Recorder of London).

Council, with others joined with them, should overlook the penal laws and put certain of them in execution. Other[s] should answer suitors; other[s] should oversee my revenues and the order of them, and also the superfluous, and the payments heretofore made; other[s] should have commission for taking away superfluous bulwarks.[47]

1. Order was given, for defense of the merchants, to send four barks and two pinnaces to the sea.[48]

4. The Earl of Westmorland, the Lord Wharton, the Lord Conyers, Sir Thomas Palmer, and Sir Thomas Chaloner were appointed in commission to meet with the Scottish ambassadors for the equal division of the ground that was called the Debatable.

6. The French ambassador declared to the Duke of Northumberland how the French King had sent him a letter of credit for his ambassador. After delivery [was] made of the letter, he declared how Duke Maurice of Saxony, the Duke of Mecklenburg, the Marquis of Brandenburg, the Count of Mansfeld, and divers other princes of Germany had made a league (sent embas *crossed out*) with his master, offensive and defensive: the French to go to Strassburg with 30,000 footmen and 8,000 horsemen, the Almains to meet with them there the 25th of this month, with 15,000 footmen and 5,000 horsemen. Also the city of Strassburg had promised them victuals; and [he] declared how the French King would send me ambassadors to

[47] This clearly marks the beginning of the King's keen and intelligent interest in reforming the administrative procedures of the Council. His views and intentions are more fully and formally set out in his memorandum dated January 15, 1553, see below, pp. 181–184. For a helpful discussion of this reform effort, terminated only by Edward's death, see F. G. Emmison, "A Plan . . . for Reorganizing the Privy Council's Work, 1552–1553," in the *Bulletin of the Institute of Historical Research*, XXXI (1958), 203–210.

[48] Against Flemish warships which had been molesting English cargo vessels.

have me into the same league. Also that the Marquis of Brandenburg and Count of Mansfeld had been privily conveyed to the
French King's presence and were again departed to levy men,
and he thought by this time they were in the field.[49]

10. He declared the same thing to me in the same manner.

9. It was consulted touching the marts, and it was agreed that it
was most necessary to have a mart in England for the enriching
of the same, to make it the more famous, and to be less in other
men's danger, and to make all things better cheap and more
plentiful. The time was thought good to have it now, because of
the wars between the French King and the Emperor. The places
[which] were thought meetest: Hull for the east parts, Southampton for the south parts of England, as appeareth by two
bills in my study. London also was thought no ill place; but it
was appointed to begin with the other two.[50]

11. The bills put up to the Parliament were overseen and certain of them were for this time thought meet to pass and to be
read; other[s], for avoiding tediousness, to be omitted and no
more bills to be taken.

15. Those that were appointed commissioners for the requests
or for execution of penal laws or for overseeing of the courts [51]
received their commissions at my hand.

18. It was appointed that for the payment of £14,000 in the end
of April there should be made an anticipation of the subsidy of

[49] The secret treaty between the German princes and Henry II was
signed at Chambord and at Friedwald in January, 1552. In March, France
threw 35,000 troops into Lorraine while the Germans gathered 30,000 men
in Franconia. Charles, though forewarned, found it too late to organize effective resistance in what was to be for him a disastrous campaign ending
with his ignominious flight over the Alps.

[50] This, too, was a matter which greatly interested the King. His proposals are more fully and cogently set out in his memorandum, *Reasons
for Establishing a Mart in England* (see below, pp. 168–173).

[51] I.e., the revenue courts.

London and of the Lords of my Council, which should go near to pay the same with good provision.[52]

20. The French ambassador brought me a letter of credit from his master and thereupon delivered [to] me the articles of the league betwixt the Germans and him, desiring me to take part in (of *in* MS.) the same league, which articles I have also in my study.

23. The merchants of England, having been long stayed, departed—in all about sixty sail, the wool fleet and all—to Antwerp. They were countermanded because of the mart, but it was too late.[53]

24. Forasmuch as the exchange was stayed by the Emperor to Lyons,[54] the merchants of Antwerp were sore afraid; and, [so] that the mart could not be without exchange, liberty was given to the merchants to exchange and rechange money for money.

A° D'NI 1552, MENSE MARTIO, 6ª CHARTA,
REGNI REGIS E. 6^i 6° ANNO

26. Harry Dudley was sent to the sea with four ships and two barques for defense of the merchants, which were daily before robbed, who, as soon as he came to the sea, took two pirates' ships and brought them to Dover.[55]

28. I did deny after a sort the request to enter into war, as appeareth by the copy of my answer in the study.[56]

[52] The King here refers to payments due in Antwerp under Gresham's refunding and repayment schedule.

[53] The Antwerp market was seriously disrupted because of the widescale war which had just broken out.

[54] I.e., the exchange of funds on Lyons.

[55] Sir Henry Dudley, a remote relation of Northumberland's, was a professional soldier. He was named Captain of Guînes in May, 1551, and Vice-Admiral on March 26, 1552. He is often confused with Northumberland's eldest son, who was killed at Boulogne in 1545, and as frequently with his fourth son, Lord Henry Dudley.

[56] No copy of the document here mentioned has been found. The English

29. To the intent the ambassador might more plainly understand my meaning, I sent Mr. Hoby and Mr. Mason to him to declare [to] him my intent more amply.

31. The Commissioners for the Debatable of the Scottish side did deny to meet, except a certain castle or pile might be first razed; whereupon letters were sent to stay our Commissioners from the meeting till they had further word.

10. Duke Maurice mustered at Arnstadt in Saxony all his own men—and left Duke August, the Duke of Anhalt, and the Count of Mansfeld—for defense of his country, chiefly for fear of the Bohemians. The young[?] Landgrave Reiffenberg and other[s] mustered in Hesse.

14. The Marquis Albert of Brandenburg mustered his men two leagues from Erfurt and after[ward] entered the same, receiving of the citizens a gift of 20,000 florins, and he borrowed of them 60,000 florins, and so came to Schweinfurt, where Duke Maurice and all the German princes were assembled.

[APRIL]

2. I fell sick of the measles and the smallpox.[57]

4. Duke Maurice with his army came to Augsburg, which town was at the first yielded to him and delivered into his hands; where he did change certain officers, restored their preachers, and made the town more free.

5. The Constable with the French army came to Metz, which

---

decision not to enter the war was probably transmitted orally to the French ambassador on March 29.

[57] The illness, contracted on April 2, was serious. The King made a good recovery within a fortnight and on April 23 was well enough to attend the celebration of St. George's Day in the Abbey (Machyn, *Diary*, p. 17). On April 28 the always observant Spanish ambassador reported that the recovery was complete (*Cal. S. P. Span., 1550–1552*, pp. 507–508). There is, however, considerable scattered evidence that Edward never fully recovered from this illness before the onset of his fatal disease.

was within two days yielded to him, where he found great provision of victuals, and that he determined to make the staple of victual for his journey.

8. He came to a fort wherein was an abbey called Gorze,[58] and that fort abide[d] eighty cannon shot, at length came to a parley, where the Frenchmen got it, won it by assault, slew all save fifteen with the captain, whom he hung.

9. He took a fort called Marange and razed it.[59]

12. The French King came to Nancy to go to the army and there found the Duchess and the young Duke of Lorraine.[60]

13. The Maréchal St. André, with 200 men of arms and 2,000 footmen, carried away the young Duke, accompanied with few of his old men, toward France, to the Dauphin which lay at Reims, to the no little discontentation of his mother, the Duchess. He fortified also divers towns in Lorraine and put in French garrisons.

14. He departed from Nancy to the army, which lay at Metz.

7. Mons. Senarpont gave an overthrow to the captain of St. Omer, having with him 600 footmen and 200 horsemen.[61]

15. The Parliament broke up, and because I was sick and not

[58] An outpost of Metz which had been fortified by the Imperialists.

[59] Marange was an outpost northwest of Metz and across the river; it fell on April 10 to Montmorency without offering serious resistance; for its location, see the map of the "Burgundischer Kreis" in *Die alten Territorien des Bezirkes Lothringen,* pt. 1, following p. 16 (vol. XXVIII of *Statistische Mittheilungen über Elsass-Lothringen* [Strassburg, 1898]).

Edward's entries for early April are drawn principally from the not particularly accurate account which he gained from the letters of Barnaby Fitzpatrick, who was attached to Henry II's entourage (see Nichols, *Literary Remains,* I, 78).

[60] Henry II joined forces with Montmorency at Metz on April 18, preparatory to moving toward Strassburg. Henry declared himself "protecteur et conservateur des personnes et biens" of Charles, the young Duke of Lorraine.

[61] Jean de Monchy, Seigneur de Senarpont, French Governor of Boulogne.

able to go well abroad as then, I signed a bill containing the names of the acts which I would have pass, which bill was read in the House.

16. Also I gave commission to the Lord Chancellor, two archbishops, two bishops, two dukes, two marquises, two earls, and two barons to dissolve wholly this Parliament.[62]

18. The Earl of Pembroke surrendered his mastership of the horse, which I bestowed on the Earl of Warwick.

19. Also he [Pembroke] left fifty of his men of arms, of which twenty-five were given to Sir Philip Hoby and twenty-five to Sir John Gates.

21. It was agreed that commissions should go out for to take certificate of the superfluous church plate to my use and to see how it has been embezzled.[63]

The French ambassador desired that, forasmuch as it was dangerous carrying of victuals from Boulogne to Ardres by land, that I would give license to carry by sea to Calais, and so from Calais to Ardres on my ground.

22. The Lord Paget was degraded from the Order of the Garter for divers his offenses, and chiefly because he was no gentleman of blood, neither of father's side nor mother's side.[64]

Sir Anthony St. Leger, who was accused by the Bishop of Dublin for divers brawling matters, was taken again into the Privy Chamber and sat amongst the Knights of the Order.

[62] This, Edward's first Parliament, had first assembled in November, 1547.

[63] The Council had on January 29, 1552, appointed a Commission to gather inventories of church plate from each county (*APC, 1550–1552,* p. 467). This difficult administrative undertaking proceeded slowly at first, not reaching its full effect until April, 1553, when all plate and ornaments not specifically required for the now severely Protestant service were ordered delivered up to the royal commissioners.

[64] Paget was the most independent, as he was probably the most able, of the then Council. His real offense had been a stubborn, if qualified, loyalty to Somerset. He was respectably, though not gently, born.

23. Answer was given to the French ambassador that I could not accomplish his desire, because it was against my league with the Emperor.

24. The Order of the Garter was wholly altered, as appears by the new statutes.[65] There were elected Sir Andrew Dudley and the Earl of Westmorland.

26. Mons. de Courrières [66] came from the Regent [of the Netherlands] to desire that her fleet might safely upon occasion take harbor in my havens. Also he said he was come to give order for redressing all complaints of our merchants.

25. Whereas it was appointed that the £14,000 I owed in the last of April (February crossed out) should be paid, by the anticipation of the subsidy of London and of the Lords, because to exchange the same oversea[s] was [a] loss of the six[th] part of the money I did so send over, stay was made thereof and the payment appointed to be made out of £20,000 Flemish which I took up there, [at] 14 per centum, and so remained £6,000 thereof to be paid there the last of May.

30. Removing to Greenwich.

28. The charges of the mints were diminished £1,400, and there was left £600.

18. King Ferdinand, Maximilian his son, and [Albert] the Duke of Bavaria came to Linz to treat with Duke Maurice for a peace, where Maurice declared his griefs.[67]

16. Duke Maurice's men received an overthrow at Ulm, where-

---

[65] The final drafts of these statutes of reorganization are in Edward's hand and are to be found in Cotton MSS., Nero, C, x.

[66] Jean de Montmorency, Seigneur de Courrières.

[67] Ferdinand, the Emperor's brother and his successor as Holy Roman Emperor, was unjustly suspected of duplicity by Charles. He had little of strength in negotiation, for Augsburg had fallen to Maurice and the Princes on April 4. Maurice did agree to an armistice to begin on May 27, but his defeat of the Emperor was, as he intended, complete before that date.

upon Marquis Albert [de]spoiled the country and gave them a day to answer.[68]

31. A debt of £14,000 was paid to the Fuggers.

MAY

1. The Steelyard men received their answer, which was to confirm the former judgment of my Council.

2. A letter was sent to the Fuggers from my Council to this effect: that I had paid £63,000 Flemish in February and £14,000 [Flemish] in April, which came to £87,000 [sic] Flemish, which was a fair sum of money to be paid in one year, (and the *crossed out*) chiefly in this busy world, whenas [money] is most necessary to be had for princes; besides this, that it was thought money should not now do him so much pleasure as at another time peradventure. Upon these considerations they had advised me to pay but £5,000 of the 45,000 I now owe and so to put over the rest according to the old interest, 14 *per cent.*, with which they desired him to take patience.

4. Mons. de Courrières received his answer, which was that I had long ago given order that the Flemish ships should not be molested in my havens, as it appeared because Frenchmen chasing Flemings into my havens could not get them because of the rescue they had. But that I thought it not convenient to have more ships to come into my havens than I could well rule and govern. Also a note of divers complaints of my subjects was delivered to him.

10. Letters were sent to my ambassadors that they should move to the princes of Germany, to the Emperor, and to the French King, that if this treaty came to any effect or end I might be comprehended in the same.

Commission was given to Sir John Gates, Sir Robert Bowes, the Chancellor of the [Court of] Augmentation[s], Sir Walter

[68] After the fall of Augsburg, only the resistance of Ulm, Nürnberg, and Strassburg separated Maurice from victory.

Mildmay, [and] Sir Richard Cotton to sell some part of the chantry lands and of the houses for the payment of my debts, which was £251,000 sterling at the least.[69]

Taylor, Dean of Lincoln, was made Bishop of Lincoln.

Hooper, Bishop of Gloucester, was made Bishop of Worcester and Gloucester.

Scory, Bishop of Rochester, was made Bishop of Chichester.[70]

Sir Robert Bowes was appointed to be Master of the Rolls.

7. Commandment was given to the Treasurers that nothing of the subsidy should be disbursed but by warrant from [the] board, and likewise for Our Lady Day revenues.[71]

14. The [Chief] Baron of the Exchequer,[72] upon the surrender made by Justice Lyster,[73] [was] made chief justice; the attorney,[74] chief baron; the solicitor general,[75] attorney; and the solicitor of the Augmentation[s] Gosnold, general solicitor; and no more solicitors to be in the Augmentation[s] Court. Also there were appointed eight sergeants of the law against Michaelmas next coming: Gawdy, Stamford, Caryll [*the rest omitted*].[76]

[69] The entry is somewhat misleading, this being only one of successive commissions empowered to sell the chantry properties. They are noted in *APC, 1550–1552*, pp. 184–185; *Cal. Pat. Rolls*, I, 135, 417–418; II, 57–58, 183; III, 347–348; IV, 354–355, 390–391, 392–393, 397–398; V, 184, 277, 411. During the fiscal year 1552–1553, upwards of £153,000 was derived by the Crown from this source. Mildmay was Surveyor-General of the Augmentations, and Sackville the Chancellor.

[70] John Taylor, John Hooper, and John Scory were all bishops of advanced Protestant persuasion.

[71] The Council wished these revenues to be held immediately available for the service of the external debt (*APC, 1552–1554*, p. 37).

[72] Sir Roger Cholmely, who was deprived and imprisoned by Queen Mary.

[73] Sir Richard Lyster, a rather pedestrian lawyer, had resigned on March 21, 1552, probably because of advanced age.

[74] Henry Bradshaw, who was also to be removed from office by Queen Mary.

[75] Edward Griffin, who was retained in office during the next reign.

[76] The eight sergeants appointed on May 19, 1552, were Thomas Gawdy,

16. The muster was made of all the men-at-arms, saving fifty of Mr. Sadler's, twenty-five of Mr. Vice-Chamberlain, and twenty-five [of] Sir Philip Hoby, and also of all the pensioners.

17. The progress was appointed to be by Portchester [Portsmouth] to Poole in Dorsetshire and so through Salisbury homeward to Windsor.[77]

18. It was appointed that money should be cried down in Ireland after a pay which was of money at midsummer next; in the mean season the thing to be kept secret and close. Also that Pirry,[78] the mint master, (should overtake *crossed out*) taking with him Mr. Brabazon, Chief Treasurer of the realm, should go to the mines and see what profit may be taken of the ore that the Almains had dug in a mine of silver; and if it would quit cost or more,[79] to go forward withal; if not, to leave off and discharge all the Almains.[80]

Also that 500 of the 2,000 soldiers there being should be cut off, and as many more as would go serve the French King or the Emperor, leaving sufficient at home. No fortifications to be

---

William Stamford, John Caryll, Robert Brooke, James Dyer (under Elizabeth a famous judge and legal historian), Richard Catlyn, Ralph Rokeby (later Chief Justice of Connaught [1570] and Master of Requests [1576]), and William Dallison.

[77] Though the King had already acquired a most formidable knowledge of the geography of his realm, he had in fact not been more than about thirty miles from London since his accession. As will be seen in subsequent entries, he profited greatly from the first of what was planned to be a series of these royal journeys.

[78] Martin Pirry, Deputy Master of the Mint in Ireland.

[79] "Quit cost": "be a return for" or "balance" (*NED*).

[80] There were silver and lead mines at Clonmine (Wexford) being worked by German miners under the supervision of a Crown agent, Robert Record. Record recommended that the Germans, who he said were disorderly, should be dismissed and Irish and English labor employed in their stead. Joachim Gundelfinger, the superintendent of the German miners, in his turn complained regarding the neglect of the workings, the starvation of three of his men, and the incompetence of Record. Though the operations seem not to have been profitable, the mines were still being worked in 1562 (*Cal. S. P. Ireland, 1509–1573*, pp. 120, 209, *et passim*).

made also yet for a time in no place unfortified; and many other articles were concluded for Ireland.

20. Sir Richard Wingfield, [John] Rogers, and [Sir Andrew Dudley] were appointed to view the state of Portsmouth, and to bring again their opinions touching the fortifying thereof.

4. The French King, having passed the straits of Lorraine, came to Saverne, four miles from Strassburg and was victualed by the country but denied of passage through their town.

3^a PAGINA CHARTAE 6^{ae}

21. Answer came from the Fuggers that for the deferring of £30,000, parcel of [£]45,000, he was content, and likewise for August pay, [just] so he might have paid him £20,000 as soon as might be.

22. It was appointed that, forasmuch as there was much disorder on the Marches on [the] Scotland side, both in vain fortifications of some places and negligent looking to other forts, the Duke of Northumberland, General Warden thereof, should go down and view it and take order for it and return home with speed. Also a pay of £10,000 to go before him.[81]

23. It was appointed that these bands of men of arms should go with me [on] this progress:

Lord Treasurer	30	Earl of Pembroke	50
Lord Great Master	25	Lord Admiral	15
Lord Privy Seal	30	Lord Darcy	30
Duke of Suffolk	25	Lord Cobham	20
Earl of Warwick	25	Lord Warden	20
Earl of Rutland	15	Mr. Vice-Chamberlain	15
Earl of Huntingdon	25	Mr. Sadler	10
		Mr. Sidney	10

[81] Northumberland, who left for the North in mid-June, being delayed by the death of his wife and of a son (Lord Ambrose Dudley), was away from the seat of power through most of the summer. He returned to southern England at the end of August.

26. It was appointed that Thomas Gresham should have paid him out of the money that came of my debts £7,000, for to pay £6,800 the last of the month, which he received the same night. 28. The same Thomas Gresham had £9,000 paid him toward the payment of £26,000 which the Fuggers required to be paid at the Paschal Mart [Easter Fair]. For he had taken by exchange from hence £5,000 and odd, and £10,000 he borrowed of the Schetz, and ten [thousand] of Lazarus Tucker. So there was in the whole [£]25,[000], of which was paid the last of April 14,[000] so the[re] remain £11,000 and £9,000, which I now made over by exchange, which made £20,000 to pay the Fuggers with.

30. I received advertisement from Mr. Pickering that the French King went from Saverne to Arromaches [Augersmache?],[82] which was yielded to him, [from] thence to Limbourg [83] and so toward Spires, his army to be about 20,000 footmen and 8,000 horsemen well-appointed, besides rascals.[84] He had with him fifty pieces of artillery, of which [there] were twenty-six cannons and six organs [85] and [a] great number of boats. From Limbourg—partly doubting Duke Maurice's meaning, partly for lack of victuals, and also because he had word that the Regent's army, of which were guides the Count of Egmont, Mons. de Rie,[86] Martin van Rossem, and Duke [Adolf] of Holest [Holstein?], to the number of 16,000 footmen and 6,000 horsemen, had invaded Champagne and fortified Aschenay [Stenay]—he

[82] Saverne lies some 30 km. to the northwest of Strassburg; Augersmache, southeast of Saarbrücken.

[83] The King called it "Leimsberg." The reference is probably to the Château of Limbourg "qui couvrait les pays d'Outre-Meuse et défendait l'entrée de la principauté de Liége," which was strongly reinforced in early April (Alexandre Henne, *Histoire du règne de Charles-Quint en Belgique*, IX [Brussels and Leipzig, 1859], 191).

[84] "Rascals": the rabble of an army (*NED*).

[85] "Organs": firearms or cannon of a particularly elaborate construction.

[86] Adrian de Croy, Comte de Rie (or Roeulx), Governor of Artois, Grand Master of Flanders.

retired homeward till he came to Striolph [Struthof?] and there commanded all unprofitable carriage[s] and men should depart to Chalons, and [he] sent to the Admiral to come to him with 6,000 Swiss, 4,000 Frenchmen, 1,500 horsemen, and thirty pieces of ordnance, meaning as it was thought to do some enterprise about Luxemburg, or to recover Aschenay [Stenay], which the Regent had fortified. There died in this journey 2,000 men for lack of good victuals. For eight days they had but bread and water, and they had marched sixty Dutch miles at the least and passed many a strait very painfully and laborsomely.[87]

19. Duke Maurice, coming from Augsburg in great haste, came this day to the first passage, called the Clouse,[88] which the Emperor had caused to be strongly fortified and victualed, a passage through a hill, cut out artificially on the way to Innsbruck, and there was a strong bulwark made hard by it which he won, after a long fight, within (no less than *crossed out*) an hour and a half by assault and took and slew all that were within; and that night he marched through that hill into a plain

[87] The entry includes much more than is to be found in Pickering's dispatch, much of which was a lamentation regarding his ill treatment and a plea to be recalled. The King's account is inexact and the geography is somewhat confused.

Very briefly, Strassburg refused to yield to Henry II and Montmorency, and the French were in no position to lay siege. A few places, among which were Hagenau and Wissembourg, were taken. The French were disturbed by reports that the Regent of the Netherlands was moving heavy forces into Luxemburg which could easily cut the supply lines and also block a retreat. They therefore fell back through Verdun, which was taken, to ward off the danger from the north by an invasion of Luxemburg. Damvillers and Montmédy were first taken, and then Yvoix capitulated. Henry II refused to surrender these places to pillage, and his principally mercenary troops mutinied, with the consequence that pitched battles were fought between French troops and the mercenaries. Thus weakened, the French fell back toward their frontiers. The expedition had, however, served its principal purpose as a diversion to assist Maurice and the rebellious German princes. And Metz remained in French hands. See below, pp. 131, 132, 133, 134–136.

[88] Ehrenberger Klause, a mountain pass south of Füssen.

where he looked for to see twelve ensigns [89] of landsknechts of his enemies. But they retired to the second strait, and yet divers of them were both slain and taken; and so that night he lodged in the plain at the entry of the second passage where [there] were five forts and one castle, which with ordnance slew some of Duke Maurice's men.

20. This morning the Duke of Mecklenburg, with three thousand footmen, cast a bridge over a river five miles beneath [a] sluice and came and gave assault behind the sluice, and Duke Maurice gave assault in the face, and the countrymen of Tyrol, for hate of the Spaniards, help[ed] Duke Maurice, so that the five forts were won by assault and the castle yielded upon condition to depart, not to serve in three months after[ward] the Emperor. In this enterprise he slew and took 3,500 persons and twenty-three pieces of artillery and 240,000 s[cutes]. The Emperor, hearing of this, departed by night from Innsbruck forty miles that night in post; he killed two of his jennets and rode continually every night; first to Brixenium and after[ward], for doubt of the Cardinal of Ferrara's army,[90] turned to Villach in Carinthia the thirtieth of May,[91] tarrying[?] for the Duke of Alva,[92] who should come to him with 2,000 Spaniards and 3,000 Italians that came from Parma. Also the Emperor delivered Duke Frederick from captivity,[93] and sent him through Bohemia into Saxony to raise a power against Duke Maurice, his nephew.

22. Duke Maurice, after that Hall (Hala *in MS.*) and divers

---

[89] "Ensigns": troops or companies.   [90] Hippolyto d'Este.

[91] The action described in these two entries deals fully and quite accurately with the dramatic battle of May 19–20, when Maurice secured and blocked the Ehrenberger Klause. Charles V, then at Innsbruck, after a futile attempt to flee to the Netherlands, was carried, ill and in pain, by litter over the Brenner Pass [Brixenium] to Villach.

[92] Fernando Alvarez de Toledo, third Duke of Alva.

[93] John Frederick, Duke of Saxony, a staunch Lutheran, had been an Imperial prisoner since the Battle of Mühlberg (1547).

other towns about Innsbruck in Tyrol had yielded, came to Innsbruck and there caused all the stuff to be brought to the market place and took all that pertained to Imperialists as confiscate; the rest he suffered the townsmen to enjoy. He took there fifty pieces of ordnance, which he conveyed to Augsburg, for that town he fortified and made it his staple of provision.[94]

7ᵃ CHARTA, Aᵒ Dᴺ¹ 1552ᵒ MENSE JUNIO
JUNE

2. Sir John Williams,[95] who was committed to the Fleet for disobeying a commandment given to him for not paying any pensions without making my Council privy, upon his submission was delivered out of prison.

4. Beaumont, M[aste]r of the Rolls, did confess his offenses, who [how] [96] in his office of wards he had bought land with my money, had lent it, and kept it from me to the [value of] £9,000 and above, more than this twelvemonth, and £11,000 in obligations; who [how], he being judge in the Chancery between the Duke of Suffolk and the Lady Powis, took her title and went about to get it into his hands, paying a sum [of] money and letting her have a farm of a manor of his and caused an indenture to be made falsely with the old Duke's counterfeit hand to it, by which he gave these lands to the Lady Powis and went about to make twelve men perjured. Also how he had concealed the felony of his man, to the sum of £200 which he stole from him, taking the money to his own hand again. For these considera-

---

[94] Bound in the *Chronicle* at this point (f. 60/f. 64) is a stray page entitled "Certain things which the Commissioners for the Requests shall not meddle withal," listing thirteen excepted matters, which may be found in the King's memorandum printed by Nichols (*Literary Remains,* II, 502–503) under the title, *Regulations for the Commissioners of Requests.*

[95] Sir John Williams, later Baron Williams of Thame, had since 1544 been Treasurer of the Court of Augmentations. He disliked and mistrusted Northumberland and was to prove an important supporter of Mary Tudor.

[96] "Who" was the ME form of the word "how," especially in Kent.

tions he surrendered into my hands all his offices, lands, and goods movable and unmovable, toward the payment of this debt and of the fines due to these particular faults by him done.[97]

6. The Lord Paget, Chancellor of the Duchy [of Lancaster], confessed how he, without commission, did sell away my lands and great timber woods; how he had taken great fines of my lands to his said peculiar profit and advantage, never turning any to my use or commodity; how he made leases in reversion for more than twenty-one years. For these crimes and other like recited before, he surrendered his office and submitted himself to those fines that I or my Council would appoint, to be levied of his goods and lands.[98]

7. Whalley,[99] Receiver of Yorkshire, confessed how he lent my money upon gain and lucre; [100] how he paid one year's revenue over with the arrearages of the last; how he bought my own land with my money; how in his accounts he had made many false suggestions; how at the time of the fall of money he borrowed divers sums of money and had allowance for it after-[ward], by which he gained £500 at one crying down, the whole sum being £2,000 and above. For these and suchlike considerations he surrendered his office and submitted to fines which I or my Council should assign him, to be levied of his goods and lands.

8. The Lords of the Council sat at [the] Guildhall in London, where in the presence of a thousand people they declared to the Mayor and brethren their slothfulness in suffering unreasonable prices of things, and to craftsmen their willfulness, etc., telling them that if upon this admonition they did not amend, I was

---

[97] See above, p. 109, and below, p. 131.   [98] See below, pp. 131, 156.
[99] See above, p. 52. Whalley was sent to the Tower on September 19; *APC, 1552–1554*, p. 126, dates it September 20.
[100] "Lucre": profit (ME).

wholly determined to call in their liberties as confiscate and to appoint officers that should look to them.

10. It was appointed that the Lord Grey of Wilton should be pardoned of his offenses and delivered out of the Tower.[101]

Whereas Sir Philip Hoby should have gone to Calais with Sir Richard Cotton and William Barnes, auditor, it was appointed [that] Sir Anthony St. Leger, Sir Richard Cotton, and Thomas Mildmay [102] should go thither, carrying with them £10,000 to be received out of the Exchequer.

Whereas it was agreed that there should be a pay now made to Ireland of £5,000, and then the money to be cried down, it was appointed that 3,000 weight which I had in the Tower should be carried thither and coined at 3 *denar.* fine, and that incontinent [103] the coin should be cried down.[104]

Also . . . of . . . tenes play should be shifted [?] to the porter's lodge.[105]

12. Because Pirry tarried here for the bullion, William Williams, assay master, was put in his place to view the mines with

[101] Grey had been imprisoned as a partisan of Somerset's in October, 1551. He was made Deputy of Calais in September, 1552, and, in the next month, commander at Guînes. At the end of the reign, as an ardent Protestant, he lent support to Northumberland's attempted coup. See above, pp. 87, 88, and below, pp. 144, 147.

[102] Thomas Mildmay, of Essex, was the brother of the more famous Sir Walter.

[103] "Incontinent": immediately (*NED*).

[104] The plan described was to coin 1,500 pounds (weight) of silver into sixpences at the English standard of fineness (S. P. Ireland, IV, 50, 51, 53: June 7–June 23, 1552).

[105] This whole entry of three lines was crossed out, probably by the King. Then another pen has rendered most of the entry quite illegible. It may well relate to an almost equally obscure entry in the Acts of the Privy Council for June 10, 1552, where "It was this day ordered that the Lord Treasurer should send for the cowper, which is in the Tower for making of plays, to deliver him." (*APC, 1552–1554,* p. 73.) It seems possible that this relates to an unknown interlude by an unknown dramatist named Cowper (or Cooper) which had caused offense to the government.

Mr. Brabazon or him who[m] the Deputy should appoint.[106]

13. Bannister and Crane—the one for his large confession, the other because little matter appeared against him—were delivered out of the Tower.[107]

16. The Lord Paget was brought into the Star Chamber and there declared effectuously his submission by word of mouth and delivered it in writing. Beaumont, who had before made his confession in writing, began to deny it again, but after being called before my Council, he did confess it again and there acknowledged a fine of his land and signed an obligation in surrender of all his goods.

17. Mons. de Courrières took his leave.

2. The French King won the castle of Rodemanche.[108]

3. Certain horsemen of the Regent's came and set upon the French King's baggage and slew divers of the carters, but at length with some loss of the Frenchmen they were compelled to retire. The French King won Mount Saint Jean.

4. The French King came to Damvillers, which was a strong town, and besieged it, making three breaches.

12. The town was yielded to him, with the captain. He found in it 2,500 footmen, 200 horsemen, 63 brass great-pieces, 300 harquebuses à croc, much victuals, and much munitions, as he did write to his ambassador.

19. It was appointed that the Bishop of Durham's matter should stay till the end of the progress.

---

[106] *Ibid.*, p. 74 (June 11, 1552); see above, p. 123 and n. 80.

[107] Almost completing the release from custody of the lesser adherents of the Duke of Somerset.

[108] Also known as Rodemachern. Barnaby Fitzpatrick was an excited witness to this action (Nichols, *Literary Remains*, I, 83). See above, p. 126, n. 87, for a brief account of the French campaign of which these June entries describe the closing phase.

20. Beaumont in the Star Chamber confessed, after a little sticking upon the matter, his faults, to which he had put to his hand.

23. It was agreed that the bands of men of arms appointed to Mr. Sidney, Mr. Vice-Chamberlain, Mr. Hoby, and Mr. Sadler should not be furnished but left off.

25. It was agreed that none of my Council should move me in any suit of land—for forfeits above £20, for reversions of leases, or any other extraordinary suits—till the state of my revenues were further known.

15. The French King came to a town standing on the river of Meuse called Yvoix,[109] which gave him many hot skirmishes.

18. The French King began his battery to the walls.

14. The townsmen of Montmédy gave a hot skirmish to the French and slew Mons. de Toge's brother and many other gentlemen of the camp.

12. The Prince of Salerno,[110] who had been with the French King to treat with him touching the matters of Naples, was dispatched in post with this answer: that the French King would aid him with 13,000 footmen and 1,500 horsemen, in the French wages, to recover and conquer the kingdom of Naples, and [that] he should marry, as some said, the French King's sister, Madam Marguerite. The cause why this Prince rebelled against the Emperor was partly the uncourteous handling of the Viceroy of Naples, partly ambition.

18. The Flemings made an invasion into Champagne, insomuch that the Dauphin had almost been taken, and the Queen, lying at Chalons, sent some of her stuff toward Paris.

[109] This castle was on the Chiers, a tributary of the Meuse.

[110] Ferdinand san Severino, who had in 1540 visited the court of Henry VIII, had been banished from the Imperial Court at Brussels by the Emperor and resided at Padua. He enjoyed great credit in Naples and some months later was in Turkey soliciting aid for the projected attack on Naples (*Cal. S. P. For., 1547–1553*, pp. 85, 233, 234, 238, 241).

12. Also another company took the town of Guise and [de]spoiled the country also.

22. Mons. de Taille [Thais] [111] was [sent] for to raise the arrear bands and legionnaires of Picardy and Champagne, to recover Guise and invade Flanders.

27. Removing to Hampton Court.

30. It was appointed that the Steads should have this answer: that those cloths which they had bought to carry over, to the sum of 2,000 cloths and odd, should be carried at their old custom, [just] so they were carried within six weeks; and likewise all commodities they brought in till Our Lady Day [March 25] in Lent next; in all other points the old decree to stand, till by a further communication the matter should be ended and concluded. [112]

The Lord Paget was licensed to tarry at London and thereabouts till Michaelmas, because he had no provision in his country.

26. Certain of the heralds—Lancaster and Portcullis—were committed to ward for counterfeiting Clarenceux seal to get money by giving of arms. [113]

23. The French King, having received divers skirmishes of the townsmen, and chiefly two—the one when they slew the French light horse lying in a village by the town, the other when they entered into the camp and pulled down tents, which two skirmishes were given by the Count of Mansfeld, governor of the town and [of] the Duchy of Luxemburg, and his three hundred

---

[111] Jean de Thais, formerly artillery master at Boulogne.

[112] *APC, 1552–1554*, p. 93 (July 8, 1552). Though, as has been noted, the Steelyard had lost their ancient privileges, they were permitted to continue on the old basis by special licenses issued from time to time until their expulsion from the realm in 1598.

[113] Both Lancaster (Fulke ap Howell) and Portcullis (Richard Withers) were degraded from office. Thomas Hawley was Clarenceux herald (Nichols, *Literary Remains*, II, 429–430).

light horse—[and] understanding by the treason of four priests the weakest part of the town, so affrayed [114] the townsmen and the Flemish soldiers that they by threatenings compelled their captain, the Count, that he yielded himself and the gentlemen prisoners, [and] the common soldiers [were permitted] to depart with white wands in their hands. This town was well fortified, victualed, and furnished.[115]

24. The town of Montmédy yielded to the French King, which before had given him a hot skirmish.

[JULY]

4. Sir John Gates, Vice-Chamberlain, was made Chancellor of the Duchy [of Lancaster].

7. Removing to Oatlands.

5. The Emperor's ambassador delivered the Regent's letter, being of this effect: that, whereas I was bound by a treaty with the Emperor made a° D'ni 1542 at Utrecht, that if any man did invade the Low Count[r]ies I should help him with 5,000 footmen or 700 crowns a day during four months and make war with him within a month after the request [was] made, and now the French King had invaded Luxemburg—desiring me to follow the effect of the treaty.[116]

7. The names of the commissioners were added and made more, both in the debts, the surveying of the courts, the penal laws, etc., and that because my Lord Chamberlain, my Lord Privy Seal, Mr. Vice-Chamberlain, and Mr. Secretary Petre went with me [on] this progress.

[114] "Affrayed": frightened.

[115] The action here described was that at Yvoix (see above, p. 132: June 15), and was based on Barnaby Fitzpatrick's letter to the King (Nichols, *Literary Remains*, II, 83).

[116] This treaty had been informally but explicitly confirmed by Paget in his long interview with the Emperor in Brussels in 1549 (*Cal. S. P. Span.*, 1547–1549, p. 416).

8. It was appointed that 50 *li.* weight of gold (bullion *crossed out*) should be coined after the new standard, to carry about this progress, which makes £ 1,500 sterling.

9. The Chancellor of the Augmentations [117] was willed to surcease his commission, given him [in] the third year of our reign.

3. Mons. de Bossu, grand Esquire to the Emperor, was made general of the army in the Low Countries, and Mons. de Praet over the horsemen.[118]

10. It was appointed here that, if the Emperor's ambassador did move any more for help or aid, this answer should be sent him by two of my Council: that [in] this progress-time my Council was dispersed; I would work by their advice and he must tarry till the matter were concluded and their opinions heard. Also I had committed the treaty to be considered by divers learned men, etc. And if another time he would press me, then answer to be made that I trusted the Emperor would not wish me in these young years, having felt them so long, to enter into them; how I had amity sworn with the French King, which I could not break; and therefore, if the Emperor thought it so meet, I would be a mean [119] for a peace between them, but not otherwise. And if he did press the treaty, lastly to conclude that the treaty did not bind me which my father had made, being against the profit of my realm and country; and to desire a new treaty to be made between me and the Emperor, which (being pressed to the Emperor in the last wars) he answered that he marveled what we meant, for we are bound (quoth[?] the Emperor) and not you. Also the Emperor had refused to fulfill it divers times,

---

[117] Sir Richard Sackville, a most competent Crown officer, did not in fact resign until late 1553, when a merging of the Court of Augmentations with the other principal revenue courts, planned in 1552, was concluded.

[118] Jean de Hennin, Count of Bossu (or Boussut), and Louis de Praet, President of the Council of the Netherlands.

[119] "Mean": mediator.

both in not letting pass horses, armor, munition, etc., which were provided by me for the wars, as also in not sending aid upon the foraging of the low country of Calais.

12. Letter was written to Sir Peter Meutas, Captain of the Isle of Guernsey, both to command him that divine service may there be used as in England, and also that he take heed to the church plate that it be not stolen away but kept safe till further order be taken.

9. The French King came to the town of Avesnes in Hainault, where, after he had viewed the town, he left it and besieged a pile called Tirloc; [120] but the bailiff of the town, perceiving his departure, gave the onset on his rearward with 2,000 footmen and 500 horsemen, and slew 500 Frenchmen. After this and the winning of certain holds of little force, the French King returned into France and divided his army into divers good towns to rest them, because divers were sick of the flux and such other diseases—meaning shortly to increase his power and so to go forward with his enterprise.

12. Frederick, Duke of Saxony, was released from his imprisonment and sent by the Emperor into his own country, to the great rejoicing of all the Protestants.[121]

5. The Emperor declared that he would [accept] none of those articles to which Duke Maurice agreed, and the King of [the] Romans also. The copy of them remains with the Secretary Cecil.

Marquis Albert of Brandenburg did great harm in the country of Franconia, burned all towns and villages about Nürnberg and compelled them to pay to the princes of his league 200,000 thalers, ten of the fairest pieces of ordnance, and 150 quintals of

---

[120] Tirloc, i.e. Trélon Castle, southeast of Avesnes. This action is more fully described in *Cal. S. P. Span., 1550–1552*, p. 557. The French fell back across the frontier after this action in an almost precipitate withdrawal.

[121] See above, p. 127.

powder. After that he went to Frankfurt to distress certain soldiers gathered there for the Emperor.

15. Removing to Guildford.

21. Removing to Petworth.[122]

23. The answer was made to the Emperor's ambassador, touching the aid he required, by Mr. Wotton and Mr. Hoby, according to the first article *supra*.[123]

24. Because the number of bands that went with me [on] this progress made the train great, it was thought good they should be sent home, save only 150 which were picked out of all the bands. This was because the train was thought to be near 4,000 horse, which were enough to eat up the country; for there was little meadow nor hay all the way as I went.[124]

25. Removing to Cowdray, Sir Anthony Browne's house.[125]

27. Removing to Halnaker.[126]

30. Whereas it had been before devised—that the new fort of Berwick should be made with four bulwarks, and for making of two of them the wall of the town should be left open on the enemy's side a great way together, which thing had been both dangerous and chargeable—it was agreed the wall should stand,

---

[122] This great house was in Crown hands from 1536 until 1557, when it was returned to the Percy family.

[123] I.e., as stated above, pp. 135–136.

[124] Seven members of the Privy Council also accompanied the King during the whole of the progress (*APC, 1552–1554*, pp. 100–101: July 23, 1552).

[125] The King noted in a letter to Barnaby Fitzpatrick that it was "a goodly house . . . where we were marvelously, yea, rather excessively, banqueted" (Nichols, *Literary Remains*, I, 80). This great pile had been built about twenty years earlier by Sir William Fitzwilliam (Earl of Southampton) and was left by him to Sir Anthony, his half brother. It may be noted that the King's letters to Barnaby provide more details of the progress than does the *Chronicle*.

[126] Near Chichester; another great house, built about forty years earlier by Thomas, Lord de la Warre.

and two slaughterhouses [127] to be made upon to scour [128] the outer curtains, a great rampart to be made within the wall, a great ditch within that, another wall within that with two other slaughterhouses, and a rampart within that again.

26. The Flemings entered in great numbers into the country of Thérouanne, whereupon 500 men of arms arose of Frenchmen and gave the onset on the Flemings, overthrew them and slew of them 1,435, whereof were 150 horsemen.

31. It was appointed upon my Lord of Northumberland's request that he should give half his fee to the Lord Wharton and make him his deputy warden there.

AUGUST

2. Removing to Warblington.[129]

2. The Duke of Guise was sent into Lorraine to be the French King's lieutenant there.

4. Removing to Waltham.[130]

8. Removing to Portsmouth.

9. In the morning I went to Chaderton's bulwark, and viewed also the town.[131] At afternoon went to see the storehouse, and there took a boat and went to the wooden tower and so to Hasleford.[132] Upon viewing of which things there were de-

[127] "Slaughterhouse": a heavily armed and fortified strong point. This is the first usage noted by *NED*.

[128] "Scour": to command an area with one's guns. The use here is earlier than that cited (1563) in *NED*.

[129] Hard by Havant, Hampshire; Warblington had very recently been conveyed by the Crown to Sir Richard Cotton.

[130] Bishop's Waltham, long the country seat of the Bishops of Winchester, had been recently surrendered by Ponet on his elevation to the see. The Crown had in turn conveyed it to William Paulet, Marquis of Winchester.

[131] Nichols suggests that the bulwark had been named for John Chaderton, master of ordnance at Portsmouth and on several occasions a member of Parliament for the town (*Literary Remains*, II, 442 n.).

[132] Identified by Nichols as a swampy area near the later Royal Naval Hospital (*ibid.*, p. 443 n.).

vised two forts to be made upon the entry of the haven, one where Ridley's tower stands, upon the neck that makes the Camber, the other upon a little neck standing on the other side [of] the haven, where stood an old bulwark of wood. This was devised for the strength of the haven. It was meant that that to town side should be both stronger and larger.[133]

10. Harry Dudley, who lay at Portsmouth with a warlike company of 140 good soldiers, was sent to Guînes with his men because the Frenchmen assembled in those frontiers in great numbers.

Eod[ie]. Removing to Titchfield, the Earl of Southampton's house.[134]

14. Removing to Southampton.[135]

16. The French ambassador came to declare how the French King meant to send one that was his lieutenant in the civil law at Paris to declare which of our merchants' matters have [been] adjudged on their side, and which against them, and for what consideration.

16. Removing to Beaulieu.[136]

The French ambassador brought news how the city of Siena had been taken by the French side on St. James's Day by one that was called the Count Perigliano [137] and other Italian soldiers, by treason of some within the town, and all the garrison

---

[133] These descriptions can easily be followed on the Ordnance Survey map.

[134] Titchfield (about two miles west of Fareham, Hampshire) had been built recently by the late Thomas Wriothesley, Earl of Southampton.

[135] More notice of the visit to Southampton may be found in the King's letter to Barnaby Fitzpatrick (*Literary Remains*, I, 81).

[136] Beaulieu (six miles northeast of Lymington, Hampshire) was a former abbey, granted by Henry VIII at the Dissolution to Wriothesley, who converted the principal building into a residence which was used by him before the building of the great house at Titchfield.

[137] Probably Niccolò Orsini, Count Pitigliano, an Italian who held a high command in the French army in Italy in this period.

of the town, being Spaniards, were either taken or slain.[138] Also how the Marshal Brissac [139] had recovered Saluzzo and taken Verucca.[140] Also how Villebon [141] had taken Turnhout and Montreuil in the Low Country.

18. Removing to Christchurch.[142]

21. Removing to Woodlands.[143]

In this month, after long business, Duke Maurice and the Emperor agreed on a peace.[144] But Marquis Albert of Brandenburg would not consent thereto, but went away with his army to Spires, and Worms, Cologne, and Trèves, taking large sums of money of all cities which he passed, but chiefly of the clergy.[145] Duke Maurice's soldiers, perceiving Marquis Albert would enter into no peace, went almost all to the Marquis' services, among which were principal[ly] the Count of Mansfeld, Baron Heideck,[146] and a colonel of 3,000 footmen and 1,000 horsemen called Reiffenberg. So that, of 7,000 which should be sent into Hungary against the Turks, there remained not 3,000. Also the Duke of Württemberg did secretly let go 2,500 of the

---

[138] The revolt of Siena began on July 17, having been precipitated by resentment because of strong fortifications which Charles V was building outside the walls. The French control thus gained, though tenuous, was not thrown off until the Imperialists starved the city into submission in April, 1555.

[139] Charles de Cossé, Seigneur de Brissac, the French commander in Italy.

[140] I.e., Verrue, between Asti and Vercelli, and across the river from Crescentino.

[141] Jean d'Estouteville, Seigneur de Villebon, a French commander who had long served with distinction in the northern area.

[142] In southwestern Hampshire.

[143] In the parish of Horton (Dorset); the seat of Sir Edward Willoughby, who had acquired it by marriage.

[144] The Treaty of Passau, August 2, 1552.

[145] The Margrave Albert had deserted his allies and had plunged into a wild attempt to overrun Franconia and to carve out a secular duchy for himself. Maurice's forces were reported to have been reduced by half by these defections (*Venetianische Depeschen*, II, 542, 548).

[146] Johann von Heideck, a colonel formerly in Maurice's service.

best soldiers in Germany to the service of Marquis Albert. So that his power was now very great.

Also in this month the Emperor departing from Villach came to Innsbruck,[147] and so to Munich and to Augsburg, accompanied with 8,000 Spaniards and Italians and a little band of a few ragged Almains. Also in this month (about the middle thereof *crossed out*) did the Turks win the city of Temesvár in Transylvania [148] and give a battle to the Christians, in which was slain Count Pallavicino [149] and 7,000 Italians and Spaniards. Also in this month did the Turks' navy take the Cardinal of Trent's two brothers, and seven galleys, and had in chase thirty-nine other[s]. Also in this month did the Turks' navy land at Terracina in the kingdom of Naples, and the Prince of Salerno set forward with 4,000 Gascons and 6,000 Italians, and the Count Perigliano [Pitigliano] brought to his aid 5,000 men of those that were at the enterprise of Siena. Also the Marshal Brissac won a town in Piedmont called Bussac[?].[150]

24. Removing to Salisbury.

26. Upon my Lord of Northumberland's return out of the North, it was appointed for the better strengthening of the Marches that no one man should have two offices, and there[fore] Mr. Strelley, Captain of Berwick, should leave the wardenship of the East Marches to the Lord Evre. And upon the Lord Conyers' resignation, the captainship of the castle of Carlisle was appointed to Sir [Ralph] Gray,[151] and the wardenship of the West Marches to Sir Richard Musgrave.[152]

27. Sir Richard Cotton made Comptroller of the Household.

[147] July 11 was the date.
[148] On July 30 (*Venetianische Depeschen*, II, 541, n. 3).
[149] Count Hippolyt Pallavicino (*ibid.*, p. 524).
[150] Probably Busca, east of St. Damian.
[151] Ralph Gray, of Chillingham, Northumberland, was in fact made Deputy Warden of the East March.
[152] Captain of Carlisle Castle.

28. Removing to Wilton.[153]

30. Sir Anthony Aucher was [ap]pointed to be Marshal of Calais, and Sir Edward Grimston Comptroller of Calais.[154]

22. The Emperor, being at Augsburg, did banish two preachers (Protestants) out of Augsburg under pretense that they preached seditiously, and left Mecardus [155] the chief preacher and six other Protestant preachers in the town, giving the magistrates leave to choose other[s] in their place that were banished.

29. The Emperor caused eight Protestant citizens of the town to be banished, of them that went to the fair at Linz, under pretense that they, taking Marquis Albert's part, would not abide his presence.

SEPTEMBER

2. Removing to Mottisfont, my Lord Sandys' house.[156]

5. Removing to Winchester.[157]

7. From thence to Basing, my Lord Treasurer's house.[158]

10. And so to Donnington Castle, beside the town of Newbury.[159]

---

[153] Conveyed in 1544 by the Crown to Sir William Herbert, now Earl of Pembroke, who had converted the conventual buildings into a magnificent residence.

[154] Grimston, a native of Suffolk, was to be taken prisoner on the fall of Calais.

[155] Mecardus, i.e., Hans Meckhart, a famous Lutheran preacher.

[156] Thomas, Lord Sandys (of the Vine) had succeeded his more famous father in 1542. Mottisfont (Hampshire) had been an Augustinian Priory.

[157] Where the King was entertained at the Bishop's Palace.

[158] Winchester's first title of peerage (Lord St. John of Basing) was derived from this ancestral family seat. Paulet had rebuilt an old castle there on a vast and sumptuous scale. The seat was two miles east of Basingstoke.

[159] Donnington Castle was the seat of the Duke of Suffolk.

12. And so to Reading.[160]

15. And so to Windsor.[161]

8ᵃ CHARTA, MED' SEPTEMBRIS, A° D'NI 1552,
A° REGNI Rˢ E. 6ˡ 6°

16. Stuckley, being lately arrived out of France, declared how that the French King—being wholly persuaded that he [Stuckley] would never return again into England because he came away without leave upon the apprehension of the Duke of Somerset, his old master—declared to him his intent that, upon a peace made with the Emperor, he meant to besiege Calais and thought surely to win it by the way of Sandhills, for having Risebank, both to famish the town and also to beat the market place; and [he] asked Stuckley's opinion. When Stuckley had answered he thought it impossible, then he told him that he meant to land in England in an angle thereof about Falmouth, and said the bulwarks might easily be won, and [that] the people were papistical; also that Mons. de Guise at the same time should enter into England by Scotland side, with the aid of the Scots.[162]

[160] Where the King stayed in an expropriated monastery, retained by Henry VIII as a royal palace (Nichols, *Literary Remains*, II, 454).

[161] Again, a stray folio (f. 69/f. 73) is bound in the *Chronicle* here, entitled "Whether the King's Majesty shall Enter into the Aid of the Emperor." It is endorsed from Windsor and is dated September 23, 6 Edward VI. The reasons for and against entering the war on the Emperor's side are noted, and a neutral position is outlined and extolled. The memorandum, not in the King's hand, is printed in Nichols, *Literary Remains*, II, 539–541.

[162] Thomas Stuckley was an engaging and an irresponsible adventurer, thought by many of his contemporaries to be an illegitimate son of Henry VIII. He served before Boulogne and in Scotland. For some time in Somerset's service, he fled abroad shortly before the Duke's arrest. He served with Henry II in the Lorraine campaign, returning to England as an agent for the French to secure information which would be of help in planning a projected attack on Calais. He at once informed Cecil of the details of his mission. The English government in its turn betrayed Stuckley by

19. After long reasoning it was determined, and a letter was sent in all haste to Mr. Morison,[163] willing him to declare to the Emperor that I, having pity, as all other Christian princes should have, on the invasion of Christendom by the Turk, would willingly join with the Emperor and other states of the empire, if the Emperor could bring it to pass in some league against the Turk and his confederates, but not to be acknown [164] of the French King; only to say that he hath no more commission, but if the Emperor would send a man into England, he should know more. This was done on intent to get some friends. The reasonings be in my desk.

21. A letter was sent, only to try Stuckley's truth, to Mr. Pickering, to know whether Stuckley did declare any piece of this matter to him.[165]

Barnaby was sent for home.[166]

23. The Lord Grey was chosen Deputy of Calais in the Lord Willoughby's place, who was thought unmeet for it.[167]

24. Sir Nicholas (Thomas *crossed out*) Wentworth was discharged of the portership of Calais, and one Cotton [168] was put into it. In consideration of his age, the said Sir Nicholas Wentworth had a hundred pound pension.

---

informing France of his confessions, which Northumberland pretended to disbelieve. Stuckley was lodged in the Tower for the remainder of the reign. In an incredible swashbuckling career, Stuckley's services were always available to the highest bidder (S. P. Dom., Edw. VI, XV, 6 [September 17, 1552], 38 [October?]; *ibid.*, XVIII, 11 [January?, 1553]; *Cal. S. P. For.*, *1547–1553*, p. 221).

[163] *Cal. S. P. For., 1547–1553*, p. 221.   [164] "Acknown": known.

[165] The Council was in fact exhibiting some evidence of panic, not knowing how to assess Stuckley's "revelations."

[166] The King had written to Barnaby Fitzpatrick on September 24, requiring his return to England (Nichols, *Literary Remains*, I, 86).

[167] This intended replacement was in fact not made at this time; see below, p. 147 (October 6).

[168] Sir Thomas Cotton, probably a younger brother of Sir Richard, Comptroller of the Household.

26. Letters were sent for the discharge of the men of arms at Michaelmas next following.

27. The young lords' table was taken away,[169] and the masters' of request, and the sergeant of arms', and divers other extraordinary allowances.

26. The Duke of Northumberland, the Marquis of Northampton, the Lord Chamberlain, Mr. Secretary Petre, and Mr. Secretary Cecil ended a matter at Eton College between the master and the fellows and also took order for the amendment of certain superstitious statutes.[170]

28. Removing to Hampton Court.

29. Two lawyers came from the French King to declare what things had passed with the Englishmen in the King's Privy Council, what and why against them, and what was now in doing and with what diligence. Which when they had eloquently declared, they were referred to London, where there should speak with them Mr. Secretary Petre, Mr. Wotton, and Mr. Thomas Smith. Where by them was declared the griefs of our merchants, which came to the sum of fifty thousand pounds, and upwards; to which they gave little answer but that they would make report when they came home because they had yet no commission, but only to declare [to] us (use *in* MS.) the causes of things done.

The first day of this month the Emperor departed from Augsburg toward Ulm, and thanking the citizens for their steadfast sticking to him in these parlous times, he passed by them to Strassburg, accompanied only with 4,000 Spaniards, 5,000 Italians, 12,000 Almains, and 2,000 horsemen, and thanking also them of Strassburg for their goodwill they bore him, that they

---

[169] Thus was disbanded the group of young nobles who had been placed in court as companions and schoolmates of the King.

[170] The commission was the second sent in this year to reform the statutes in terms of the Reformation legislation, but the College was able to stand fairly fast on the statutes laid down by its royal founder, Henry VI.

would not let the French King come into their town, he went to Wissembourg and so to Spires and came thither the 23rd of this month. Of which thing the French King [when] advertised summoned an army to Metz and went thitherward himself, sent a pay of three months to [the] Marquis Albert and the Rhinegrave and his band, also willing him to stop the Emperor's passage into these Low Countries and to fight with him.[171]

27. The matter of the Debatable [Ground] was agreed upon according to the last instructions.[172]

6. Duke Maurice, with 4,000 footmen and 1,000 horsemen, arrived at Vienna, against the Turks.

21. Marquis Hans of Brandenburg came with an army of 13,000 footmen and 1,500 horsemen to the Emperor's army, and many Almain soldiers increased his army wonderfully. For he refused none.

OCTOBER

3. Because I had a pay of £48,000 to be paid in December and had as yet but £14,000 beyond sea to pay it withal, the merchants did give me a loan of £40,000, to be paid by them the

[171] Charles, in a notable recovery of his fortunes, had marched from the Tyrol to Augsburg, while Alva coming down from the North had secured the important bridge at Strassburg. At Ulm the Emperor, though ill, determined to lead his now formidable army by way of Strassburg to the Netherlands, sweeping aside the French in his path. But he was repeatedly delayed by his own illnesses, and it was not until the end of October that he and Alva laid siege to the now heavily fortified city of Metz.

It will be observed that from about this point forward Edward VI was increasingly concerned with the fortunes of this phase of the war between France and the Empire. Interestingly, the information available from the English ambassadors abroad was both very sparse and very inaccurate for these weeks. The King was gaining fairly detailed and on the whole accurate information from other sources, the most important of which was the French ambassador in London.

[172] On November 17, 1552, this long disputed border settlement was attained, Sir Thomas Dacre and Sir Richard Musgrave acting as the English commissioners.

last of December and to be repaid again by me the last of March. The manner of levying this loan was of[f] the cloths after the rate of 20s. of[f] a cloth. For they carried out at this shipping 40,000 broadcloths. This grant was confirmed the 4th day of this month by a company assembled of 300 Merchant Adventurers.[173]

2. The bulwarks of earth and boards in Essex, which had a continual allowance of soldiers in them, were discharged, by which was saved presently £500, and hereafter £700 or more.

4. The Duke [of] Alva and the Marquis of Marignano [174] set forth with a great part of the Emperor's army, having all the Italians and Spaniards with them, toward Trèves, where the Marquis Albert had set ten ensigns of lance knights [175] to defend it, and tarried himself with the rest of his army at Landau beside Spires.

6. Because Sir Andrew Dudley, Captain of Guînes, had indebted himself very much by his service at Guînes, also because it should seem injurious to the Lord Willoughby that for the contention between him and Sir Andrew Dudley he should be put out of his office, therefore it was agreed that the Lord William Howard should be Deputy of Calais and the Lord Grey Captain of Guînes.[176]

Also it was determined that Sir Nicholas Strelley should be captain of the new fort at Berwick, that Alexander Brett [177] should be porter, and one Rokesby should be marshal.

7. Upon report of letters written from Mr. Pickering—how that

---

[173] The details of this agreement are set out in S. P. Dom., Edw. VI, XV. 13 (October 13, 1552).

[174] Gian Jacomo de Medicis, Marquis of Marignano, an Imperial general.

[175] Apparently a corruption (*NED*) for "landsknechts."

[176] Lord Howard served as commander of Calais until Queen Mary appointed him Lord Admiral, in which capacity he served from 1554 to 1573.

[177] Brett, then a commander of London cavalry, lent his support to the insurgents in Wyatt's rebellion and was shortly afterward hanged.

Stuckley had not declared to him, all the while of his being in France, no one word touching the communication afore specified and declared, and also how Mr. Pickering thought and certainly advertised that Stuckley never heard the French King speak no such word, nor never was in credit with him or the Constable, save once when he became an interpreter between the Constable and certain English pioneers—he was committed to the Tower of London. Also the French ambassador was advertised how we had committed him to prison for that he untruly slandered the King our (my *crossed out*) good brother (as other such renegades do daily the same). This was told him to make him suspect the English renegades that be there. A like letter was sent again to Mr. Pickering.

8. The Seigneur de Villandry [178] came in post from the French King with this message: First, that although Mr. Sidney's and Mr. Winter's matters were justly condemned, yet the French King (because they both were my servants, and one of them about me) was content *gratuito* to give Mr. Sidney his ship and all the goods in her, and Mr. Winter his ship and all his own goods.[179] Which offer was refused, saying we required nothing *gratuito*, but only justice and expedition. Also Villandry declared that the King his master wished that an agreement were made between the ordinances and customs of England and France in marine affairs; to which was answered that our ordinances were nothing but the civil law, and certain very old additions of the realm; that we thought it reason[able] not to be bound to any other law than their old laws, which had been of long time continued and no fault found with them. Also Vil-

[178] Claude le Breton, Seigneur de Villandry (d. 1556), finance minister under Francis I.

[179] William Winter, with his brother, George, was an English merchant trading principally to the Levant (*Cal. S. P. For.*, *1547–1553*, p. 254), as well as Surveyor of Ships in the royal service (see above, p. 36). Sidney, also an English merchant whose ship and goods had been seized by the French, has not been certainly identified.

landry brought forth two new proclamations which for things to come were very profitable for England, for which he had a letter of thanks to the King his master. He required also pardon and releasement of imprisonment for certain Frenchmen taken on the seacoast. It was shown him [that] they were pirates; how some of them should by justice be punished, some by clemency pardoned; and with this dispatch he departed.

10. Removing to Westminster.

11. Horne, Dean of Durham,[180] declared a secret conspiracy of the Earl of Westmorland [in] the year of the apprehension of the Duke of Somerset—how he would have taken out treasure at Middleham [181] and would have robbed his mother and sold £200 [of] land and, to please the people, would have made a proclamation for the bringing up of the coin, because he saw them grudge at the fall. He was commanded to keep this matter close.[182]

6. Mr. Morison, ambassador with the Emperor, declared to the Emperor the matter of the Turks before specified; whose answer was, he thanked us for our gentle offer and would cause the Regent to send a man for the same purpose to know our further meaning in that behalf.[183]

---

[180] Horne had been appointed Dean of Durham in November, 1551, moving at once to a thorough reform of the cathedral clergy and services. Shortly after this revelation he was appointed by Northumberland as Bishop of Durham to succeed the deprived Tunstall (see above, p. 101, and below: October 15). Horne aroused Northumberland's intense dislike by refusing to accept the see because of the circumstances of Tunstall's deprivation. An exile under Mary, Horne was appointed Bishop of Winchester in 1560.

[181] Middleham: Neville properties in Yorkshire.

[182] This entry is the principal authority for this alleged conspiracy. Westmorland was nonetheless continued as a Privy Councillor and served as ambassador in Scotland. On the King's death he was a ready and warm supporter of the claims of Mary Tudor.

[183] *Cal. S. P. For., 1547–1553*, p. 222; Alfred Katterfeld, *Roger Ascham. Sein Leben und Seine Werke* (Strassburg, 1879), pp. 195–202.

149

11. Mr. Pickering declared to the French King, being then at Reims, Stuckley's matter, confession, and the cause of his imprisonment; who, after protestation made of his own good meaning in the amity and of Stuckley's ingratitude toward him, lewdness, and ill demeanor, thanked us much for this so gentle an uttering of the matter, that we would not be led with false bruits and tales.

15. The Bishop Tunstall of Durham was deprived of his bishopric.

In this month Mons. de Rie, Martin [van] Rossem, and an army of Flemings (while the French [King] had assembled his men of war in Lorraine, had sent the Constable to the army which lay four leagues from Verdun, the Duke of Guise with 7,000 men to Metz, and the Maréchal St. André to Verdun) razed and [de]spoiled between the river of Somme and Oise many towns and villages, as Noyon, Roye, Chauny, Nesles, Folembray, a new[ly] built house of the King's, etc., insomuch that the French King sent the Admiral of France [184] to help the Duke of Vendôme against that army. There was at this time that reigned a great plague in sundry parts of France, of which many men died.

20. A man of the Earl of Tyrone's was committed to the Tower because he had made an untrue suggestion and complaint against the Deputy and the whole Council of Ireland. Also he had bruited certain ill bruits in Ireland, how the Duke of Northumberland and the Earl of Pembroke were fallen out, and one against another in the field.[185]

17. The Flemings, and the Englishmen that took their parts, assaulted by night Hamleteu; the Englishmen were on the walls, and some of the Flemings also, but by the cowardice of a great part of the Flemings the enterprise was lost and many men

[184] Claude d'Annebaut, Baron de Retz and de la Hunaudaye.
[185] *APC, 1552–1554,* p. 192 (December 12, 1552).

slain. The number of the Flemings was 4,000; the number of the men within Hamleteu, 400. The captain of this enterprise was Mons. de Vendeville, Captain of Gravelines.[186]

6. Mons. de Bossu entered Trèves with a Flemish army to the number of 12,000 footmen and 2,500 horsemen Burgundians, without any resistance, because the ensigns there left by Marquis Albert were departed, and thereupon the Duke of Alva and the Marquis of Marignano marched[?] toward Metz; the Emperor himself and the Marquis Hans of Brandenburg, having with him the rest of his army, the 9th day of this month departed from Landau toward Metz. Monsieur de Bossu his army also joined with him at a place called Zweibrücken or Deuxponts.

23. It was agreed that, because the state of Ireland could not be known without the Deputy's presence, that he should in this dead time of the year leave the governance of the realm to the Council there for the time and bring with him the whole estate of the realm, whereby such order might be taken as the superfluous charge might be avoided, and also the realm kept in quietness and the revenue of the land better and more profitably gathered.[187]

25. Whereas one George Paris,[188] Irishman, who had been a practiser[189] between the Earl of Desmond and other Irish Lords and the French King, did now, being weary of that matter, practise means to come home and to have his old lands in Ireland again; his pardon was granted him and a letter written

---

[186] Vendeville may be identified as François Destourmel, Seigneur de Vendeville. Hamleteu is the King's phonetic rendering of Ambleteuse (Newhaven), formerly part of the system of fortifications in the Boulogne area. The English official papers are singularly silent on this action.

[187] *Cal. S. P. Ireland, 1509–1573*, p. 128.

[188] See above, p. 108, n. 23, and below, pp. 152, 153, for further particulars on this somewhat elusive and wholly unreliable agent.

[189] "Practiser": from "practise," to negotiate or treat (*NED*).

151

to him from my Council in which he was promised to be considered and helped.

There fell in this month a great contention among the Scots. For the Carrs slew the Lord of Buccleuch in a fray in Edinburgh, and as soon as they had done, they associated to them the Lord Home and all his kin. But the Governor [190] thereupon summoned (his *crossed out*) an army to go against them. But at length, because the Dowager of Scotland favored the Carrs and Homes, and so did all the French faction—the French King also having sent for 5,000 Scottish footmen and 500 horsemen for his aid in these wars—the Governor agreed [that] the 5,000 footmen under the leading of the Earl of Cassilis, and 500 light horsemen, of which the Carrs and Homes should be captains, should go with such haste into France that they might be in such place as the French King would point them to serve in by Christmas, or Candlemas [February 2] at the furtherest. And thus he trusted to be well rid of his most mortal enemies.

27. The Scots, hearing that George Paris practised for pardon, committed him to ward in Stirling Castle.

25. Mons. de Rie, having burned in France eighteen leagues in length and three leagues in breadth, having burned, pill[ag]ed, sacked, and razed the fair towns of Noyon, Roye, Nesles, and Chauny, the King's new house of Folembray, and infinite other villages, bulwarks, and gentlemen's houses in Champagne and Picardy, returned into Flanders. [191]

23. The Emperor in his person came to the town of Metz with his army, which was reckoned 45,000 footmen, as the bruit went, and 7,000 horsemen. The Duke of Alva with a good band went to view the town, upon whom issued out the soldiers of the town and slew of his men about 2,000 and kept him [in] play

[190] I.e., the Earl of Arran.

[191] This brilliantly conceived diversionary expedition from Flanders was designed to prevent the further concentration of French forces for the relief of the besieged city of Metz.

till the main force of the camp came down, which caused them
to retire with loss. On the French party was the Duke of Nemours [192] hurt on the thigh. There was in the town as captain
the Duke of Guise, and there were many other great lords with
him, as the Prince of Roche-sur-Yon,[193] the Duke of Nemours,
the Vidame of Chartres, Pietro Strozzi, Mons. Châtillon, and
many other gentlemen.

[NOVEMBER]

5. Mons. de Villandry returned to declare how the King his
master did again offer to deliver four ships against which judgment had [been] passed. He said the King would appoint men
to hear our merchants at Paris, which should be men of the best
sort. He said likewise how the King his master meant to amend
the ordinance, of which amendments he had brought articles.

7. These articles were delivered to be considered by the Secretaries.

9. Certain [men] were thought to be sought out by several
commissions, viz., whether I was justly answered of the plate,
lead, iron, etc., that belonged to [the] abbeys; whether I was
justly answered [of] the profit of alum, copper,[194] fustians,
etc., which were [ap]pointed to be sold; and suchlike articles.[195]

12. Mons. Villandry received answer for the first article as he
did before: how I meant not by taking freely so few to preju-
dice the rest. For hearing of our merchants' matters at Paris by
an inferior council we thought both too dilatory after these long
suits and also unreasonable, because the inferior council could

---

[192] Jacques de Savoie.

[193] Charles de Bourbon, brother of Louis de Bourbon, Duke de Montpensier.

[194] "Copar" in the MS.; "copes" could be meant.

[195] Several such commissions were appointed, with wide powers of invest-
igation and recovery for the Crown.

undo nothing (though cause appeared) which had been before judged by the higher council. And as for the new ordinances, we liked [them] in effect as ill as their old and desired none other but the old accustomed which have been used in France of late time and be yet continued between England and the Low Country. Finally, we desired no more words, but deeds.

4. The Duke d'Aumale, being left in Lorraine—both to stop the Emperor's provision, to annoy his camp, and to take up the stragglers of the army—with a band of 400 men of arms, which is 1,200 horse and 800 light horse, hearing how Marquis Albert [of Brandenburg] began to take the Emperor's part, sent first certain light horse to view what they [could]. Those vaunt-couriers [196] lighted on a troop of 500 horsemen, who drove them back till they came to the Duke's person. Whereupon the skirmish grew so great that the Marquis, with 12,000 footmen and 1,000 horsemen, came to his men's succor, and so the Duke's part was discomfited, the Duke himself taken, and hurt in many places. Mons. de Rohan [197] was also slain, and many other gentlemen slain and taken. This fight was before Toul, into which fort escaped a great part of the light horse.[198]

6. Hesdin [Heding *in* MS.] town and castle was taken by Mons. de Rie. The castle was reckoned too well stored of all things and rendered either by cowardice or treason. The battery was very small and not suitable.[199] The most was that the captain, Mons. Genlis, was with one of the first shots of the cannon slain, and his lieutenant with him. In this month Fernando [di] Gonzaga besieged St. Martin's in Piedmont.[200]

[196] "Vaunt-couriers": scouts.   [197] René, Vicomte de Rohan.

[198] Albert's account of the action is in Druffel, *Briefe und Akten*, II, 806–807.

[199] "Sautable" in the MS. The first use of the word in this sense noted by *NED* is 1582.

[200] St. Martin's is near Turin and three leagues distant from Ivrea (*Mémoires du Sieur François de Boyvin, Chevalier, Baron Duvillars*, vol. XXIX of Petitot's *Collection complète des mémoires relatifs à l'histoire de France*,

18. There was a commission granted out to Sir Richard Cotton, Sir John Gates, Sir Robert Bowes, and Sir Walter Mildmay, to examine the account of fall of money by the two proclamations.[201]

20. The Lord Ogle leaving the wardenship of the Middle Marches, because my Lord Evre's land lay there, he [Lord Evre] was made Deputy Warden there with the fee of 600 marks, and Sir Thomas Dacre of the East [West *is meant*] Marches with the fee of 500 marks.

24. Thomas Gresham came from Antwerp hither to declare how Mons. de Longin, treasurer to the Emperor of Flanders, was sent to him from the Regent with a certain packet of letters which the Burgundians had taken in Boulognois [country], coming from the Dowager of Scotland, the effect whereof was how she had committed George Paris, the Irishman, to prison because she had heard of his meaning to return into England; how she had found the pardon he had, and divers other writings; and how she had sent O'Connor's son into Ireland to comfort the Lords of Ireland. Also he showed certain instructions, a° 1548, upon the Admiral's fall, given to a gentleman that came hither, that if there were any heir of the Admiral's faction he should do his utmost to raise an uproar.[202]

29. Harry [Sir Francis] Knollys was sent in post into Ireland with a letter to stay the Deputy if he met him in Ireland, be-

[Paris, 1823], p. 145). Brissac described it as a little post, capture of which would give him the right bank of the "Dora Baltea" which runs north of Ivrea (Charles Marchand, *Charles Ier de Cossé, Comte de Brissac* [Paris, 1889], p. 208).

[201] The two proclamations mentioned were dated May 6 and July 9, 1551; see above, pp. 62 and 71.

[202] This diplomatic exchange is more fully described in two long dispatches from the Queen Regent to the Emperor (*Cal. S. P. Span., 1550–1552*, pp. 601–603, 605–606: December 9 and 15, 1552); and see above, pp. 108, 151, 152. The reference to the "Admiral" is to Thomas Seymour, who was executed in 1549.

cause of this business, and that he should seem to stay for his own affairs and prolong his going from week to week, lest it be perceived. Also he had with him certain articles concerning the whole state of the realm, which the Deputy was willed to answer.

30. There was a letter of thanks written to the Regent and sent to Mr. Chamberlain to deliver [to] her, for the gentle overture made to Thomas Gresham by the treasurer Longin. He was also willed to use gentle words in the delivery of the letters, wishing a further amity; and for recompense of her overture, to tell her of the French King's practise for 5,000 Scottish footmen and 500 horsemen, and also how he takes up by exchange at Lübeck an £100,000, whereby appears some meaning that way, the next spring.

28. The Lord Paget was put to his fine of £6,000, and £2,000 diminished, to pay it within the space of [blank] years at days limited.[203]

[203] Paget was pardoned on the condition of the conveyance of lands to the Crown with an annual worth of £200 and the payment of £1,000 by Christmas, 1552, and an additional £1,000 by Christmas, 1553. In April, 1553, the amount remaining was remitted and he was restored to favor.

The King's *Chronicle* ends on this somber note of the undeserved political and financial persecution by Northumberland of perhaps the ablest and certainly the most honorable of all those left in Edward's Council.

THE POLITICAL PAPERS

I. Discourse on the Reform of Abuses in Church and State (April?, 1551) [1]

THE governance of this realm is divided into two parts: one ecclesiastical, (another *altered to*) the other temporal.

The ecclesiastical consists in (prea *crossed out*) setting forth the word of God, continuing the people in prayer, and the discipline. The setting forth of the word of God consists in the good discreet doctrine and example of the teachers and spiritual officers. For as the good husbandman makes his ground good and plentiful, so does the true preacher with doctrine and example (set forth *crossed out*) print and [en]grave in the people's mind the word of God, that they at length become plentiful. (Wherefore the *crossed out*) Prayers to God also must be made continually of the people and officers of the church to assist them with His grace. And those prayers must first with good consideration be set forth and faults therein be amended; next, being set forth, the people must continually be allured to hear them. For discipline: it were very good that it went forth and that those that did notably offend in swearing, rioting, neglecting of God's word, or suchlike vices, were duly punished, so that those that should be the executors of this discipline were men of tried honesty, wisdom, and judgment. But because those bishops who should execute—some for papistry, some for ignorance, some for age, some for their ill name, some for all these—are men unable to execute (justice *crossed out*) discipline, it is

[1] The original may be found in the British Museum, Cotton MSS., Nero, C, x, 113 ff. We have supplied the title; the MS. has no heading.

159

therefore a thing unmeet for these men. Wherefore it were necessary that those that were appointed to be bishops or preachers were honest in life and learned in their (sermons *crossed out*) doctrine, that by rewarding of such men other[s] might be allured to follow their good life. As for the prayers and the divine service, it were meet [that] the faults were drawn out, as it was appointed, by learned men, and so the book to be established,[2] and all men willed to come thereunto, to hear the service, as I have put in remembrances in articles touching the statutes of this Parliament. But (as *crossed out*) for discipline, I would wish no authority given generally to all bishops, but that commission be given to those that be of the best sort of them, to exercise it in their dioceses.

This much generally for religion.

TEMPORAL REGIMEN

The temporal regimen consists in well-ordering, enriching, and defending the whole body politic of the commonwealth, and every part of the whole, so one hurt not the other. The example whereof may be best taken of a man's body. For even as the (hand helpeth the *altered to*) arm defends, helps, and aids the whole body, chiefly the head, so ought servingmen and gentlemen chiefly and suchlike (crafts *altered to*) kind of people be always ready to [the] defense of their country, and chiefly of their superior and governor, and ought in all things [to] be vigilant and painful for the increasing and aiding of their country. And forasmuch as they in serving their king and country have divers great and manifold (harms that *altered to*) charges, even as the arm doth many times bear great stresses for defense of the head and body, (therefore *crossed out*) having no kind of way to enrich (itself *crossed out*) themselves, neither by (selling *altered to*) merchandise, neither by handicraft, neither

---

[2] I.e., the recently promulgated Book of Common Prayer, already under revision.

by husbandry, (hath the stomach *crossed out*) as the arm does decoct [3] no meat itself, nor engenders no blood, therefore even as the stomach, liver, and lights, which parts engender the blood, does send nourishment to the arms and legs, sufficient to strengthen the part, even so (doth *altered to*) must the artificers (merchants and husbandmen *crossed out*) so use their gain in working, and so truly and justly make that that they work, the merchants must so sell their wares and so labor to bring in strange commodities, the husbandmen must pay such rent and so sell things that come of the increase of the ground, that the hands and the legs, that is to say, the states (of nobles *crossed out*) of gentlemen (I mean *crossed out*) and of servingmen may well do the commonwealth that service [which] they ought to do. And as the gentlemen and servingmen ought to be provided for, so ought not they neither have too much as they have in France, where the peasantry is of no value, neither yet meddle in other occupations. For the arms and legs do never draw the whole blood from the liver, but leave it sufficient to work on, neither do meddle in any kind of engendering of blood. No, nor no one part of the body does serve for two occupations. Even so, neither the gentleman ought to be a farmer, nor the merchant an artificer, but to have his art particularly. Furthermore, no member in a well-fashioned and whole body is too big for the proportion of the body. So must there be in a well-ordered commonwealth no person that shall have more than the proportion of the country will bear. For as it is convenient to enrich the country, so is it hurtful immoderately to enrich any one part.

I think this country can bear no [4] merchant to have more land

---

[3] "Decoct": "to boil so as to extract the soluble parts" (*NED*, citing 1545).

[4] The King originally wrote: "I think this country can bear no (. . . *defaced*) above £8,000 no wer[?] wel that." All this was recast by the King in the form indicated above, including certain deletions which cannot be read. The deletions almost certainly referred to the permissible income of the nobility and gentry, a subject on which it would have been interesting indeed to have had the King's views.

than £100,[5] no husbandman or farmer worth above £100 or
£200, no artificer above 100 marks, no laborer much more than
he spends. I speak now generally and in such cases may fail in
some one particular. But this is sure: this commonwealth may
not bear one man to have more than two farms, than (two
altered to) one benefice, than 2,000 sheep, and one kind of (living *altered to*) art to live by. Wherefore, as in the body no part
has too much or (occupieth *crossed out*) too little, so in a commonwealth ought every part to have *ad victum et non ad
saturitatem.* (But idle *crossed out*) And as there is no part ad-
mitted in the body that does not work and take pain, so ought
there no part of the commonwealth to be but laborsome [6] in his
vocation. The gentleman ought to labor in service in his country; the servingman ought to wait diligently on his master; the
artificer ought to labor in his work, the husbandman in tilling
the ground, the merchant in passing the tempests; but the vagabonds ought clearly to be banished, as is the superfluous hu-
mor in the body, that is to say, the spittle and filth which, because it is for no use, is put out by the strength of nature. This is
the true ordering of the state of a well-fashioned commonwealth: that every part do obey one head, one governor, one
law, as all parts of the body obey the head, (and *crossed out*)
agree among themselves, and one not to eat another up through
greediness, but that we see that order (be an *crossed out*),
moderation, and reason bridle the affections. But this is most of
all to be had in a commonweal well-ordered, that the laws and
ordinances be well executed, duly obeyed, and (uncorruptly
altered to) [ad]ministered without corruption. Now, having seen how things ought to be, let us first see how now they be

[5] This passage in original draft read: "No merchant to have more (worth
altered to) land than £30,000 (*crossed out and* £100 *substituted*)." But
it appears almost certain that a cipher was added in another hand increasing £3,000 to £30,000.

[6] "Laborsome": this most useful—and now archaic—word as here used
appears to be the first instance cited by the *NED*.

ordered, and in what state they stand now, and then go forward to seek a remedy.

The first point in ordering the commonwealth we touched was that the gentlemen, noblemen, and servingmen should stand stoutly to [the] defense of their superior and governor and should be painful in ordering their country; which thing, although in some part and the most part be well (thanks be to God), yet in some parts is not absolutely, which I shall show hereafter particularly. But the second point, for maintenance of the state and of nobles[se] of landed men, is ill looked to. For that state of gentlemen and noblemen which is truly to be termed the state of noblesse (is *crossed out*) has alone not increased the gain of living. For merchants have enhanced their wares; farmers have enhanced their corn and cattle, laborers their wages, artificers the price of their workmanship, mariners and boatmen their hire for service, whereby they recompense the loss of things they buy; but the most part of true gentlemen (I mean not these farming gentlemen, nor clerking knights) have little or nothing increased their rents; yet their housekeeping is dearer, their meat is dearer, their liveries dearer, their wages greater, which thing at length, if speedy remedy be not had, will bring that state into utter ruin (*quod absit*). The artificers work falsely, the clothiers use deceit in cloth, the masons in building, the (smiths *crossed out*) cloakmakers in their cloaks, the joiner in his working of timber, and so forth all other[s] almost, to the intent they would have men come oftener to them for amending their things and so have more gain, although at the beginning they take out of measure.[7] The merchants adventure not to bring in strange commodities but loiter at home, send forth small hoys with two or three mariners, occupy exchange of money, buy and sell victuals, steal out bullion, corn,[8] victuals, wood, and suchlike things out of the realm, and sell (it *crossed out*) their wares unreasonably. The hus-

---

[7] "Out of measure": excessively.   [8] The word could be "coine."

bandmen and farmers take their ground (to *crossed out*) at a small rent and dwell not on it, but let it to poor men for treble the rent they (pay *crossed out*) take it for, and sell their flesh, corn, milk, butter, etc., at unreasonable prices. The gentleman, constrained by necessity and poverty, becomes a farmer, a grazier, or a sheepmaster; the grazier, the farmer, the merchant become landed men and call themselves gentlemen, though they be churls. Yea, the farmer will have ten farms, some twenty, and will be a peddler merchant; the artificer will leave the town and for his more pastime will live in the country; yea, and more than that, will be a justice of [the] peace and will think scorn to have it denied him, so lordly be they nowadays. For now they are not content with 2,000 sheep, but they must have 20,000 or else they think themselves not well [off]; they must [have] twenty mile square [of] their own land, or full of their farms, and four or five crafts to live by is too little, such hellhounds be they. For idle persons there were never, I think, more than [there] be now; the wars (men think) is the cause thereof—which persons can do nothing but rob and steal. But slack execution of the laws has been the chiefest sore of (them *crossed out*) all. The laws have been manifestly broken, the offenders punished, and either by bribery or foolish pity escaped punishment. The dissension and disagreement, both for private matters and also in matters of religion, has been no little cause, but the principal [cause] has been the disobedient and contentious talking and doing of the foolish and fond people, which for lack of teaching have wandered and broken, willfully and disobediently, the laws of this realm. The lawyers also, and [the] judges, have much offended in corruption and bribery. Furthermore, they do nowadays much use to forestall not only private markets of corn and victuals, whereby they enhance the price thereof, but also send to the sea to aboardships and take the (corn *crossed out*) wine, sugar, dates, or any other wares, and bring it to London where they sell [at] double the price. What shall I say of those that buy and sell offices of trust, that impropriate benefices, that destroy timber, that—not considering the sustaining of men of their [corn]—turn till-ground to pasture, that use excesses in apparel, in diet, and in building; of enclosures of wastes and commons; of those that cast false and seditious bills—but that the thing is so tedious, long, and lamentable to entreat of the particulars that I am weary to go any further in the particulars. Wherefore I will cease, having told the worst, because the best will save itself.

Now I will begin to entreat of a remedy. The ill in this commonwealth, as I have before said, stands in deceitful working of artificers, using of exchange and usury, making vent with hoys only into Flanders, conveying of (gold *crossed out*) bullion, lead, bell metal, copper, wood, iron, fish, corn, and cattle beyond sea[s], enhancing of rents, using two arts to live by, (that artificers *crossed out*) keeping of many sheep and many farms, idleness of people, disobedience of the lower sort, buying and selling of offices, impropriating benefices, turning till-ground to pasture, exceeding in apparel, diet, and building, enclosing of commons, casting of ill and seditious bills.

These (faults *altered to*) sores must be (amended *altered to*) cured with these medicines or plasters: 1. Good education; 2. Devising of good laws; 3. Executing the laws justly, without respect of persons; 4. Example of rulers; 5. Punishing of vagabonds and idle persons; 6. Encouraging the good; 7. Ordering well the customers; 8. Engendering friendship in all the parts of the commonwealth. These be the chief points that tend to order well the whole commonwealth. And for the first, as it is in order first, so it seems to be in dignity and degree. For Horace says very wisely, *Quo est imbuta recens servabit odorem testa diu.* With whatsoever thing the new vessel is imbued it will long keep the savor, says Horace, meaning that for the most part men be as they be brought up, and that men keep longest the savor of their first bringing-up. Wherefore, seeing that it seems so necessary a thing, we will show our device therein. Youth must be brought up—some in husbandry, some in working, graving, gilding, joining, printing, making of cloths—even from their tenderest age, to the intent they may not, when they come to man's estate, loiter as they do nowadays (and be brought up in *crossed out*) and neglect, but think their travail sweet and honest. And for this purpose would I wish that artificers and other[s] were either commanded to bring up their sons in like trade or else have some (schools *altered to*) places appointed [for] them in every good town where they should be apprentices and bound to certain kind[s] of conditions. Also that those vagabonds that take children and teach them to beg should, according to their demerits, be worthily punished.

This shall well ease and remedy the deceitful working of things, disobedience of the lower sort, casting of seditious bills, and will clearly take away the idleness of people.

2. Devising of good laws. I have showed my opinion heretofore what statutes I think most necessary to be enacted this (Parlia *crossed out*) session. Nevertheless I would wish that beside them, hereafter, when time shall serve, the superfluous and tedious statutes were brought into one sum together and made more plain and short, to the intent that men might the better understand them, which I think shall much help [9] to advance the profit of the commonwealth.

3. Nevertheless, when all these laws be made, established, and enacted, they serve to no purpose except they be fully and duly executed. By whom? By those that have authority to execute. That is to say, the noblemen and the justices of [the] peace. Wherefore I would wish that after this Parliament were ended, the noblemen, except a few that should be with me, went to their countries and there should see the statutes fully and duly

[9] "Which I think shall much help" is our rendering of what seems to be written, "wich I thing shal moch help."

executed, and that those men should be put from being justices of [the] peace that be touched or blotted with those vices that be against these new laws to be established. For no man that is in fault himself can punish another for the same offense. *Turpe est doctori cum culpa redarguit ipsum.* And these justices being put out, there is no doubt for the execution of the laws.[10]

[10] The discourse ends thus, evidently unfinished.

II. *Reasons for Establishing a Mart in England* (March 9, 1552) [1]

THE reasons and causes why it is now most necessary to have a mart in England:

1. Because our vent of cloths might be open in all wars.

2. Because our merchants' goods might be out of danger of strangers, without fear of arresting for every light cause.

3. Because it would much enrich the realm. For as a market enriches a town, so does a mart enrich a realm.

4. Because for a need round sums of money might be of them borrowed that haunt the mart.

5. Because we should have a great multitude of ships [of] strangers to serve in the wars.

6. Because all strangers' goods, when war is made, should be in our danger.

7. Because we should buy all things at the first hand of strangers, whereas now the Spaniards sell to the Flemings their wares, and the Flemings to us.

8. Because the towns toward the seaside should be much more populous.

9. Because, whereas now they bring tapestry, points, glasses, and laces, they would then bring in bullion and other substantial merchandise, to the intent to have our cloth and our tin.

10. Because we should take from our enemies their power and

[1] The manuscript of this memorandum may be found in Cotton MSS., Nero, C, x, 85 ff.

make that they should borrow no money of merchants but when we list—at least, no great sum of money.

The causes why this time is most commodious to erect a mart in:

1. The wars between the French King and the Emperor, and the ships of either side, make the Italians, Genoese, Portuguese, and Spaniards to forbear their trade to Antwerp. *ij.* The Frenchmen, the Steads, the Sprusses [Prussians?], and ships of Eastland [the Baltic], being against the Emperor, will not come neither. *iij.* The French King invading Lorraine and fearing Flanders. *iiij.* And the Almains lying on the river of Rhine stop the course of merchandise out of Italy to Antwerp (and also Frankfurt Mart *added*). *v.* The putting of men of war in the town [Antwerp] makes the merchants to forbear their traffic and to look to their lives. *vj.* The breach of the last tempest is like[ly], they say, to make the channel uncertain and the haven nought. *vij.* The stop of the exchange to Lyons will make many Flemings bankrupt. These things will decay the marts of Antwerp and Frankfurt. But those nations cannot live without a vent. Therefore they will now most willingly come hither if they had a free mart.

2. It were an easier matter to come to Southampton for the Spaniards, Bretons, Gascons, Lombards, Genoese, Normans, and Italians than to go to Antwerp.

3. It were easier for the merchants of the Eastland, the Sprusses, the Danes, Swedes, and Norwegians to come to Hull than to Antwerp.

4. Southampton is a better port than Antwerp.

5. The Flemings have allured men to make a mart there with their privileges, having but very little commodities. Much easilier shall we do it, having cloth, tin, sea coal, lead, bell metal, and such other commodities, as few realms Christian have the like, nor they when they began had no such opportunity.

169

How the mart will be brought to pass:

1. First, our merchants are to be stayed from a mart or two under pretense that they abstain because of the imposition.

2. Then proclamation must be made in divers places of the realm where merchants resort, that there shall be a free mart kept at Southampton with these liberties and customs: 1. The time of the mart to begin after Whitsuntide and to hold on five weeks, by which means it shall not let [2] St. James's Fair at Bristol nor Bartholomew Fair in London. 2. All men coming to the mart shall have free going and free coming, without arresting, except in cases of treason, murder, or felony. 3. For the time of the mart all sorts of men shall pay but half the customs they do in other places of the realm. 4. No shipping shall be from any other place from South Wales to Essex during that time. 5. In the shires of Hampshire, Wiltshire, Sussex, Surrey, Kent, Dorsetshire, etc., no bargain shall be made of wares during that time but in the mart town. 6. A court to correct offenders, with liberties thereto. 7. Some one commodity must be assigned to the mart, or some one kind of cloth. 8. The Merchants of the Staple must be bargained withal, and contented with some honest offer, to the intent by their liberties they may not let the mart. 9. Some more liberties must be given to the inhabitants of Southampton, and if money may be spared, some must be lent them to begin their trade withal. 10. Our ships on the sea must look as well as they may, observing the treaties, to the safeguard of the merchants when they come. 11. If this prove well, then may another be made at Hull, to begin after Stourbridge Fair, to the intent they may return before the great ices come on their seas.

The discommodities and lets to the mart to be kept in England:

1. Because strangers lack access hither by land, which they have at Antwerp.

[2] "Let": hinder.

2. The ill working of our cloths, which make them less esteemed.

3. The abundance of our cloths in Flanders will make them less sought for here.

4. The merchants have established their dwelling places at Antwerp.

5. That other nations will stay their coming hither for a while by the Emperor's commandment.

6. The denial of the request of the merchants of the Steelyard will somewhat let the mart, if it be not looked to.

7. The poverty and littleness of the town of Southampton.

8. The goodliness of the Rhine.

The remedies and answers thereunto:

TO THE FIRST POINT

1. At this time, when the mart should begin at Southampton, the French King and the Almains shall stop the intercourse by land so that nothing shall come that way but in great danger.

2. When war shall be made against us, then our navy may defend them.

3. As the town of Southampton lacks the commodity [3] of access of merchandise by land, so it has this commodity: that there can be no access of enemies by land, which may be at Antwerp, and men think will be this year, which [is] a great safety to the merchants.

4. The traffic that comes by land will not much diminish the mart, for it is only almost the Venetians' traffic, who shall much easilier come hither by sea than to Antwerp and with less danger of the seas.

TO THE SECOND POINT

1. The ill making of our cloths will be meet to be looked on this Parliament, and order thereupon to be given. The matter is

---

[3] "Commodity": advantage.

come to some ripeness already; the upper house hath one bill, and the nether house has another in good forwardness.[4]

2. As ill as they be made, the Flemings do at this time desire them wonderfully, offering rather to pay the imposition of the Emperor than to lack them.

TO THE THIRD POINT

1. It were very necessary that the ships that [shall] be (now *altered to*) hereafter going were stayed till further consideration be had of them, if (they be not already gone *altered to*) the mart were come to some ripeness.

2. The cloths hereafter might be bought up with our money here and conveyed to Southampton, to be there uttered [5] at the mart time; and so it shall help the mart very well.

TO THE FOURTH [POINT]

1. The danger of their lives, which they now fear very much, will make them seek another harbor to rest in more safely.

2. They came from Bruges to Antwerp only for the English commodities, although they were [settled at Bruges.]

3. They have a great commodity to come to Southampton, and a great fear of spoiling to drive them from Antwerp.

4. The merchants never assign to themselves such a mansion, but for more gain they will leave that and take another.

TO THE FIFTH POINT

1. The Emperor is so driven at this time to his shifts that neither he shall be able to attend the stay of many from coming to the mart; neither, if he were able to attend, he could, I think, do it now—the Flemings being put in such fear as they be of the loss of all they have.

2. The Flemings, and the Spaniards which be under him, can

[4] The measures were passed as 5 & 6 Edward VI, cs. 6, 7, 8, 22.
[5] "Uttered": sold or vended.

hardlier be without us than we without them, and therefore they would hardly be brought to forbear our traffic.

TO THE SIXTH POINT

1. It were good the Steelyard men were for this time gently answered and that it were seen whether, by any gentle offer of some part of their liberties again, they might be brought to ship (at Newcastle *crossed out*) their wares to the mart. The Frenchmen also, I think, would easily be brought to come hither, having now none other traffic but hither. These two nations would suffice to begin a mart for the first part.

TO THE SEVENTH POINT

1. It is not the ability of the English merchants only that makes the mart, but it is the resort of other nations to some one place when they do exchange their commodities one with another. For the bargaining will be as well amongst the strangers themselves, the Spaniards with the Almains, the Italians with Flemings, the Venetians with the Danes, etc., as other nations will bargain with us.

2. The merchants of London, of Bristol, and other places, will come thither for the mart time, and traffic.

3. The merchants will make shift enough for their lodging.

4. There may some of these cloths that (should now go out *altered to*) shall go out hereafter be bought with my money and so carried to Southampton to be there uttered.

TO THE EIGHTH POINT

1. Bruges, where the mart was before, stood not on the river of Rhine, nor Antwerp does not neither stand on that river.

2. Frankfurt Mart may well stand for a Fair for High Almain, although Southampton [may] serve for all nations that lie on the seaside. For few of those come to Frankfurt Mart.

III. *Memorandum as to Ways and Means* (Summer, 1552) [1]

PAYMENTS of (wa[r?] *crossed out*) debts beyond seas........
£200,000

My debts owing me....	100,000	
The subsidy............	80,000	£200,000
Church plate superfluous	20,000	

I think this way best, because it shall make things to be looked for that else would peradventure be lost, as church plate, which as men say is daily conveyed away; and so the bullion may remain still and the land not sold, which if it were to be spent were better bestowed hereafter on those that have served than sold to auditors or penmen [2] who, having store of money, would buy it.

£20,000 in the household
10,000 of the mints
10,000 of Michaelmas rent

The treasure I have of	£100,000
The bullion	34,000
The land	3,000
The fustians .... (34,000 *altered to*)	14,000

[1] The manuscript is to be found in the Lansdowne MSS., 1236, f. 21. We have supplied the title. It is endorsed at f. 21b:

N. XL (in an unknown hand)
36 K. Edw^rdes Memoryall (in Cecil's hand)

and is further endorsed, possibly in Strype's hand:

A° 1552
11 The Kings Memorials
no. 11

[2] "Penmen": scriveners or notaries. The use is much earlier than that first cited in this sense (1612) in the *NED*.

174

Ways and Means

The forfeits, which, being asked of those persons that have willingly devoured their neighbors and broken the law, will do much good.

The arrearages of the surveyors and auditors of the courts shall be left for a treasure, or not dismembered by these payments.

IV. *Memorandum for the Council* (October 13, 1552) [1]

A SUMMARY OF MATTERS TO BE CONCLUDED

1. How a mass of money may be gotten to discharge the sum of £300,000 both for discharge of the debts, and also to get £50,000 of treasury money for all events.

2. Diminishing of the charges of the pensioners' table, the Lord Privy Seal's, the physician's, and the master's of [the] household, giving them reasonable recompense.[2]

3. Redeeming the leases pertaining to the liveries at Westminster, Waltham, Reading, and St. Albans.[3]

4. Discharging in the Admiralty.

5. Provision to be made for the wardrobe whereby the charge may be the less.

6. Discharge of the posts.

7. Discharge of certain bulwarks on the seaside which be thought superfluous.

---

[1] This manuscript is also to be found in the Lansdowne MSS., 1236, ff. 19–20. We have supplied the title for the paper, which bears only the heading *A summary of matters to be concluded.* At the top left (f. 19a) is written, "A 1552," probably in Strype's hand. The memorandum was endorsed in Cecil's hand "[The] Kynges Mat. Memoryall 13:Octob.1552," to which has been added in a later hand (probably Strype's) the further endorsement "LXXXI" and "no. 10."

[2] The allowances for three such court groups had already been abolished on September 27, 1552 (see above, p. 145).

[3] I.e., to reclaim the leases on these large and formerly monastic properties.

8. Discharging (700 *altered to*) 1,000 men in Ireland more than be yet.

9. Discharge of (500[?] *altered to*) 500 men at Berwick when the fort shall be reared (and 200 at Guînes for this winter *added*).

10. Bringing the Augmentation Court into the Exchequer, and likewise the Court of First Fruits and Tenths, and saving all those fees that may be spared.[4]

11. Examining whether by their patents they have portage money allowed them (and if they have it, how they got it *added*).

12. Discharging the superfluous fees in the Duchy (the Augmentat *crossed out*) and the Wards (and also in the mints *crossed out*).[5]

13. Gathering and coining of the church plate.

14. Sale of certain lands of chantries (colleges, houses, and Beaumont's[6] lands to the sum of £5,000 *added*).

15. Bringing in the remnant of (my *altered to*) the debts.

16. Taking accounts of all those that have had to do with (my *crossed out*) money since the 36th year of K. H. 8.

17. The stay of lead.[7] (*Added, possibly in Strype's hand,* Sr. Th. Gresham's.)

---

[4] This anticipates the report of the commission appointed to consider the merging of the Court of Augmentations and certain other revenue courts into a single revenue agency (see above, pp. xxviii–xxix, and below, pp. 181–184).

[5] I.e., in the Duchy of Lancaster and in the Court of Wards, both being revenue courts, incidentally, whose merger in the Exchequer was contemplated.

[6] John Beaumont, Master of the Rolls, had been deprived and heavily fined for corruption and abuses in office (see above, pp. 109, 128, 131).

[7] Sir Thomas Gresham in August, 1552, had recommended, among other devices, that the King take into his own hands the staple of lead, thereby controlling the European market.

18. The sale of the bell metal.[8]

19. The execution of penal laws touching horses, plows, (poor folk *crossed out*) for riots, oppressions, (wod *crossed out*) planting and grafting of trees, for the [as]size of wood and billet, forestalling and regrating.[9]

20. The offenses and forfeits of the merchants of the Steelyard.

21. The calling of a Parliament for to get some subsidy, in respect of (my *crossed out*) defense of the Englishmen that be robbed by the Frenchmen.[10]

22. Sale of certain jewels to the sum of £15,000.

23. Examining how the sale of the fustians is made,[11] and also of the copper.

(24. The borrowing of the merchants' cloths *crossed out*.) [12]

25. The borrowing of the staplers [*crossed out, but rewritten as No. 24*].

26. Guidotti's obligations to be pursued.[13]

27. Taking order for the mines in Ireland.

---

[8] There was a considerable amount of bell metal in royal hands, not only from expropriated and razed monasteries but from that yielded when church bells in Devonshire and Cornwall, used for signaling in the rising of 1549, were ordered to be taken down and expropriated.

[9] The King is here concerned more with social than with fiscal policy. The statutes referred to are those, still in effect, though largely unenforced, which sought to prevent further enclosures of arable land, excessive emparking, and further rise in prices.

[10] Edward's second Parliament was convened on March 1, 1553.

[11] Gresham had in August, 1552, been obliged to buy fustians costing £6,000 from the Fuggers in Antwerp as the condition of the renewal of large royal debts still outstanding there.

[12] See above, pp. 146–147, for the details of this forced loan from London merchants, imposed in order to meet obligations in Antwerp.

[13] See above, pp. 20, 24.

Memorandum for the Council

FOR RELIGION

1. A catechism to be set forth for to be taught in all grammar schools.[14]

2. An uniformity of doctrine to which all preachers should set their hands to.

3. Commissions to be granted to those bishops that be grave, learned, wise, sober, and of good religion, for the executing of discipline.

4. To find fault with the slothfulness of the pastors and to deliver [to] them articles of visitation, willing and commanding them to be more diligent in their office and to keep more preachers.

5. (The amending *altered to*) The abrogating of the old canon law and establishment of a new.[15]

6. The dividing of the bishopric of Durham into two, and placing of men in them.[16]

7. The placing of Harley into the bishopric of Hereford.

8. The making of more homilies.

9. The making of more injunctions.

10. The placing of one in a bishopric in Ireland which Turner of Canterbury has refused.[17]

[14] This catechism, the work of Alexander Nowell, was in hand and was published shortly thereafter. Three editions appeared in 1553.

[15] For further details, see above, p. 110.

[16] One see was to be at Durham and the other at Newcastle, while a considerable proportion of the revenues of the great see were to be gathered to the Crown.

[17] On Turner's refusal, for lack of knowledge of the Irish language, John Bale, the famous Protestant scholar and polemicist, was appointed to the see of Ossory.

King Edward VI

1. The fortifying of Portsmouth.

2. The fortifying of Berwick to be accomplished.

3. The reparation of Beaucastle in Tyndal.[18]

4. Fortification at the Black Bank.[19]

5. Amending the pier of Dover.

6. Amending Sandwich haven.

7. Repairing of Dover castle and haven.

8. Amending the jetty at Calais.

9. Fortifying of (Risebank *altered to*) Newnhambridge.[20]

10. Making of storehouses at Guînes.

11. To strengthen the havens of Falmouth and Dartmouth.

12. The making of more great ordnance of the copper in the Tower and the bell metal.

13. Provision for more armor.

14. Provision for more piques, harquebuts, staves, bowstaves, bills, etc.

(15. The establishment *crossed out*.)

15. Sending commissioners to view the state of the realm for keeping of great horses, whether they do observe the statute made concerning the same.

16. The device of two marts, one at Hull, another at [South]-ampton.[21]

17. To bring more arts into the realm so that all may not stand by clothing.

[18] In Cumberland on the Scottish border.

[19] The Black Bulwark, an outpost of the Dover fortifications, is possibly meant.

[20] Both places were fortified works near Calais (see above, pp. 35, 49, 55, 143).

[21] As proposed in the King's earlier memorandum (see above, pp. 168–173).

V. Certain Articles Devised and Delivered by the King's Majesty for the Quicker, Better, and More Orderly Dispatch of Causes by His Majesty's Privy Council (January 15, 1553) [1]

First, His Majesty wills, that all suits, petitions, and common warrants delivered to his Privy Council be considered by them (on the Mondays in the morning *inserted*), and answered also on the (Mondays *altered to*) Saturdays at afternoon, and that (that *altered to*) those day[s], and none others, be assigned to that purpose.

Secondarily, that, in answering of those suits and bills of petition, heed be taken that so many of them as pertain to any court of His Majesty's laws be as much as may be (by them *crossed out*) referred to those courts where by order they are triable. (Such as cannot be ended without them be with expedition determined *added*.)

Thirdly, that, in making of those warrants for money that pass by them, it be foreseen that those warrants be not such as may already be dispatched by warrant dormant, lest by means of such warrants the accounts should be uncertain.

Fourthly, His Majesty's pleasure is, that on the Sundays (provided that on Sundays they be present at common prayer *added in margin*) they intend the public affairs of this realm, they dispatch answers to letters for the good order of the realm and make full dispatches of all things concluded the (last *crossed out*) week before.

---

[1] The original is in Cotton MSS., Nero, C, x, ff. 86–89.

[The following were added by the King:]

17. That all warrants for reward above £40 and for his business or affairs above £100 pass not but under his signature.

18. That no private suit be intermeddled with the great affairs, but heard on the Mondays alone.

19. If there be under four, and a matter of expedition arise, they shall declare it to the King's Majesty and before him debate it, but not send answer without it require wonderful haste.

[Endorsed by the King:]

For the Council,
15 Januarij, 1552 ⁰ [1553]
R.R.E.6 ¹ 6 ⁰

VI. *Notes on the English Occupation of France in the Reign of Henry VI* (Undated) [1]

JOHN, DUKE OF BEDFORD, 1427 ET 28 [2]

[5] Earls in Normandy.

6 Barons.

74 Knights.

Of which Knights the Earl of Ormonde's son after [earl], the Earl of Arundel's brother after earl, three Barons' sons, eight bannerets, sixty-one knights bachelors.

Gien: [3] 3 barons, 2 bannerets, 6 knights.

Lords of France that came in:

3 Dukes, John of Burgundy, Philip of Burgundy, Duke of Cleves.

7 Barons.

19 Knights.

The revenue of the realm of France, beside allowances to offi-

---

[1] The original is in Cotton MSS., Nero, C, x, ff. 94–97. We have supplied the title, the document bearing no heading. The first page has been damaged.

[2] Bedford was the King's eldest uncle. Henry VI was still a child in 1427–1428, having been born in 1421. Bedford, whom Parliament had named Protector, was much in France in these months as the leader of an Anglo-French coalition now seeking to deal with the French resurgence inspired by Joan of Arc. The young King was taken to France on his first state visit in 1430, but so far had English power receded that he was detained for some months at Rouen while an attempt was made to clear the way to Reims, where it was planned to crown him. The coronation took place instead at Paris on December 16, 1430.

[3] Gien, on the Loire to the east of Orleans.

cers, buildings, and reparations, and other necessar[y] charges, is 129,240 francs; which, reckoning 9 francs to the pound English (as then it was), came to £14,360 ([E]nglish), out of which was paid in pensions by the treaty 50,040 francs,[4] which make Eng[lish] £5,560, also to counselors attending upon the Regent 20,520 francs, which is Eng[lish] £2,280. To officers in the law, keepers of records, of houses, wardrobes, gardens, lions, (etc. *crossed out*), to heralds, workmen, ambassado[rs], posts, and to the Earl of Warwick for laying siege to Pontorson[5] 79,410 francs, which make English £8,823 6s.8d. Item for keeping of twenty-five fortresses in France allowed to the captains 45,550 francs, which is English £5,061 and one franc over. *Summa totalis* of the charge being 175,000 fr., that is to say £19,444 8s.10d.ob.q., exceeds the revenue, which is but 129,240 fr., £14,360, by the sum of 46,561 fr.: *id est,* £5,173 8s.10d.ob.q. besides 8,000 francs which came by a new crew,[6] so that the whole overcharge is £6,062 2s.10d.ob.q.[7]

The revenue of the Duchy of Normandy, together with a subsidy granted by the three estates of 160,000 fr., amounts in the year of Our Lord 1433 (*corrected from* 1434) to the sum of 320,000 francs, which make English £35,555 and 5 francs odd.

Out of which in special payments by treaties, pensions, officers of the law, heralds, messengers, etc., 123,600 (137,633 *crossed out*) francs, which is English £13,733 6s.8d. Item for soldiers' wages and garrisons 250,260 francs, which is English £27,806 13s.4d. So that the overcharge of Normandy comes to 53,860 francs, which makes English £5,984 and 4 francs odd.[8]

Memorandum. There were 57 captains of fortresses, and they had 367 lances on horseback, of which were 4 knights bannerets and 20 knights bachelors. They had 389 lances afoot and 2,415

---

[4] I.e., by the Treaty of Troyes.   [5] Pontorson in Manche.

[6] "Crew": an augmentation of the military force in France.

[7] The total and hence the debit balance are not correctly stated, though the franc conversions are correct save for one trifling error.

[8] This calculation is correct.

archers. The wages of a lance afoot lacked somewhat of 6*d.* a day and was more than 5[*d.*]*ob.* The archers had every year near about £6 16*s.* As for the lances on horseback, because there be certain bannerets and knights that had more than the rest, it cannot be perfectly judged what they had. But it should appear they had after the rate of 14*d.* by the day, and so there is left £141 to be distributed upon the knights' wages.

The revenue of the county of Maine and city of Maine was 56,200 (5600200 *crossed out*) francs, which is English £6,244 and 4 francs odd, the year of Our Lord God 1434.

Out of which [was] paid to 121 lances on horseback, 34 lances afoot, and 510 [*corrected from an illegible figure*] archers in 4 garrisons, of which one was kept but seven months, and had in one lance on horseback two on foot, and 30 archers, the sum of 55,362 fran[cs], which is English £6,151 6*s.*8*d.* Item paid to judges, bailiffs, counselors 725 fr., which makes English £80 and 5 francs, so that the overcharge of Maine was 112 francs, that is to say, £12 6*s.*8*d.* English.

Notandum. That the Regent in recompense[?] of service gave away land to the value of 60,000 francs. Also in those garrisons, and also there was no difference of wages betwixt the ensign-bearer, whiffler,[9] [and] mustermaster. No man had more wages one than another, except he were a captain of a fort, a knight, or a lord.

Sir John Fastolf's counsel: [10]

That the offer made by the French at Arras,[11] which was that

[9] "Whiffler": an armed attendant charged with keeping public order, especially on public occasions or processions.

[10] The famous soldier was in 1423 appointed Regent in Normandy and Governor of Anjou and Maine. In 1429 Fastolf relieved Orleans in a great victory at Rouvray but lost favor after his defeat at Patay in June, which is satirized in Shakespeare's *Henry VI.* Fastolf raised the siege of Vaudemont in 1431. He remained in Normandy until 1440, when, at the age of sixty-two, he retired from military service. See above, p. xxxii, for a note on Edward's use of sources emanating from Fastolf.

[11] Concluded in 1434. Fastolf was one of the English commissioners responsible for negotiating the treaty.

Henry the Sixth should enjoy peaceably the Duchy of Normandy as of the French King, should be refused.

Ratio 1ª. Because the title to France by this treaty should be lost. 2ª. Because the King should be said to be of no power. 3ª. Because the French, seeing advantage, would break and win Normandy. Better were it for us to take our advantage.

2. If the King will no war, then certain foreign princes, to [be] assigned equally by both parties, to take up the matter and not to stand to the enemy's limitation.

3. If war be to be made, then this way to be followed:

1. First, no siege to be laid (for *crossed out*) except upon some notable strait passage or way, whereby as much land may be conquered withal as will bear the charges thereof. For laying of sieges spends men, money, and [or?] time, and wins little country.

2. That two noblemen be sent each with 700 spears, and they to march severally ten leagues in distance, and upon necessity to join, and to burn and waste the country as they go, sparing nothing. For, offer being made to the French that men of war should only meddle with men of war and not spoil the country, they refused it. Also they, because they have been rebels to Harry the Sixth, must in no wise be spared.

Part of Sir John Fastolf's counsel:

3. That 500 spears besides the garrisons be left in Normandy, both to spoil, waste, and subdue the countries of Anjou, Maine, Chartreine,[12] Brittany, as also to succor and relieve the garrisons if any invasion should be made. These numbers of 1,900 spears to be kept only these months: July, August, September, October, November.

4. That the sea be strongly kept, and that the towns of Normandy and England put to their helping hands.

---

[12] So in MS.; Chartrain is presumably meant, an area which today includes parts of the departments of Eure-et-Loire and Seine-et-Oise.

5. That no sanctuary should serve traitors, conspirators, or rebels.

6. Because Flanders is under the Duke of Burgundy, who favors the French, that alliance be made with Venice or Genoa for uttering our cloths.

7. That the great towns of Normandy be better fortified.

8. That the (realm *altered to*) Duchy of Normandy be governed by Englishmen and not too much by Frenchmen-born.

9. If siege be to be laid to any place, then an army to be levied, both to succor the siege and also to resist the enemy if he should invade another way.

FINIS

Articles desired by Richard Duke of York, (in *crossed out*) for the governance of France when he (desired th *altered to*) received the same by indenture 18° H^i.6^i.

1. To have like power or commission as the Duke of Bedford had.

2. To have three of these nine, of every estate one, to be of the Council of France.

The Bishop of Lincoln	The Viscount of Beaumont
The Bishop of Norwich	The L. Fanhope
The Bishop of Salisbury	The L. Hungerford
	Sir Ralph Botiller
	Sir John Stourton
	Sir John Popham [13]

3. (Item in time *crossed out*) To have £20,000 readily, truly, and at days paid to him, out of England in time of war. If truce came, then to rebate the greatness of that charge; likewise if

[13] They may be briefly identified, in order, as: Marmaduke Lumley, Thomas Brouns, William Aiscough; John Beaumont (the first Englishman to bear the title of Viscount), John Cornwall (Baron Fanhope), Walter Hungerford (Baron Hungerford); and the three knights (all soldiers) as listed. We supply "Beaumont" in the text; the MS. reads "Bemô" (edge of page).

towns were to be besieged and great armies levied, then to be augmented to him.

4. Item, for his own diet he desired 36,000 francs, which is £4,000 English.

5. He desired 6 great guns, 4 dd. of stones of Maidstone, 12 great fowlers likewise furnished, 12 last of saltpeter, 12 gunners, 2 master gunners, and 12 yeoman gunners, 1,000 spears, 4,000 bows, 12,000 sheaves of arrows, 200 gross of strings, 200 long panes of ordnance, 2,000 of lead, with carriage for the same.

6. He desired in (cause *altered to*) case he should besiege Harfleur or Dieppe, [that] a navy might be sent of 2,000 men, both to let the herring fish, which is a great comfort and victualing to Dieppe, and also to give free passage for Englishmen that would traffic to Rouen.

7. He desired license to carry victuals to such towns as by siege or otherwise should have need, out of England, paying therefor.

8. He required to have a good band of knights and squires, of such as might be forborne and entreated to go.

9. If he die in service, then no account to be asked of him of that receipt of money.

10. If any of these articles be broken, and the King certified thereof, then the said Duke to leave his regency and come into England.

11. Because divers men having [the] keeping of castles in France for term of life were not resident thereon, order to be taken that if he were not resident another should be [ap]pointed to his place.

12. If mischance fall by battle or rebellion, the said Duke doing his devoir,[14] that it be not laid to his charge.

13. To have such letters as he should think good under the King's great and privy seal.

FINIS

[14] "Devoir": one's duty.

BIBLIOGRAPHY

[This list includes works found helpful in identifying foreign names as well as works actually cited.]

Acts of the Privy Council of England. Ed. by J. R. Dasent. New series, Vols. II (1547–1550), III (1550–1552), IV (1552–1554). London, 1892.

Aimond, Charles. *Les rélations de la France et du Verdunois de 1270 à 1552*. Paris, 1910.

Aumale, M. le Duc d'. *Histoire des Princes de Condé pendant les XVIe et XVIIe siècles*. 7 vols. Paris, 1863–1896.

Babinger, Franz, "Das Ende der Arianiten," in *Sitzungsberichte der bayerischen Akademie der Wissenschaften*, "Phil. hist. Klasse," 1960, No. 4.

Bellay, Martin et Guillaume. *Mémoires*. Ed. by V. L. Bourilly and F. Vindry. 4 vols. Paris, 1908–1919.

Bibliothèque Nationale. *Catalogue de la Collection Dupuy*. Ed. by Léon Dorez. Paris, 1928.

Brantôme, Pierre de Bourdeille, Seigneur de. *Oeuvres complètes*. Ed. by Lodovic Lalanne. 11 vols. Paris, 1864–1882.

"Brief Discours du Siège de Metz," in *Archives curieuses de l'histoire de France*. Ed. by L. Cimber and F. Danjou. Ser. 1, vol. 3. Paris, 1835. Pp. 117–138.

Calendar of the Patent Rolls Preserved in the Public Record Office, Edward VI. Ed. by R. H. Brodie. 6 vols. London, 1924–1926.

Calendar of State Papers, Foreign Series, of the Reign of Edward VI, 1547–1553. Ed. by W. B. Turnbull. London, 1861.

191

Bibliography

Calendar of the State Papers Relating to Ireland . . . 1509–1573. Ed. by H. C. Hamilton. London, 1860.

Calendar of . . . State Papers, Relating to . . . Spain. Vols. IX (1547–1549), X (1550–1552). Ed. by M. A. S. Hume and Royall Tyler. London, 1912–1914.

Calendar of State Papers . . . Relating to . . . Venice. Vol. V (1534–1554). Ed. by Rawdon Brown. London, 1873.

Commentaires et lettres de Blaise de Monluc Maréchal de France. Ed. by Alphonse de Ruble. 2 vols. Paris, 1864. The *Commentaires* were also published in Michaud and Poujoulat's *Nouvelle collection des mémoires pour servir à l'histoire de France.* Ser. 1, Vol. 7. Paris, 1838. Pp. 3–383.

Correspondance politique de M. de Lanssac (Louis de Saint-Gelais). Ed. by Ch. Sauzé. Vol. 33 of *Archives Historiques du Poitou.* Poitiers, 1904.

Correspondance politique de Odet de Selve Ambassadeur de France en Angleterre (1546–1549). Ed. by Germain Lefèvre-Pontalis. Paris, 1888.

Decrue, Francis. *Anne Duc de Montmorency . . . sous les Rois Henri II, François II et Charles IX.* Paris, 1889.

Desjardins, Abel. *Négociations diplomatiques de la France avec la Toscane.* 6 vols. Paris, 1859–1886.

Die alten Territorien des Bezirkes Lothringen. Pt. I. Vol. XXVIII of *Statistische Mittheilungen über Elsass-Lothringen.* Strassburg, 1898.

Druffel, A. von, ed. *Briefe und Akten zur Geschichte des sechzehnten Jahrhunderts.* 4 vols. Munich, 1873–1896.

Elton, G. R. *The Tudor Revolution in Government.* Cambridge, 1962.

Emmison, F. G., "A Plan . . . for Reorganizing the Privy Council's Work, 1552–1553," in *Bulletin of the Institute of Historical Research,* XXXI (1958), No. 84.

Ganier, G. *La politique du Connétable Anne de Montmorency.* Le Havre, n.d.

Henne, Alexandre. *Histoire du règne de Charles-Quint en Belgique.* Vol. IX. Brussels and Leipzig, 1859.

"Histoire Particulière de la Court du Roy Henri II," in *Archives*

Bibliography

curieuses de l'histoire de France. Ed. by L. Cimber and F. Danjou. Ser. 1, Vol. 3. Paris, 1835. Pp. 275–306.

Inventaire sommaire des archives du Département des Affaires Etrangères. Correspondance Politique. Vol. I. Paris, 1903.

Katterfeld, Alfred. *Roger Ascham. Sein Leben und seine Werke.* Strassburg, 1879.

Langenn, F. A. von. *Moritz, Herzog und Churfürst zu Sachsen.* 2 vols. Leipzig, 1841.

Lennel, F. *Histoire de Calais.* 2 vols. Calais, 1910.

Machyn, Henry. *The Diary of Henry Machyn . . . 1550 to 1563.* Ed. by J. G. Nichols. Camden Society, Vol. XLII. London, 1848.

Marchand, Charles. *Charles Ier de Cossé, Comte de Brissac.* Paris, 1889.

Mémoires de François de Lorraine, Duc d'Aumale et de Guise . . . pendant les années 1547 à 1561. Ed. by Michaud and Poujoulat, *Nouvelle collection des mémoires pour servir à l'histoire de France.* Ser. 1, Vol. VI. Paris, 1839. Pp. 1–539.

Mémoires de la vie de François de Scepeaux, Sire de Vieilleville. Ed. by Michaud and Poujoulat, *Nouvelle collection des mémoires.* Ser. 1, Vol. IX. Paris, 1838. Pp. 7–400. Another edition by M. Petitot, *Collection complète des mémoires relatifs à l'histoire de France.* Vols. XXVI–XXVII. Paris, 1822.

Mémoires du Sieur François de Boyvin, Chevalier, Baron Duvillars. Ed. by Michaud and Poujoulat, *Nouvelle collection des mémoires.* Ser. 1, Vol. X. Paris, 1838. Pp. 3–390. Another edition by M. Petitot, *Collection complète des mémoires.* Vol. XXIX. Paris, 1823.

Notices sur les deux sièges de Metz de 1444 et 1552. Ed. by F. Verronnais. Metz, 1844.

"Papiers des Pot de Rhodes, 1529–1648," ed. by Hiver de Beauvoir, in *Mémoires de la Commission Historique du Cher,* II. Bruges and Paris, 1864. Pp. 75–283.

Rabutin, François de. *Commentaires des dernières guerres en la Gaule Belgique, entre Henri Second du nom . . . et Charles Cinquiesme.* Ed. by Michaud and Poujoulat. Ser. 1, Vol. 7. Paris, 1838. Pp. 393–610.

Romier, Lucien. *La carrière d'un favori. Jacques d'Albon de Saint-André.* Paris, 1909.

Bibliography

Rowse, A. L. *Tudor Cornwall.* London, 1941.

Ruble, Alphonse de. *François de Montmorency.* Paris, 1880.

Salignac, Bertrand de. *Le siège de Metz par l'Empereur Charles V, en l'an 1552.* Ed. by Petitot, *Collection complète des mémoires.* Vol. XXXII. Paris, 1823. Pp. 255–406.

Teulet, Alexandre. *Relations politiques de la France et de l'Espagne avec l'Écosse au XVIᵉ siècle.* Vol. I. *"Correspondances françaises, 1515–1560."* Paris, 1862.

Tudor Royal Proclamations. Ed. by P. L. Hughes and J. F. Larkin. Vol. I. New Haven, 1964.

Venetianische Depeschen vom Kaiserhofe. Ed. by Gustav Turba. Vol. II. Vienna, 1892.

Vindry, Fleury. *Les ambassadeurs Français permanents au XVIᵉ siècle.* Paris, 1903.

Vitalis, Alexandre. *Correspondance politique de Dominique du Gabre . . . Trésorier des armées à Ferrare (1552–1554).* Paris, 1903.

Wriothesley, Charles. *A Chronicle of England during the Reigns of the Tudors.* Ed. by W. D. Hamilton. Camden Society, New series, Vols. XI, XX. London, 1875, 1877.

Zeller, Gaston. *La réunion de Metz à la France (1552–1648).* 2 vols. Paris, 1926–1927.

INDEX

INDEX

Index

Index

Braye, John, Lord, 25, 27, 61, 91, 93, 98, 103
Bremen, 48, 95
Brend, John, 93
Brett, Alexander, 147
Brézé, Artus de Maillé, Seigneur de, and de Maillé, 29
Bridgwater, 15
Brissac, Charles de Cossé, Seigneur de, 140, 141
Brittany, 188
Bromley, Sir Thomas (Privy Council; Chief Justice of Common Pleas), 110
Brooke, ——, 86
Brooke, George, Lord Cobham (Deputy of Calais), 25, 30, 31, 47 n., 52, 70, 71, 98, 100, 124
Brooke, Robert (Recorder of London), 113, 123 n.
Broughty Castle, 8, 12
Browne, Sir Anthony (Privy Council), 4
   his son (also Sir Anthony), 56, 90, 103, 105, 106, 137
Browne, George, Bishop of Dublin, 102, 119
Bruges, 111
Bruno, Dr. John, 27 n.
Brunswick, Duke of, 27
Bryan, Sir Francis, 7, 8
Buccleuch, Lord of, see Scott, Sir Walter
Bucer, Martin, xxiv, 53
Burgh, William, Baron, 98
Burgundy:
   troops of, 151, 155
   Dukes of (temp. H. VI), 185, 189
Burke, Richard, second Earl of Clanricard, 104
Burnet, Bishop Gilbert, xiii, xiv–xv
Bussac (Piedmont), 141
Butler, Thomas, tenth Earl of Ormonde, 61, 105

Calais, 23, 25, 27, 29, 34, 35, 41, 43, 45, 46, 47, 49, 53, 55, 62, 66, 104, 119, 130, 136, 142, 143, 144, 147, 180
Cambridge, xi, 53–54
Canterbury, Archbishop of, see Cranmer, Thomas
Cape Gris-Nez, 13 n.
Capua, Leo Strozzi, Prior of, 82, 86
Carey, ——, 103, 105
Carinthia, 127
Carlisle, 141
Carr, James, 51
Carr family, 152
Caryll, John, 110, 122
Cassilis, Earl of, see Kennedy, Gilbert
Castiglione, Camillo di Gonzaga, Count of, 78
Catherine (Parr), Queen, 6, 107 n., 112 n.
Cawe(s) Mills, 51
Cecil, Sir William (Privy Council; Principal Secretary, 1550–1553), xx, xxviii, 39, 46, 82, 86, 88, 90, 110, 136, 143 n., 145
Chaderton, John, 138
Chaloner, Sir Thomas, 58, 73–74, 105 n., 114
Chalons, 132
Chamberlain, Lord Great, see Parr, William (1550)
Chamberlain, of the Household, see Darcy, Thomas (1551–1553); and FitzAlan, Henry (1546–1550)
Chamberlain, Sir Thomas (ambassador to the Regent of the Netherlands), 44, 156
Champagne (France), 85, 112, 125, 132, 152
Chancellor, Lord, see Goodrich, Thomas (1552–1553); and Rich, Richard (1547–1552)
Chandlers (of London), 103
Chantry lands, sale ordered, 121–122
Charing Cross, 100
Charles V, Holy Roman Emperor:

199

Index

Constable of France, *see* Montmorency, Anne de

Conyers, Lord John, 53, 106, 114, 141

Cook, Dr. William (Master of Requests), 41, 43, 110

Cooke, Sir Anthony, 110

Cornhill, 94

Cornwall, John, Baron Fanhope, 189

Cornwall (county), 178

Corso, Captain Peter, 77

Cotton, Sir Richard (Comptroller of the Household, 1552–1553), 90, 104, 122, 130, 138 n., 141, 144 n., 155

Cotton, Sir Robert Bruce, xiv

Cotton, Thomas (brother of Sir Richard), 144

Cotton, Sir Thomas (son of Sir Robert), xiv

Council, *see* Privy Council *and* Trent

Coup d'état, against Somerset, 17–19

Courrières, Jean de Montmorency, Seigneur de, 120, 121, 131

Courtney, Mr., 103, 105, 106

Coverdale, Miles, Bishop of Exeter, 78, 110

Cowdray Castle, 90 n., 137

Cox, Dr. Richard, xi–xii, 3, 110

Crane, William, 89, 92, 95, 97–99, 131

Cranmer, Thomas, Archbishop of Canterbury, 3, 5, 28 n., 56, 110

Croft, Sir James (Lord Deputy of Ireland, 1551–1553), 52, 57, 77

Cromwell, Gregory, second Baron, 98

Croydon (co. Surrey), 63

Culpepper, Alexander, 71

Dacre, Sir Thomas, 146 n., 155

Dacre, Sir William, third Baron Dacre "of the North," 7, 12, 44

Dalkeith, 8

Dallison, William, 123 n.

Damvillers, 126 n., 131

Darcy, Sir Arthur, 91

Darcy, Thomas, Lord, of Chiche (Lord Chamberlain of the Household, 1551–1553), 18, 20, 50, 57, 98, 100, 124

Dartmouth, 180

Day, George, Bishop of Chichester, 23, 82, 83, 84, 86

Debatable lands, 51, 106, 114, 117, 146; *see also* Scotland

Debt, royal, 30, 106, 107, 109, 111, 113, 120, 125, 174, 176; *see also* Economic affairs

Denmark, 50, 52

Dennis, Sir Maurice, 25, 29

Depopulation, 163–165

Deptford, 25, 31, 36, 70, 106

Derby, Earl of, *see* Stanley, Edward

Derbyshire, 101

Desmond, Earl of, *see* FitzGerald, James

Deuxponts, 151

Devereux, Walter, first Viscount Hereford, 98

Devonshire, 13, 15, 101, 178 n.

Dieppe, 43 n., 69, 79, 95, 190

Digby, Anthony, 103, 105, 106

Donnington Castle, 142

Doria, Andrea, 42, 45–47, 65–66

Dorset, Marquis of, *see* Grey, Henry

Douglas, Lady Margaret, 93, 94

Dover, 23, 25, 26, 43, 70, 180

Dragut, Arraiz, 42, 45, 46, 65–66

Drury, Thomas, 103, 105

Dublin, Archbishop of, *see* Browne, George

Dudley, Lord Ambrose, 103, 105, 106

Dudley, Sir Andrew (brother of John Dudley), 5–6, 8, 12, 18, 106, 120, 124, 147

Dudley, Sir Henry (Vice-Admiral), 116, 139

Dudley, John, Earl of Warwick,

Index

Index

Hammes, 49, 55

Hammond, Lawrence, 88, 93, 97, 99, 100

Hampshire, 12, 41, 101, 139

Hampton Court, x, 17, 18, 20, 32, 33, 72, 78, 83, 91, 92, 145

Hanse towns, 58 n., 133; *see also* Merchants *and* Steelyard

Harfleur (France), 190

Harley, John, Bishop of Hereford, 101, 179

Harwich, 6

Hasleford, 138

Hastings, Francis, second Earl of Huntingdon, 98, 100, 124
wife of, 93

Heath, Nicholas, Bishop of Worcester, 82 n., 83, 84, 86

Heathfield (co. Kent), 32 n.

Heideck, Baron Johann von, 140

Henry II, King of France, xxi, 6, 13, 23, 26, 30, 38
wife of, 37, 132
sister of, 132
daughter of, *see* Elizabeth
sons of, *see* Angoulême
see also Charles V *and* France

Henry VI, King of England, xxxiii, 185, 188

Henry VIII, King of England, x, xx n., 3, 4, 24 n.

Herbert, William, first Earl of Pembroke, 12, 24, 34–35, 36, 39, 50, 81, 86, 93, 94, 98, 99, 100, 119, 124, 142 n., 150
wife of, 92, 112

Hereford, Viscount of, *see* Devereux, Walter

Hertford, Earl of, *see* Seymour, Edward

Hertfordshire, 12

Hesdin, 83, 154

Hoby, Sir Philip, 17, 60, 63, 76, 80, 82, 109, 111, 113, 117, 119, 123, 130, 132, 137

Holcroft, Sir Thomas, 9, 89

Holland, 66

Holstein, Duke Adolf of, 125

Home family, 51 n., 152

Home Castle, 8, 12

Honiton (co. Devon), 13–15

Hooper, John, Bishop of Gloucester, 40, 110, 122

Hopton, Robert, 105

Horne, Robert, Dean of Durham, 149

Horse, Master of, *see* Dudley, John; *and* Herbert, William

Howard, Sir George, 103

Howard, Thomas, third Duke of Norfolk, 3
daughter of, *see* Richmond, Mary, Duchess of

Howard, Lord William, first Baron Howard of Effingham, 91 n., 103, 147

Howell, Fulke ap, 133 n.

Hull, 104, 115, 180

Hunaudaye, *see* Annebaut, Jean d'

Hungary, Queen of, *see* Mary, Queen Dowager of Hungary

Hungerford, Lord Walter, 189

Hungerford, Sir Walter, 105

Hunsdon (co. Herts), 42

Huntingdon, Earl of, *see* Hastings, Francis

Huntly, Earl of, *see* Gordon, George

Husbandmen, status of, 160–162

Hyde Park, 75

Ibrachan, Donough, Baron of, 104

Injunctions:
against superstitious ceremonies, 6
more required, 179

Innsbruck, 126, 127, 128, 141

Interim, The, 47

Ireland:
administration of, 9, 38, 46, 52, 66, 77, 104, 109, 123, 130, 150, 151
mines in, 178
see also 39, 41, 42, 51, 54–55, 57, 64 n., 155

Ireland, Lord Deputy of, *see* Bellingham, Sir Edward (1548–1549); Croft, Sir James

205

Index

Index

Index

Parma, 65 n., 74, 77, 102
Parr, Catherine, 6, 107 n., 112 n.
Parr, William, Earl of Essex, Marquis of Northampton (Great Chamberlain, 1550; Privy Council), 4, 15, 18, 30, 34, 36, 50, 59, 60, 61, 63, 66, 67, 68, 74, 76, 78, 87, 91, 93, 94, 98, 99, 100, 101, 134, 145
wife of, 92, 93
Parris, George van, 28 n., 58 n.
Partridge, Sir Miles, 87, 89, 99, 108 n., 109
Passau, treaty of, 140 n.
Paston, Mr., 103
Path, The (Cockburnspath), 7
Paulet, William, Earl of Wiltshire, Marquis of Winchester (Privy Council; Great Master of the Household, 1545–1550; Treasurer, 1550–1553), 50, 58, 59, 86, 91, 92, 94, 96, 97, 100, 101, 124, 138 n., 142
wife of, 93
"Pauncy" (ship), 6
Peckham, Sir Edmund (Treasurer of the Mint; Privy Council), 49 n., 81 n.
Peers, John, 89
Pembroke, Earl of, see Herbert, William
Perigliano, Count, see Pitigliano, Niccolò Orsini, Count
Périgueux, Bishop of, 75
Perne, Andrew, 101
Perrot, Sir John, 103, 106
Petitt, Thomas, 35 n.
Petre, Sir William (Principal Secretary, 1544–1553; Privy Council), xxx, 17, 21, 25, 30, 31, 34, 39, 41, 78, 103, 110, 134, 145
Petworth (co. Sussex), 137
Philip II, King of Spain, 63 n.
Picardy, 133, 152
Pickering, Sir William, 53, 57, 59, 60, 75, 107, 112, 125, 144, 147–148, 150
Piedmont, 79, 82, 85, 141, 154
Pinkie, battle of, 6–8, 87 n.
Pirry, Martin, 123, 130

Pitigliano, Niccolò Orsini, Count, 139, 141
Pleshey (co. Essex), 64 n.
Ponet, John, Bishop of Rochester and of Winchester, 38, 58, 110, 138 n.
Pontorson, siege of, 186
Poole (co. Dorset), 89, 123
Popham, Sir John, 189
Portcullis Herald, 133
Portsmouth, 89, 97, 123, 124, 138, 180
Portugal:
    Infante of, 27
    Emmanuel I, King of, 27 n.
Powis, Lady Anne, 109, 128
Poynings, Sir Adrian, 86
Praet, Louis de, 135
Prices:
    attempts to control, 49, 81, 96, 103, 129–130
    problem of, 163–165
    see also Economic affairs
"Primrose" (ship), 70
Privy Council:
    additions to, 25, 29
    proposals for reform of, 181–184
    see also xviii, xix, xxvii–xxxi, 4, 17, 29, 44, 55, 56, 67, 76, 84, 93, 116, 129, 131, 135, et passim
Privy Seal, Lord, see Russell, John
Proclamations, 29, 45, 46–47, 49, 62, 64, 70, 71, 73, 81, 86, 96, 155
Progress, royal (1552), 123, 137–143 passim
Protector, Lord, see Seymour, Edward
Prussia, Albert the elder of Brandenburg, Duke of, 94
Purton's bulwark, 35

Radcliffe, Henry, second Earl of Sussex, 91, 98
Radcliffe, Thomas, Lord Fitzwalter, 61, 91, 93, 103, 105, 106
Rangone, Count Pallavicino, 33
Reading (co. Berks), 14, 42, 143

Index

Rebellions:
threats of, 12–13, 28, 37, 41, 59, 78
in the West of England, 13–15
in East Anglia, 15–16
Record, Robert, 123 n.
Redman, John, 54
Reed, Sir Richard, 41 n., 110
Regent, *see* Mary, Queen Dowager of Hungary
Reid, Robert, Bishop of Orkney, 57 n.
Reiffenberg, Frederick von, 117, 140
Reims (France), 118, 150
Religious policy, xxii, xxiv–xxv
Act of Uniformity, 10
Act for ordinations, 19
order for preaching, 25
heresy, executions for, 28, 58
reform of service, 37, 49
chaplains at large appointed, 101
commission to revise canon law, 110
expropriation of church plate, 119, 177
chantry lands, sale of, 121–122, 177
reforms needed, 159–160, 179
Rhinegrave, Philip Francis, 9, 31, 146
Rich, Richard (Lord Chancellor, 1547–1552; Privy Council), 30, 41, 44, 78, 84, 101, 102
Richmond, Mary (Howard), Duchess of, 93, 94
Richmond, 33, 48, 72, 73, 76
Ridley, Nicholas, Bishop of London, 23, 28, 37, 39, 40, 56, 110
Ridley's Tower, 139
Rie (or Roeulx), Adrian de Croy, Count of, 125, 150, 152, 154
Risebank, 35, 49, 143, 180
Risings, *see* Rebellions
Robsart, Amy, 33 n.
Robsart, Sir John, 33
Rochepot, François de Montmorency, Seigneur de, 21, 24
Rochester, Bishop of, *see* Ponet,

John; Ridley, Nicholas; *and* Scory, John
Rochester, Robert, 76, 78
Roche-sur-Yon, Charles de Bourbon, Prince de, 153
Rodemanche Castle, 131
Rogers, Sir Edward, 18, 91
Rogers, John, 34, 52, 124
Rohan, René, Viscount of, 154
Rokeby, Ralph, 123 n.
Rolls, Master of, *see* Beaumont, John; *and* Bowes, Sir Robert
Romford (co. Essex), 37
Ross, Bishop of, *see* Panter, David
Rouen, 48
Roxburgh, 8, 22, 23
Roye (France), 150, 152
Russell, John, first Earl of Bedford (Keeper of the Privy Seal, 1542–1555; Privy Council), 13, 14, 18, 21, 34, 40, 50, 94, 98, 103, 106, 124, 134
wife of, 93
Rutland, Earl of, *see* Manners, Henry
Rutlandshire, 12
Rye (co. Sussex), 70

Sackville, Sir Richard, 122 n., 135 n.
Sadler, Sir Ralph (Master of the Wardrobe; Privy Council), 8, 50, 109, 124, 132
St. Albin, ——, 95
St. André, Jacques d'Albon, Seigneur de, Marshal of France, xxiii, 69–73 *passim*, 75, 112, 118, 150
St. Andrew's (Scotland), 38
St. James's field, 100
St. John, Lord, of Basing, *see* Paulet, William
St. Leger, Sir Anthony (Lord Deputy of Ireland, 1540–1547, 1550–1551, 1553–1556), 9, 40, 42, 57, 66, 102, 119
St. Martin's (Piedmont), 154
St. Michael, Order of, 62, 66, 72–73, 84

Index

St. Omer, 118
Salerno, Ferdinand san Severino, Prince of, 132, 141
Salisbury, Bishop of (temp. H. VI), 189
Salisbury (city), 123, 141
Saluzzo, 85, 140
Sancerre, Louis de Bueil, Count of, 112
Sandhills (Calais), 143
Sandingfield (Calais), 49
Sandwich, 180
Sandys, Thomas, Lord (of the Vine), 142
Sassy, Seigneur de, see Bochetel, Guillaume
Saverne, 124, 125
Saxony, Dukes of, see John Frederick and Maurice
Scepperus, Corneille, M. d'Eecke, 40, 41, 44, 66
Schetz, Jasper, 111, 125
Scheyve, Jean, 25 n., 80 n.
Schweinfurt, 117
Scilly Isles, 35
Scory, John, Bishop of Rochester and of Chichester, 110, 122
Scotland:
 war with, 6–10
 French intervention in, 6–10, 54
 border defenses of, 10, 12, 40, 41, 43, 44, 45, 52, 53, 58, 66, 83, 98, 124, 137–138, 141, 155, 177, 180
 peace concluded with, 21–23, 26, 28, 73–74
 diplomatic relations with, 38, 51–52, 106–107, 117, 146, 147
 Emperor's peace with, 50
 commissioners from and to, 57–58, 65
 unrest in, 44, 124, 152
 see also 24, 29, 31, 34, 43, 84, 89–92, 93–94; Debatable lands; and Mary, Queen Mother of Scotland
Scott, Sir Walter, Lord of Buccleuch, 152

Secretary, Principal, see Cecil, Sir William (1550–1553); Paget, Sir William (1543–1548); Petre, Sir William (1544–1553); Smith, Sir Thomas (1548–1549); and Wotton, Dr. Nicholas (1549–1550)
Senarpont, Jean de Monchy, Seigneur de, 118
Seymour, Alexander, 99
Seymour, Anne, 32
Seymour, David, 88, 91
Seymour, Edward, 22, 33
Seymour, Edward (Duke of Somerset, Lord Protector), xxi, xxiii, xxxiii, 4, 5, 6, 7, 8, 17, 18, 19, 24, 28, 30, 32, 34, 35–36, 40, 41, 42, 50, 59, 72, 78, 87–91 passim, 102, 109, 143, 149
 charges against, 92–93
 trial of, 96–100
 execution of, 107
 daughter of, see Seymour, Anne
 sons of, see Seymour, Edward; and Seymour, John
Seymour, Jane, Queen of England, x, 3, 18 n.
Seymour, John, 88
Seymour, Thomas, Baron Sudeley (Lord High Admiral, 1547–1549; Privy Council), xxiii, 4, 5, 6, 10–11
Sharington, Sir William, 11, 25, 29
Sheen, 32, 75 n.
Sheffield, Lord Edmund, 4, 15
Shoreditch, 94
Shrewsbury, Earl of, see Talbot, Francis
Sicily, 77, 79, 85
Sidney, Sir Henry, 25, 75, 86, 97, 103, 106, 124, 132
Siena, 139, 141
Sion House, 40
Sipier, Philibert de Marcilly, Seigneur de, 77
Skinner, Anthony, 110
Smith, Sir Clement, 56
Smith, Dr. Richard, 6
Smith, Sir Thomas (Principal Sec-

211

Index

Smith, Sir Thomas (*cont.*)
retary, 1548–1549), 19 n., 60
Social reforms, proposals for, 163–167
Solicitor General, *see* Griffith, Edward; *and* Gosnold, John
Somerset, Duke of, *see* Seymour, Edward
Somerset, William, third Earl of Worcester, 61, 98
Somme (River), 150
Soranzo, Giacomo, 66
Southampton, Earl of, *see* Wriothesley, Thomas
Southampton (co. Hants), 115, 139, 180
Southwell, Sir Richard (Privy Council), 19
Southwick Priory, 90 n.
Spain, troops of, 78, 140, 141, 145, 147
Spinola, Captain Paolo Baptista, 14
Spires (Germany), 125, 140, 146, 147
Stafford, Sir Robert, 105
Stafford, Sir William, 86, 103
Stamford, William, 110, 122
Stanhope, Sir Michael, 89, 92, 104, 108 n.
Stanley, Edward, third Earl of Derby, 22 n., 98
Stanley, Henry, Lord Strange (son of Earl of Derby), 22, 32, 93, 99
Star Chamber, 131, 132
Steads, *see* Hanse towns
Steelyard, 107, 108, 112, 113, 121, 133 n., 173, 178
Stenay, 125, 126
Stirling Castle, 152
Stourton, Charles, seventh Baron, 98
Stourton, Sir John, 189
Stradling, Sir Thomas, 95
Strange, Lord, *see* Stanley, Henry
Strangers, congregations of, 37, 58, 59
Strassburg, 38, 114, 121 n., 124, 126 n., 145

Strelley, Sir Nicholas, 53, 141, 147
Strozzi, Leo, Prior of Capua, 82, 86
Strozzi, Pietro, 74, 82, 153
Struthof, 126
Stuart, Robert, 62
Stuckley, Thomas, 143, 144, 148, 150
Sudeley, Baron, *see* Seymour, Thomas
Suffolk, Dukes of, *see* Brandon, Charles; Brandon, Henry; *and* Grey, Henry
Suffolk (county), 29 n., 101
Sultan (Sulaymán I), 42 n.
Superantio, *see* Soranzo, Giacomo
Surrey (county), 63, 91
Sussex, Earl of, *see* Radcliffe, Henry
Sussex (county), 12, 32 n., 37, 41, 90, 101
Sweating sickness, outbreak of, 71–72
Sweden, diplomatic relations with, 24, 26–27

Talbot, Francis, fifth Earl of Shrewsbury, 10, 22 n.
Talbot, Lord George, 22
Tavannes, Gaspard de Saulx, Seigneur de, 112
Taylor, John, Bishop of Lincoln, 110, 122
Taylor, Rowland, 110
Temesvár (Transylvania), 141
Terracina, 141
Thais, Jean de, 133
Thames (River), 32, 36, 66, 71
Thermes, Paul de la Barthe, Seigneur de, 65, 74, 75, 77
Thérouanne, 138
Thirlby, Thomas, Bishop of Norwich, 23, 57–58
Thomas, William, xx, 25
Thomond, Earl of, *see* O'Brien, Murrough
Throckmorton, Sir Nicholas, xx n., 91
Tiberio, Captain Francisco, 10
Titchfield (co. Hants), 42 n., 139

Index

Westminster Hall, 5, 97
Westmorland, Earl of, *see* Neville, Henry
Whalley, Richard, 52–53, 129
Wharton, Thomas, Baron, 98, 114, 138
White, John, 90
Wight, Isle of, 89
Wilford, Sir James, 9, 12
William of Worcester, xxxi–xxxii
Williams, Sir John, 128
Williams, William, 130
Willoughby, Sir Edward, 140 n.
Willoughby, William, first Baron Willoughby of Parham, 47, 106, 144, 147
Wilton, 142
Baron of, *see* Grey, William
Wiltshire, Earl of, *see* Paulet, William
Wiltshire, 12, 41
Winchester, 142
Bishops of, *see* Gardiner, Stephen; *and* Ponet, John
Windsor, William, second Baron, 98
Windsor, 3, 5, 10, 17, 18, 33, 40, 41, 42, 78, 82, 123, 143
Wingfield, Sir Anthony (Comptroller of Household, 1550–1552; Privy Council), 20, 78, 93
Wingfield, James, 89
Wingfield, Sir Richard, 124
Winter, William (King's Surveyor

of Ships and merchant), 36, 51 n., 148
Wissembourg, 126 n., 146
Woking, 42, 45
Wokingham, 78
Woolwich, 70
Wool-winders, proclamation concerning, 30
Worcester, Bishop of, *see* Heath, Nicholas; *and* Hooper, John
Worcester, Earl of, *see* Somerset, William
Worcestershire, 12
Worms, 140
Wotton, Dr. Nicholas (Principal Secretary, 1549–1550; Privy Council), 18, 46, 56, 90, 137, 145
Wriothesley, Thomas, Earl of Southampton (Lord Chancellor, 1544–1547; Privy Council, 1547), 42, 139
Wroth, Sir Thomas, 18
Württemberg, Duke of, 140

York, Sir John, 48, 54, 83
York, Richard, Duke of, 189
York (city), 83
Yorkshire, 13, 101, 129
Yvoix, 126 n., 132, 134 n.

Zouche, Richard, tenth Baron la, 98
Zweibrücken, 151